REBEL WRITERS

The Accidental Feminists: Shelagh Delaney,
Edna O'Brien, Lynne Reid Banks, Charlotte Bingham,
Nell Dunn, Virginia Ironside, Margaret Forster

By Celia Brayfield

BLOOMSBURY CARAVEL
LONDON · OXFORD · NEW YORK · NEW DELHI · SYDNEY

BLOOMSBURY CARAVEL
Bloomsbury Publishing Plc
50 Bedford Square, London, WC1B 3DP, UK

BLOOMSBURY, BLOOMSBURY CARAVEL and the Diana logo are trademarks of
Bloomsbury Publishing Plc

First published in Great Britain 2019
This edition published 2019

A catalogue record for this book is available from the British Library

Library of Congress Cataloguing-in-Publication data has been applied

ISBN: HB: 978-1-4482-1749-6; eBook: 978-1-4482-1751-9

2 4 6 8 10 9 7 5 3 1

Typeset in Perpetua Std by Deanta Global Publishing Services, Chennai, India
Printed and bound in Great Britain by CPI Group (UK) Ltd, Croydon CR0 4YY

To find out more about our authors and books visit www.bloomsbury.com
and sign up for our newsletters

This book is dedicated to
Joan Barker

AUTHOR'S NOTE

This biographical study focuses on writers whose work contributed to radical social changes more than two generations ago. They challenged many aspects of the world in which they grew up and to present their work accurately, it is also necessary to portray that world and their responses to it as they appeared at the time. Readers may be distressed by some of the events described, and the language the writers chose, particularly in Chapters 7 and 10.

CONTENTS

INTRODUCTION

In London in 1958 a play written by a 19-year-old redefined women's writing in Britain. It also began a movement that would change women's lives. The play was *A Taste of Honey* and the author, Shelagh Delaney, was the first of a succession of very young women who wrote about their lives with an honesty that dazzled the world. Some of their work is shocking, even today, because much about their lives was shocking in reality. They rebelled against sexism, inequality and prejudice and in doing so also rejected masculine definitions of what writing and a writer should be. After Delaney came Edna O'Brien, Lynne Reid Banks, Charlotte Bingham, Nell Dunn, Virginia Ironside and Margaret Forster to challenge traditional concepts of womanhood in their novels, films, television, essays and journalism.

Not since the Brontës had a group of writers been united by such a burning need to tell the truth about what it was like to be a girl. These authors were astonishingly young, some still teenagers when they started to write. Equally astonishing is that they wrote about the same things but could hardly have come from more different backgrounds. The pampered daughter of a multi-millionaire had the same yearning for a different way of life as a girl from a rat-infested Northern slum. A high-achieving Oxford graduate and a failed actress shared the same sense of being motherless and resolved to find a better way of creating a family. An ex-debutante and a sophisticated art student felt the same feeling of abandonment as they drifted from party to party, wondering what love might be while fighting off predatory males. Their characters all feel the instinct to revolt against their destiny as the narrator of Nell Dunn's *Poor Cow,*

who says, 'I can't bear the thought of all those women around me –
all doing the same things – washing their husband's shirts, changing
their babies, doing the shopping – the everyday life – the sight of a
shopping basket almost turns my guts'.[1]

There are many connections between these women but founding
a literary movement was the last thing on their minds, which makes
it all the more remarkable that they spoke with one voice. They
shared an inner place, the territory of girlhood, rather than such
traditional literary landscapes as Paris cafés or Oxford common
rooms. Their work is full of joy and humour but is not afraid to
confront the darker aspects of their lives, the violence, tragedy
and injustice they experienced. And it is constructive, in that their
characters are all looking for better ways to live, all proposing new
roles for women, new family structures, new ways to express love.

These writers did not create a literary movement consciously.
They were isolated young women who shared values and perceptions
but lacked the self-regard to see themselves as cultural crusaders.
Nor was that role bestowed on them by the media, as it was on their
contemporaries, the Angry Young Men, although this book argues
that their work was far more influential. They were beneficiaries
of a genre created by the publishing industry which gave them
platforms without understanding quite how subversive their work
would prove to be. It is delicious to reflect that the men who
thought they were merely exploiting a passing trend in publishing
were unknowingly laying the foundations of second-wave feminism.

There were some links between the Rebel Writers. The two
youngest of this group, Charlotte Bingham and Virginia Ironside,
had lived in the same area of London, on the edge of Chelsea since
childhood. Some formed relationships after their start of their
writing careers. Edna O'Brien and Nell Dunn moved into the same
street in a riverside inner-suburb of London and sat out in their
gardens on summer evenings talking about writing. They became
friends and were still meeting for lunch, sometimes with Margaret
Drabble, at the time this book was written. So something of the

shape of a traditional literary movement can be made out in this story, although the Rebel Writers never met together over years to share their writing and define a creative stance as did The Inklings in pre-war Oxford or the Beat Generation in 1950s America

Thematically the work of these writers is remarkably unified in its passionate statements about love, sex, marriage and its provocative challenge to accepted ideas of class and race. It is also prescient in imagining a new, diverse society and foreshadowing the idea of the urban family.

In the mid-1950s British intellectual life was dominated by privileged and Oxbridge-educated men. Evelyn Waugh, born in Hampstead and the son of a publisher, educated at public school and Oxford, veteran of military service and married into the aristocracy, provided the template for his generation. The famous observation by one of their number, the critic Cyril Connolly, that 'There is no more sombre enemy of good art than the pram in the hall', expressed the disdainful misogyny of their values, in which family life was almost an unmentionable obscenity. The women writers who were accepted in this milieu, among whom Brigid Brophy and Iris Murdoch were the most notable, fitted the mould of academic intellectuals who blended inoffensively into the prevailing atmosphere of a gentlemen's club while Doris Lessing was admired as a post-colonial voice, a self-evident outsider who posed no threat to the status quo. Many of the rising generation of young male writers, the Angry Young Men, were easily assimilated into the institutions, both formal and informal, that excluded women. Indeed, Kingsley Amis and John Osborne were soon members of the Garrick Club, a London institution that to this day does not admit female members. Female figures barely featured in British writing of this period except as the 'property' of the male characters who, like Kingsley Amis's *Lucky Jim*, occasionally fretted over, 'the awful business of getting on with women'.[2]

One of the many ideas that the elite discounted was the notion that writing might be a way of earning a living. Margaret Drabble, an author who firmly distances herself from Chelsea and all that it implies, remembers that when she told her Cambridge careers advisor that she wanted to be a novelist, he told her she would need to, 'marry a rich man'. Mass-market fiction was dismissed as deplorable content-free entertainment and the artistic, political and financial potential of television and film were largely denied.

FEMALE IN THE FIFTIES

A young woman in Britain in the fifties was living in a country that had not yet recovered from World War II, either economically, physically or socially. The authors in this study were all born on the eve of conflict which, in Europe, began in 1939 when Britain declared war on Germany. Their early childhoods were all shaped by the war itself, after which they grew up in the drawn-out desolation, disruption and austerity of the post-war decade. In *The White Bus*, a short story Shelagh Delaney wrote in the late sixties, she described her home neighbourhood:

> To get to where I lived I had to walk through a part of the city that was being demolished... Whole rows of evacuated houses had been left standing waiting for the bulldozers. Shop signs creaked. It was like a ghost town in a cowboy picture. Windows had been smashed and doors removed. I saw uncarpeted stairs and empty rooms. All around this deserted place the new city sheered up higher than ever before.[3]

Britain's visible devastation was matched by emotional damage. After years of danger, fear and instability people comforted themselves with nostalgia for the domestic security they imagined had existed before the war. Europe and America were gripped by an intense yearning for an ideal family life, for peace, harmony and comfort, for a happy marriage, healthy children and a predictable existence. In her 1975 book *A Woman's Place*, which recorded the social history of women through the twentieth century, the writer Ruth Adam characterised post-war Britain as a nation sharing a, 'passion of affection for the ordinary things of home life'.

In the post-war years, young women, millions of whom had been conscripted to work in factories or essential services on pain of imprisonment, now aspired to the status of housewife and were as eager as their husbands to start a family, giving birth to the baby boom generation. Young people married at a record rate. With just over 400,000 weddings in 1947, the number of happy couples almost equalled the number of wartime deaths.

Home and family were dreams shared by the hundreds of thousands of citizens who were still living in temporary flat-pack dwellings thrown together for people who had been bombed out of their homes. They had fresh memories of the food rationing, which did not end until 1953. Supporting this new normal were retrogressive expectations of gender. This had not been a concern when women workers were needed in factories and public services as well as in military roles during the war, but by the 1950s the roles of women and men were rigidly defined, perhaps more so than before.

The full-time wife and mother was a central image in the picture of an ideal family, burnished in new forms of media such as advertising and women's magazines, projected in glorious Technicolor in the movies and supported by the legal and social framework of the country. Some women commentators observed that, 'A cult of Homemaking and Motherhood is fostered by the press and propaganda. The sentimental glorification which these activities receive may flatter housewives but sometimes the glorification has a suspicious air of persuasion.'[4] But few listened. Second-wave feminism was still more than a decade away.

In 1958, when Shelagh Delaney made her debut, only about 30 per cent of married women in Britain worked and those women earned only 56 per cent of a man's wage for the same job. Disapproval of working mothers had developed into the most-debated moral issue of the day, and one-parent families were condemned as the cause of youth crime, low academic achievement and poor public health. Only 2 per cent of women went to university and at Oxford and Cambridge they were segregated into women's colleges, while medical schools operated a quota system, taking only 13 per cent of women students. There were no women judges, no women bank managers, few women CEOs and of the 630 members of Parliament elected in 1955 only twenty-four were women.

For working-class women the glossy ideal of a wife in a cocktail apron, welcoming her husband home while surrounded by domestic appliances and fresh-faced, obedient children, was farcically unrelated to the reality of their lives. In her family memoir, *Hidden Lives*, Margaret Forster recalled the 'drudgery' of her mother's daily routine. She woke every day before sunrise and her first task was to rake out and light the coal-fired stove that was the house's only heating. With three children, she cooked three meals a day for them and their father, washed all the family's clothes by hand on three days of the week, kept their council house spotless and, having no refrigerator, made a daily logistical exercise out of shopping on her husband's meagre wages. Having time to sit down and read a letter from her sister was an afternoon treat, although acting as counsellor, nurse and midwife to the neighbourhood seldom left much time for such a luxury. The family wore second-hand clothes, their only means of transport was a bicycle and they enjoyed a holiday in a seaside caravan in Britain once every three years.

Even over their own bodies, women in 1950s Britain had little control. Contraception was only available on medical prescription and only then for married women – or middle-class single women who were confident enough to find a sympathetic doctor and persuade him that they were engaged to be married. Oral contraception was not legally available until 1961. Abortion was illegal, but was nevertheless widely carried out and often fatal for the mother, as two of the ten stories in Nell Dunn's *Up the Junction* reveal. In a lecture given in 1963, the chair of the Family Planning Association,

Margaret Pyke, estimated the number of illegal abortions in Britain at almost 110,000 a year.[5]

Most other aspects of life were also outside women's control. A woman could not open a bank account or apply for a mortgage unless a man, usually her husband or father, stood as the guarantor of the account. A married woman also had to reveal her earnings to her husband, who was the only person who could legally sign her tax return: thus Edna O'Brien's husband was able to appropriate her earnings. For the young writers who are the subject of this book, a further restriction was that the age of majority – at which a person could vote or enter into a legally binding contract – was twenty-one, which meant that an adult, again most often a husband or father, needed to sign contracts on behalf of the minor. Thus the fathers of Charlotte Bingham and Virginia Ironside, and Shelagh Delaney's producer, Gerry Raffles, were able, to some extent, to protect the writers' interests. The age of consent, at which a person could legally have sex, remains in Britain now as it had been fixed in 1885 – at sixteen. Thus, Jo and her boyfriend in *A Taste of Honey*, who conceive when she is fifteen, were breaking the law.

Divorce was difficult, expensive and frightening. The Royal Commission on Marriage and Divorce, which reported in 1956 after five years of investigation, was set up to advise the government on family law. In the event, it was more concerned with protecting marriage as an institution than with the wives, mothers and children who might be suffering from desertion or abuse. In the parliamentary debates following the Commission's report, one speaker suggested that, rather than making divorce easier or cheaper, it was more important to protect young men from the terrible suffering caused by marrying a woman who could not cook.[6]

These restrictions were bolstered by censorship, both official and cultural. There was widespread outrage across 1950s British society that these young women should dare to talk about their experiences. Edna O'Brien was informed that copies of *The Country Girls* had been burned by a priest in a churchyard near the family parish of

Tuamgraney and her first six novels were officially banned by the Irish Censorship of Publications Board. On the whole, the critics disparaged the books that these women wrote. Both the authors and their editors sanitised many of the texts to avoid prosecution under the Obscene Publications Act. Bizarrely, official censorship of the theatre was enacted not by the government, but by a division of the Royal Household, the Lord Chamberlain's Office, whose principal concern was to protect audiences from characters who were clearly homosexual. When *A Taste of Honey* was staged, this Office considered the portrayal of a gay man in detail and with some distaste.

CHELSEA – THE PLACE TO BE

Chelsea, the borough of south-west London that became one of the world's most fashionable places in the sixties, was home at some point to four of the Rebel Writers and connected to the rest in their writing or their lives. They were part of a decisive cultural shift in the capital, which was largely played out in the streets of Chelsea. In the fifties, this borough was a neglected patchwork of tenements, bomb sites and peeling stucco-fronted terraces, but it had a certain bohemian heritage. It was bordered to the east by the luxurious mansions of Belgravia, to the south by the river Thames – where the gracious grounds of the Royal Hospital (famous for its much-loved red-coated Chelsea Pensioners) meet the riverside Embankment. To the west of the Royal Hospital the stature of the buildings declined over a mile or so until the World's End estate – once a Victorian slum – where the decaying artisan cottages blended into the even more grim backstreets of Fulham. To the north of Chelsea lay the handsome terraces of Kensington, but this area in turn declined into the grimy dilapidation of Notting Hill, the major focus of settlement by immigrants from the Caribbean and the site of race riots in 1958. Chelsea's main artery is King's Road, which runs west from Sloane Square to the riverside at Fulham, a straight road apart from a sharp chicane at World's End, as if to tell the traveller that they are entering a danger zone as they move from Chelsea into Fulham. In the period spanned by this study, King's Road was transformed from an unremarkable minor traffic route to the main artery of 'swinging' London, lined with funky boutiques, crowded with fashionable young people every Saturday and crammed with outrageous custom cars once a month.

Writers, artists and actors had made homes in Chelsea for centuries. Once just a charming village on the Thames, it was swallowed by urbanisation in the nineteenth century but never achieved uniform prosperity. In the late nineteenth-century Chelsea began to be settled by painters and sculptors in need of cheap studio space. They gathered at the determinedly bohemian Chelsea Arts Club in Old Church Street and lived alongside ordinary working families. But it remained an economically mixed part of London – to this day the tenements built by housing trusts sit beside white-pillared garden squares and the 1970s brutalist towers of the World's End estate look down on the imposing eighteenth-century houses of Cheyne Walk.

Suddenly, in the middle of the fifties, Chelsea became the crucible of Britain's artistic and cultural regeneration. At Sloane Square, where the underground station had been slowly rebuilt following its destruction by a bomb in 1940, the nineteenth-century Royal Court Theatre had been closed for almost twenty years when it was leased by the English Stage Company in 1956. This radical new entity, led by two directors – Tony Richardson and George Devine – intended to establish a writer's theatre that would become part of the intellectual life of the country, in contrast to the well-padded bourgeois dramas and frothy comedies playing in the West End.

The Royal Court Theatre was also the birthplace of a male literary movement that was the contemporary of the young women writers of this book. The fourth play produced at the theatre was *Look Back in Anger* by an unknown writer, John Osborne. As described in a later chapter, the play's publicist, looking for a phrase to describe its combination of social realism and nihilistic rage, came out with the description 'angry young man'. In the press Osborne was quickly and randomly linked to other contentious writers, whether serious social realists, anti-establishment ranters or outright chancers, including Kingsley Amis, Alan Sillitoe, John Braine, Arnold Wesker and Colin Wilson. The Angry Young Men became the first literary movement to be a media construct.

The work of the Rebel Writers was part of a seismic shift in British culture. The sensation caused at the Royal Court immediately pulled the artistic energy of London southwards. A few blocks away, in Kensington, the Royal College of Art opened its new building in 1960, where David Hockney, Peter Blake and R.B. Kitaj exhibited together in their degree show a year later. Both Virginia Ironside's parents taught at the Royal College of Art and her mother, against the opposition of her more traditional colleagues, famously launched the generation of fashion designers who were soon selling alongside Bazaar, the boutique where the fashion designer Mary Quant sold her first mini-skirt. The Chelsea dynamic was not only about new artists and new ideas. It was about new young audiences and a new definition of culture that gave pride of place to the popular while challenging the values of the traditional.

WOMEN, YOUTH AND LANGUAGE

The premise of this book is that this group of writers was remarkable for their own youth and their focus on the experiences of young women. Perhaps it is more remarkable that young women's voices were ever missing from the cultural register. Girls have an edge with writing. They are better at language than boys. A great many research studies have noted that the genders process language differently and this difference leads girls them to perform better than boys in academic tasks in which language skills are key. An influential study at Northwestern University, USA[7] used magnetic resonance imaging to look at the way girls and boys responded to language and found striking differences; in essence, much more of a girl's brain was active in processing language. Later studies have suggested an intensely female dimension to this phenomenon, in that female hormones improve girls' performance still more,[8] which suggests that at puberty a girl's relationship to language will become more intense. There is, in short, a neurophysiological reason why teenage girls read so obsessively.

Added to this biological aptitude are social and cultural forces which make it more likely that a girl will be more at home in the world of language. A study by the Centre for Arts and Cultural Studies at Princeton University noted that in America a cluster of social imperatives would discourage a boy but reward a girl for sitting down with a book. As adults, women heavily outnumber men as readers generally. In 2009 a study of 2000 British people[9] found that 48 per cent of women, but only 26 per cent of men, were avid readers who said they couldn't put a book down. New media and new social patterns seem to have intensified women's dominance in literature, with the overwhelming majority of book group members and book bloggers being female. Women are particularly heavy readers of fiction; in Britain, a woman is 2.5 times more likely to read a novel than a man and the publishing industry refers to this as the 'fiction gap'.

With such clear biological, cultural and commercial dominance on their side, it is more surprising that novels by young women were ever rare than that they suddenly, and briefly, became a hot phenomenon in the sixties. There is clear evidence that patriarchal values in publishing and the media favour male authors in many different ways, and that the exclusion of women writers from publishing lists and review pages still takes place. The annual study by *Vida: Women In Literary Arts*, reporting in 2016, found that about two-thirds of authors published and of authors reviewed, were men. Locally things were even worse. The *London Review of Books* had 'the worst gender disparity', with women representing only 18 per cent of reviewers and 26 per cent of authors reviewed.

In contrast, the *New York Times Book Review* was at parity on reviewers and at 44 per cent of women authors reviewed.

Small wonder, then, that the writers in this study did not set out to seek conventional literary success. When novels are rated by sales rather than critical acclaim, the picture is similar. This is the zone in which Stephanie Meyer is slugging it out with Stephen King and James Patterson. In the fifties and early sixties around 30 per cent of the authors in the *New York Times* Best Seller list were women. In the 2010s, the proportion is just below 50 per cent, with a decisive shift towards parity happening in the 1990s. Much of this is accounted for by the decline in popularity of male-oriented genres such as adventure or spy thrillers and the rise of genres read by both men and women, of which those classified as 'literary/other' have seen the highest gain. However, when male and female authors are compared on sales, books by men outsold those by women substantially, over a period in which overall sales by all writers had risen dramatically. Accounting for this is the fact that, while both genders prefer books by authors of the same sex, women will read both male and female authors, whereas men show resistance to reading books by women. A study by Goodreads[10] found that in the first year of publication, 80 per cent of a female author's audience will be women, but that women will also make up 50 per cent of a male author's audience.

The youngest characters created by the writers in this study are Caithleen/Kate in *The Country Girls* trilogy, seen from the age of eight, and the 15-year-old Jo in *A Taste of Honey*. The youngest authors, Delaney, Bingham and Ironside, were under twenty years of age when they made their debuts. This was extremely young, although a small number of women writers, some of whom also appear in this study, were first published their twenties in the post-war period. This group includes Penelope Mortimer, at twenty-nine, Emma Smith at twenty-five and Elizabeth Jane Howard at twenty-four, who were published in the late 1940s, followed by Brigid Brophy at twenty-four in 1953. Ten years later Margaret Drabble also made her debut at twenty-four, followed by Ann Quinn at twenty-eight in 1964. For the most part their work was decisively literary, and their themes not related to those of the Rebel Writers, although *The Millstone*, Drabble's third novel, shares the focus on single motherhood and is considered in that chapter.

A CHARMING LITTLE MONSTER

The literary sensation who opened the doors of the publishing industry to young women writers in the fifties appeared in Paris. Françoise Sagan's first book, *Bonjour Tristesse,* was published in 1954 when she was just eighteen years old. Born Françoise Quoirez, she was the adored youngest daughter of a successful and innovative electrical engineer and had grown up during World War II, at her grandparents' home deep in the rural department of the Lot, in south-west France. In 1950, despite disappointing exam results, she got a place at the Sorbonne university in Paris, where she met another young woman who was absorbed by literature: Florence Malraux, the only daughter of two radical writers, Clara and André Malraux, by then divorced. Florence recalls that Sagan, 'had read all Stendhal, and then Flaubert, Faulkner, Hemingway, Camus, Fitzgerald and a little Malraux. She had been colonised by literature'. Florence Malraux shared her own passion for Dostoevsky and Tolstoy as well as stories of dinner with Albert Camus. 'There was a bit of narcissism in our attraction for each other. People took us for two sisters'.

The friendship gave Sagan both literary focus and an insight into the French publishing industry. When she returned to university after the summer holidays in 1953, she told Florence that she had just finished a novel. It had taken her six weeks to write *Bonjour Tristesse* in longhand in a blue notebook, and then to type it out with one finger. She gave the manuscript to Florence as they shared a bus ride across Paris and at 2 a.m. her friend rang to say, 'It's all right. You are a writer'.

Françoise sent the manuscript to three publishers and put her date of birth on the title page. One of the three, René Julliard, who had the reputation of a showman with a gift for publicising his authors, reacted immediately and sent her a telegram asking her to meet him the next morning at 11 a.m. Françoise, never an early riser, suggested 5 p.m. She asked for an advance of 25,000 francs. Julliard offered her double. The deal was done and her parents, anxious about the family reputation, suggested she pick a pseudonym. She chose Sagan after the Princesse de Sagan, a character in Proust's *À La Recherche de Temps Perdu*.

Bonjour Tristesse was an instant critical and commercial success, selling 350,000 copies in France alone in its first year, with publishers from around the world bidding for the foreign rights. A Hollywood film followed in 1958, starring Jean Seberg, Deborah Kerr and David Niven and directed by Otto Preminger, whose masterpiece it is considered. A month after the book appeared it was awarded the *Prix des Critiques* and its 'unquestionable' literary merit was praised by the chair of the judges, the 70-year-old Nobel laureate François Mauriac, on the front page of France's leading mid-market newspaper, *Le Figaro*.

Bonjour Tristesse concerns a 17-year-old girl, Cecile, who amuses herself on a long hot family holiday in the south of France by trying to manipulate her handsome, charming and widowed father. She seduces and discards her own boyfriend, befriends her father's young mistress and goes to war against an older woman, a friend of her late mother, with whom her father falls in love. Eventually her rival commits suicide. There is no suggestion of empathy in Cecile, or any clue that she may be grieving for her own mother. Instead she expresses only an unfeeling selfishness.

It is no surprise that Cecile's heartless hedonism and the extended descriptions of a middle-aged man's irresistible allure were exactly what a middle-aged male publisher would consider acceptable in the work of a young female author. The story is a flattering flirtation with the ageing patriarchy that merely curtseys to feminism in suggesting that a young woman might have – and even enjoy – sex. Nevertheless, the novel's portrayal of teen sexuality was considered both profound and outrageous. Sagan was hailed as the new Colette. Looking back thirty years later, she mused:

> It was inconceivable that a young girl of seventeen or eighteen should make love, without being in love, with a boy of her own age and not be punished for it. People couldn't tolerate the idea that the girl should not fall madly in love with the boy and not be pregnant by the end of the summer. It was unacceptable, too, that a young girl should have the right to use her body as she will, and derive pleasure from it without incurring a penalty.[11]

In case the French establishment should be concerned that a young woman who had once been expelled from school for hanging Molière in effigy should have any genuinely revolutionary instincts, Sagan was photographed by the hugely popular weekly gossip magazine *Paris Match*, dressed in an apron while putting some tasty dish in a brand new oven. However compromised she may have been as a feminist, Francoise Sagan was living proof that a man could make his fortune in publishing by betting on a teenage girl.

So, when the 20-year-old Shelagh Delaney met the press in London after the success of *A Taste of Honey*, she was variously dubbed an 'Angry Young Woman' or Britain's 'answer to Françoise Sagan'. As we shall see when considering the reception of these young female writers and their subsequent careers, they were initially supported by such earlier successes. The gate-keepers of the cultural industries that produced their work were banking on audiences that had already been identified. What they missed, however, was that this group of writers would, in fact, be far more successful as subversives.

PART ONE

SEVEN WRITERS

I

INNOCENCE & EXPERIENCE

What a disparate bunch. A sales assistant, two housewives, a television reporter, a typist, an art student and a teacher. The heads of the households in which they grew up were a bus-driver, an alcoholic, a doctor, a titled spymaster, an artist, a factory worker and a multimillionaire baronet. These seven writers could not have come from more different backgrounds. It is remarkable that, whether they were born into extreme wealth or dire poverty; educated minimally or in the finest universities in the world; raised by supportive or neglectful families; they expressed the same opinions, had the same experiences and felt the same powerful need to speak out. In all other respects, their ambitions varied almost as much as the circumstances of their lives. Variously, they wrote because they wanted social justice or understanding, to make people think, to entertain, to annoy their parents or simply for the sake of being a writer.

For most, artistic innovation – arguably the traditional aim of a literary talent – was not a major ambition, or so these women claimed when interviewed. As this book will show, it was the very nature of our writers to challenge literary conventions. The world of literature, at the time of their debuts, was so thoroughly colonised by the patriarchy that these writers saw no merit in its accepted values. Instead, they became forerunners of the theory of *l'écriture féminine*, asserting the validity of their own experience and challenging the masculine mould of fiction. They were also the harbingers of profound social changes which were to follow their treatment of the themes of class, race, gender and sexuality.

1958: SHELAGH DELANEY AND *A TASTE OF HONEY*

Sheila Delaney was born on 25 November 1938 in one of the most deprived areas of Britain. Salford, part of the conurbation that is now Greater Manchester, was a post-industrial slum, a warren of run-down terraces that appeared in the top three in national statistics for infant mortality and deprivation diseases such as rickets and scurvy. In the week in which Delaney was born the town enthusiastically subscribed to National Rat Week,[1] an anti-vermin initiative that seemed to do little for Salfordians' environmental health. A century earlier, Salford's 'wretched [...] miserable and filthy' living conditions had traumatised Friedrich Engels, who worked in a cotton mill there in 1842 and later wrote the *Communist Manifesto* of 1848 with Karl Marx.

Hellish as it was, Engels saw Salford in its heyday, when the area teemed with textile workers, miners and dockers, but by 1938 these industries had collapsed, leaving mass unemployment, even worse living conditions and a toxic legacy of pollution in both the air and the ground. World War II in which heavy German bombing known as the 'Salford Blitz', demolished 2,000 homes and damaged ten times that number, added to a vortex of deprivation which persists in some parts of the region to this day.

Delaney was still a baby on the eve of the World War II. Her father, a bus driver, was conscripted but wounded in North Africa and invalided out of the army, so he could at least share with his wife and children the chaos of the war years. After the war, a slum clearance programme, during which 22,000 homes were demolished, forced the family to move frequently. Delaney later recalled that she, 'went to about five different schools between the ages of five and nine'.[2] Destined to be tall and slender, she was so thin at the age of eleven that she was sent for a short time to a children's convalescent home at Lytham St Annes, an establishment run by nuns who confiscated her pen and forbade writing and reading, except for the Bible.

The rebellious instinct that was to assert itself often in Delaney's life inspired her to defy the nuns and start writing. As a teenager she carried a notebook everywhere, making her family's neighbours wary. Her fractured early education had left her without formal examination passes but with an obvious intelligence and social maturity that both teachers and fellow pupils felt made her a 'natural leader'[3] even though she was often late and frequently broke school rules. Her route to underachievement seemed to have been confirmed when she was sent to a run of the mill school, but her teachers and her father lobbied the Education Committee, with the result that Delaney spent two years at the more academic Pendleton Grammar School, before leaving at the age of sixteen.[4]

A series of unskilled and short-lived jobs followed while she immersed herself in the cultural life of the Manchester area, from participating in amateur drama groups to a stint as an usherette at the Manchester Opera House. She continued to write in private, although, 'the general reaction to my announcement that I intended to try and write for a living was one amounting to hysteria'.[5] In 1957 Delaney's father died. Early in 1958, she wrote to Joan Littlewood, the legendary director and champion of avant-garde theatre in London, at the Theatre Royal Stratford East, sending a play and explaining, 'A fortnight ago I didn't know the theatre existed, but a young man, anxious to improve my mind, took me to the Opera House in Manchester and I came away after the performance having suddenly realised that at last, after nineteen years of life, I had discovered something that meant more to me than myself'.[6]

She had good reason to hope that Littlewood would respond to the work. The director was a passionate communist, a champion of working-class voices in every form and lover of British music-hall (equivalent to American vaudeville). In addition, her first husband – the poet and singer Ewan McColl – was also a Salfordian. Littlewood had begun her artistic career with him in Manchester and was dedicated to community and political theatre, to improvisation and the use of working-class language. Indeed, the play instantly appealed to her. She heard echoes of music-hall patter in the exchanges between Delaney's characters. John Bay, an actor in Littlewood's Theatre Workshop company. who was to take the part of the mother's boyfriend in the play, was more cynical about its appeal, saying, 'Teenage sex, a black baby on the way and a queer boyfriend. She's not so dumb'.

Indeed, Delaney's letter, when set against the evidence of her people who knew her at the time, suggests that, at the age of nineteen, she was not quite the unsophisticated natural genius for which she was taken by her early admirers, but an astute self-mythologist and, as a writer, an accomplished auto-didact. The 'young man' she wrote of was a fellow pupil at her grammar school, Harold Riley, a protégé of L.S. Lowry who later became a distinguished artist. He remembers many visits with Delaney to cinemas and theatres and conversations in which she spoke as one who was, 'steeped in' knowledge of the theatre.[7] Two years earlier, when she was just sixteen, Delaney had made contact with Manchester's Library Theatre, where she watched rehearsals and sought career advice from the director. The decision to send the play to Littlewood itself suggests both ambition and sophistication. Delaney's self-mythologising was especially evident when she adopted the Irish spelling of her first name, Shelagh, perhaps inspired by Littlewood's acclaimed staging of *The Quare Fellow* by the Irish playwright Brendan Behan in 1956.

Littlewood pioneered the workshop style of direction in British theatre, in which text was viewed as a starting point rather than a blueprint. She would develop the performances with the actors in her Theatre Workshop company. With *A Taste of Honey* Littlewood decided that the characters, particularly Helen, the mother, should deliver their lines music-hall style, as asides to the audience, which completely transformed Delaney's original script during the performance. While she was struck by the inherent comedy of some of the exchanges between characters but concerned at what she saw as a disjointed narrative. Declaring 'Jazz will solve it,' Littlewood used music from a jazz trio to link the scenes. In spite of these changes, when Delaney was invited to London to stay with Littlewood and her partner Gerry Raffles and see the production, Littlewood said later, 'I don't think she noticed the difference between her draft and the company's adaptation'.[8]

A Taste of Honey is a play of two acts, four scenes and five characters. The core of the drama is the relationship between Jo, a schoolgirl of fifteen when the play begins, and her mother, Helen — a raucous forty-something good-time girl who has relied on a series of boyfriends for support and, in the first act, is about to marry one of them. Mother and daughter bicker, squabble and verbally abuse each other tirelessly. Jo is in love with a young black man, a naval rating who promises to marry her when his tour of duty ends. By the second act Jo is pregnant, estranged from her mother and, with no sign of her boyfriend, is living amicably with a gay man, Geof, while supporting herself as a barmaid. Helen comes crashing back into her life and, at the end of the play, is threatening to take over, oust her daughter's friend and dominate her life once more. The energy and humour of the dialogue and Jo's brutal realism give the play a momentum that takes the place of dramatic events.

A Taste of Honey ran at the Theatre Royal, Stratford East from 27 May 1958 until it transferred to the West End in February 1959. It was immensely successful, with full houses every night and critics stunned, shocked but admiring. Writing in the establishment periodical the *Spectator*, the left-wing critic Alan Brien, who would later be married to the feminist journalist Jill Tweedie, wrote:

> *A Taste of Honey* is a boozed, exaggerated, late-night anecdote of a play which slithers unsteadily between truth and fantasy, between farce and tragedy, between aphrodisiac and emetic. It is written as if it were a film script, with an adolescent contempt for logic or form or practicability on stage...

Twenty, ten or even five years ago, before a senile society begin to fawn upon the youth which is about to devour it, such a play would have remained written in green longhand in a school exercise book on the top of a bedroom wardrobe ... This is not so much dramaturgy as anthropology, demonstrated by a genuine cannibal.[9]

Like many others, O'Brien ascribed what he saw as the play's faults to Delaney's youth and gender. The possibility that the unstructured form was a conscious challenge to traditional dramatic narrative did not seem to have occurred to these critics.

The novelist Colin MacInnes, admired for his portrayal of the emerging diversity of London and the bohemian character of the Notting Hill area, wrote that it was, 'the first play that I can remember about working class people that entirely escapes being a 'working class play': no patronage, no dogma – just the thing as it is, taken straight'.[10] Kenneth Tynan in *The Observer* showered it with praise, noted that the play had faults but in conclusion called Delaney 'nineteen years old and a portent'.

In the audience were admirers as disparate as the prima ballerina Margot Fonteyn and the Irish poet Louis MacNeice. Graham Greene, one of Britain's most celebrated novelists at the time, overheard Littlewood complaining about Delaney's dilapidated typewriter and promptly bought her a new one. Nineteen-year-old Delaney was fêted, invited to all the best social gatherings, interviewed, filmed and captured on camera by some of the greatest photographers of the day. The same level of adulation that had been given to Francoise Sagan now threatened to overwhelm her.

Delaney signed a two-year contract which Littlewood, whose (civil and professional) partner Gerry Raffles explained would 'protect her from the trouble that Brendan Behan got himself into by signing up with the first agent who came along. But I hope, when all the fuss has died down, some literary agent will be sufficiently interested in Shelagh to take her in hand and help her in many ways which I cannot. When that time comes I shall not stand in her way'.[11]

Despite this profession of paternalistic altruism, the contract was also intended to keep Delaney away from the Royal Court Theatre in Chelsea, which Littlewood regarded as a faux-socialist rival. Raffles was aware that the Royal Court, now the home of the Angry Young Men and the launch pad for the theatre revolution taking place in Britain, had approached Delaney and offered itself for the play's transfer. As Delaney was under contract, Raffles could rebuff them and instead A Taste of Honey went into the West End, to the very traditional Wyndham's Theatre.

Delaney was awarded the Charley Henry Foyle New Play award in 1958, presented – condescendingly – by the actor and dramatist Emlyn Williams. The reader for the Arts Council, conceded that the work had, 'a certain strength in its crudity' and Delaney was awarded a bursary of £100, with a further modest guarantee to the production, a remarkable grant by a supposedly autonomous government body that had refused to fund Robert Bolt and Samuel Beckett around the same time.[12] In the event the show turned around the perilous fortunes of the Theatre Royal Stratford East and made a profit of £7,047 3s 6d, of which 10 per cent was returned to the Arts Council.

For Delaney these sums were soon overshadowed by the transfer takings from Wyndham's and the profits of the Broadway production that followed in 1960, jointly estimated at £300 a week. The Broadway version was directed by Tony Richardson and the cast included 34-year-old Joan Plowright as Jo and 36-year-old Angela Lansbury as her mother, Helen. Plowright came fresh from success in John Osborne's second play for the Royal Court, The Entertainer, and was to marry her co-star in that production, Britain's leading actor, Laurence Olivier, in 1961. Lansbury, who was struggling in Hollywood at the time, was drawn to this unglamorous stage role as it was, 'truly female'[13] and written by a woman. Male playwrights, she felt, seldom wrote dialogue the way women actually talk, or had female characters think the way women do. It was to prove a pivotal moment in Lansbury's career, showcasing the emotional power that won her the leading role of a more glamorous middle-aged diva in the iconic Broadway musical, *Auntie Mame,* for which she won the New York Drama Critics Award in 1961.

Honey's film rights were also sold immediately, to Woodfall Film Productions – the company formed by the same director, Tony Richardson, for £20,000. As co-founder of the English Stage Company at the Royal Court, – he had directed *Look Back in Anger* as both a play and a film. Littlewood's biographer, Peter Rankin, is one of several authorities who have described the relationship between Gerry Raffles, Joan Littlewood and the teenage playwright as 'a parent-daughter relationship'.[14] She lived with them when she was in London but, in contrast to the close and mutually protective relationship that Delaney had with her real-life family, this connection became turbulent very quickly and took the same conflicted tone as her relationships with earlier authority figures. The temperature rose to the point where every connection between them became a point of conflict. Delaney wanted to buy a sports car. Raffles forbade it – remember Delaney was still legally a minor – and they argued. She wrote to Joan, describing the exchange.

> I had a very interesting telephone conversation with Gerry the other week but as he started to speak to me in a language that was arrogant, pompous, witless and ham-fisted I soon cut the cackle short on that one and tried to contact you ... I have never liked being told what to do and I've no intention of starting to like it now.[15]

She turned twenty-one in 1959, the legal age of majority at that time, and her contract with Raffles and Littlewood was due to expire a year later. When Littlewood suggested that more work was needed on her second play, *The Lion in Love*, Delaney reacted petulantly. There were rumours of an affair with Brendan Behan and she had been openly 'snogging' Cedric Price, the visionary young architect with whom Littlewood was also involved, in the back of a car when Littlewood was a passenger in the front. [16] The relationship with her parents-in-theatre foundered, Delaney chose Chelsea and her second play was destined for the Royal Court.

The career trajectory of this young playwright is now regarded as a model of the difficult route that many female artists have navigated. As this book will consider in later chapters, the unquestioning support that was given to Delaney's male contemporaries, who were, at least initially, backed through failures and false starts, was not available to her, not least because she rejected the advice of Littlewood and Raffles. That advice was not wholly altruistic. And an artist can never be taken as a talent alone, but always as an entire being whose creative gifts are developed along with their human character. Delaney was certainly volatile, outspoken and over-confident, but so were most of her male contemporaries. There seem to be two points of difference; the men did not suffer for their arrogance and their investors, monetary or creative, were far more loyal though their early setbacks.

1960: EDNA O'BRIEN AND *THE COUNTRY GIRLS*

'By the time I was born, we were no longer rich,' wrote Edna O'Brien in her autobiography, *Country Girl*, in which she describes how her family land in Ireland had been sold by her alcoholic father. Their house was already gone – he had proudly told the family how he had joined with the local IRA to burn down his ancestral home after a rumour suggested that it was to be used as a barracks for the Black and Tans (the notoriously brutal police recruited largely in England to combat the IRA in the Irish war of Independence). The blackened ruin, wallpaper still peeling from the ballroom walls, was not far from the family's new home, a small modern villa surrounded by a few fields in the village of Tuamgraney in

County Clare – a place which O'Brien has said had a, 'pathological, indelible' effect on her.

Born in 1930, O'Brien's early memories were of wild creatures in the woods and a bailiff she once found in the kitchen when she got home from the village school. Tuamgraney and its sister village of Scariff are a bleak straggle of low buildings situated on marshy land close to Lough Dergh in eastern County Clare. An elaborate Art Nouveau-style monument to fallen members of the IRA is the finest construction in the parish, while the village churches used for week-to-week worship are grim, prim little buildings, each surrounded by a graveyard. The parish also contains the oldest church in continuous use in Ireland, dedicated to St Cronin. Across the lough, veiled by rain or mist, is Inis Cealtra or 'Holy Island', home to the ruins of an ancient religious settlement that includes the church of St Caimin, built at the command of Ireland's 10th century king, Brian Boru.

The ancient, mystical sites seem something apart from the neat and unadorned homes of the village. There has been little wealth and much tragedy here. During the potato famines in the nineteenth century, called the 'Great Hunger', the workhouse in Scariff was crammed to capacity. The graveyard at St Cronin's had to be extended and then more land bought for mass graves. An estimated 7,000 people, about one in eight of the population, died, meaning that every family in the area lost relatives.

A hundred years later, the tiny village had twenty-seven bars and O'Brien's father drank heavily every day. 'It was foolish to expect [him] to come home sober,' O'Brien wrote in *Country Girl*.[17] On one occasion he tried to tear off her mother's clothes, believing she had hidden money in her underwear, and then shot at her with a revolver, after which the police arrived and he was taken to a nearby monastery to detox in the care of the monks. He made the journey in a taxi to hide the shame of his condition, although in such a small community it can hardly have been a secret.

During World War II, Ireland remained a neutral country and as a child O'Brien seemed to have been unaware of the conflict and the food shortages which were one of its consequences. Her family was poor in every way and books were a rare and controversial treasure in the house. 'My family was radically opposed to anything to do with literature. Although Ireland has produced so many great writers, there is a deep suspicion about writing there. Somehow they know that writing is dangerous, seditious'. The books in O'Brien's house were mostly prayer books and religious anthologies, although her widowed aunt had a copy of *War and Peace* and asked her to write down the Russian names for her so she could remember them. At the village school she wrote childish stories and plays but after she moved to a convent school at the age of thirteen a fluctuating religious fervour overtook her until the call of the world outside led her to study hard and pass her final exams a year early.

Following her older brother and sister, O'Brien moved to Dublin when she was seventeen, marvelling at the monuments, the grand buildings, the glowing dress shops and the street lighting. Her family determined that she should train as a pharmacist, which meant a paid apprenticeship in a chemist's shop and evening lectures. Through her sister, Eileen, a secretary in the railway company, O'Brien was also invited to write a weekly column in their house magazine, which she was told should be 'light-hearted and of interest to women'.[18] She wrote under a pen name and 'the image of a vamp with bobbed hair and a cigarette holder, supposed to be a likeness of me, featured at the top of each of these nonsensical jottings'. Fashion notes and tips on pancake making went down well, but, tiny as this platform was, she used it to her advantage. In one column, she asserted on little evidence that 'Monsieur Dior and Monsieur Fath and all the Monsieurs who count are concentrating this year on fashions for men,' and went on to namecheck half a dozen well-dressed men about Dublin, beginning, 'Michael MacLiammoir is always spectacular in black.' The great actor, dramatist and co-founder of

Dublin's Gate Theatre could only have been complimented, even by a humble house magazine.

O'Brien began to visit the bar frequented by the staff of the *Irish Times* and offered articles to newspapers, full of joy when an account of her visit to a seaside resort was accepted as 'people at home would read it and my mother might forgive my literary aspirations'.[19] She began to meet writers and intellectuals. For fourpence at a second-hand book stall, she bought a copy of *Introducing James Joyce* by T.S. Eliot, 'and carried it with me everywhere, even to pharmacy lectures'. From Joyce she learned that a writer could depict their own life, and as the city, in all its glamour and misery, impressed itself on her memory she began to look back on her childhood from a new perspective.

She met her husband, Ernest Gébler, then a successful, if conflicted, author of historical novels, through a mutual friend and gradually adopted the ways of Dublin's bohemian set, moving in with him and eventually getting married – following the intervention of her outraged parents – a month before her first child, Carlo, was born. A second son, Sasha, followed two years later.

Ian Hamilton,[20] an editor at the London publisher Hutchinson, met Gébler on a scouting trip to Dublin and suggested that his career would flourish if he and his family moved to London, which they did in 1958, living in the outer suburb of Wimbledon.

Gébler's first novel, *The Voyage of the Mayflower* (1950), had been a bestseller on a scale seldom seem even today. It sold 5 million copies and was adapted into a Hollywood film starring Spencer Tracy. In the aftermath of this phenomenon, Gébler despised popular success and was struggling to write anything that satisfied him. His wife's descriptions of him sleeping until the early afternoon then shutting himself in his study for hours suggest a man suffering from depression. As a literary figure, however, Gébler had an immediate entrée into London literary society which his young wife shared to some extent. Nevertheless, O'Brien felt intensely lonely and alienated by the city.

I felt bewildered and lost—an outsider. So in a sense *The Country Girls,* [my first novel] which I wrote in those first few weeks after my arrival, was my experience of Ireland and my farewell to it.

But something happened to my style which I will tell you about. I had been trying to write short bits, and these were always flowery and over lyrical. Shortly after I arrived in London I saw an advertisement for a lecture given by Arthur Mizener [author of a book on F. Scott Fitzgerald, *The Far Side of Paradise*] on Hemingway and Fitzgerald. You must remember that I had no literary education, but a fervid religious one. So I went to the lecture and it was like a thunderbolt [...] and I couldn't believe it – this totally uncluttered, precise, true prose, which was also very moving and lyrical. I can say that the two things came together then: my being ready for the revelation and my urgency to write. The novel wrote itself, so to speak, in a few weeks. All the time I was writing it I couldn't stop crying, although it is a fairly buoyant, funny book. But it was the separation from Ireland which brought me to the point where I had to write.[21]

Ian Hamilton, who was by now her husband's editor, paid O'Brien a very small advance of £50 for *The Country Girls*, which was jointly published in 1960 with Knopf in New York. As O'Brien's memoir makes clear, the book was commissioned on the basis of Hamilton's attraction to her which she repulsed after her husband overheard a 'tender' telephone conversation between them. As a married woman she could not open her own bank account and so had to endorse the advance cheque and all subsequent payments to Gébler, who paid them into his own account.

The Country Girls became an instant sensation and commercial success. The novel, about two young girls who grow up in a small village in Ireland, go to a convent school and then move to Dublin to, 'live. Drink gin. Squeeze into the front of big cars and drive up outside big hotels', is both overtly and thematically autobiographical. 'Two girls discovering what life's about,' was how

O'Brien described it at the time. The novel's lyrical nature-writing and crystalline observation recreate her the landscapes of Ireland and her own home life, as does the pervading terror of the narrator, Caithleen's, drunken father. Caithleen and her friend Baba, far from being pious, obedient and bookish schoolgirls like O'Brien had been, are expelled from their convent for writing a note that suggested a nun and a priest had sex. From the age of eight, Caithleen drifts into a long and almost chaste relationship with 'Mr Gentleman', a married man who grooms her from childhood. In Dublin he pursues her, and they begin a hopeless, unconsummated love affair, then make plans to run away to England. On the last page of the novel he sends a telegram crying off and ending, 'must not see you'.

Like Delaney's play, O'Brien's first novel was at once lauded and controversial. Film rights were sold to Woodfall and a minor British literary award followed. Although the novel contains no erotic scenes it was a *success de scandale* as well as *d'estime*. O'Brien was feted in London, while her husband, upon reading it, announced he would never forgive her, 'the death-knell of the already ailing marriage'.

1960: LYNNE REID BANKS AND *THE L-SHAPED ROOM*.

Lynne Reid Banks was working at Independent Television News (ITN) as what was then called a 'girl reporter' when she began her first novel. Founded in 1955, this was Britain's first commercial television news operation and Banks and her colleague, Barbara Mantel, were the first female news reporters on British television. ITN was a dynamic new enterprise that set out to challenge the deferential tone of the state broadcaster, the BBC. Banks's colleagues included the Olympic athlete Christopher Chataway and a young former lawyer, Robin Day, who was to become the foremost screen journalist of his generation. While Day's inquisitorial interviewing style was applauded, the two women were not expected to work

on political stories and argued, unsuccessfully, for stories of more
significance than the 'soft stuff' to which they were confined.

When testing a teleprompter[22] one day, Banks needed some
sample text and so began to type on the device's keyboard. 'It was
unplanned [...] I typed the first few words of the book, which I
didn't know was a book at all, it was just a sentence, which led on to
another sentence, and halfway down the page I discovered that this
girl was going to have a baby. [...] I had no plan, no design'. While
Banks makes much of this random beginning, she had in fact already
begun her writing career, with three plays, *It Never Rains* (1954), *All
in a Row*, (1956) and *The Killer Dies Twice* (1956), of which the first
had been produced by the BBC.

Banks was born in London in 1929. Her father was a doctor and
her mother an actress. A decade later, with the outbreak of war, she
and her mother were evacuated to Saskatchewan in Canada for their
safety and stayed for five years. Banks has identified her time there
as the source of inspiration for the children's book she wrote many
years later, *The Indian in the Cupboard*. She also drew on Canada for
her 2014 autobiographical novel, *Uprooted – A Canadian War Story*.

> Since my mother was evacuated with me, I was very happy and
> though we were poor, I hardly noticed it, except that I couldn't
> have trendy clothes. I didn't really realise what the war meant,
> or the terrible things that had been happening, until I got back
> to England, at the very formative age of fifteen. I found my city
> in ruins and learned what had been happening to my family, left
> behind and, in Europe, to the Jews. I felt like a deserter.[23]

She was particularly moved by the images of the victims of Nazi
concentration camps, so horrific that they were not officially
released until after the war was over, emotions which were to have
a profound effect on her later life.

At eighteen Banks decided that she wanted to become an actress
and attended first the Italia Conti Stage School and then the Royal

Academy of Dramatic Art. After graduating, she spent some years in repertory theatre, on which she was able to draw for Jane, her protagonist in *The L-Shaped Room* and then followed several of her contemporaries on the path from acting to news broadcasting. Because she had already had some success as a playwright when she began *The L-Shaped Room*, she also had a literary agent, Ursula Winant at Richmond, Towers & Benson.

It took Banks two years to complete the novel and she has said she used it as a therapeutic contrast to her own personal life at the time, which seemed so much less troubled when she had spent a few hours with an unmarried mother in a rundown bedsit. She struggled to write the concluding scenes. 'I think it was Edna O'Brien who said, "nobody can finish a book without getting drunk. Somebody had given me a bottle of slivovitz."'[24] The book was accepted by Chatto & Windus, which she described as, 'one of the greatest thrills of my life'.

The novel's protagonist is Jane, a woman of twenty-eight who has given up an unsuccessful acting career – so far, so autobio-graphical – to work in the press office of a small and exclusive London hotel. With her thirtieth birthday approaching she is worried that she has never been in love and decides to reconnect with a boyfriend from earlier in her life. They make love but it is a miserable experience and neither sees the event as a renaissance of their relationship. A few weeks later she suspects that she is pregnant.

Everything Jane does next is motivated by her sense of shame. More time passes before she abruptly tells her widowed father, with whom she lives, that she is pregnant. Offended and shocked, he orders her to leave their home. Although able to afford to live in a good area, she chooses to rent a disgusting attic room infested with bedbugs in Fulham – at that time a deprived inner London suburb at the western edge of Chelsea. She falls in love with another tenant, Toby, a struggling writer, but alienates him and he disappears. The other occupants of the house – John, a black guitarist; Mavis, a retired wardrobe mistress and another Jane, one of the streetwalkers who live in the basement – offer her help and support. She loses her job, and then, when her immediate boss tracks her down and offers her money, she burns the cheque. She eventually accepts the support of an elderly aunt.

Rational, unsentimental but buffeted by storms of emotion, Jane argues with herself, observes herself, amazes herself when her instincts assert themselves. Twice she is offered the means to an abortion, but refuses this too. Slowly she forms the intention of having the baby and bringing 'him' up alone (at this point she imagines the child to be a son). A son he proves to be, and after the birth both her lovers return and proceed to fight over her. Her father also seeks her out and is reconciled and her aunt, whom Banks admits is a *deus ex machina* figure, dies and leaves her a house in her will. So, Jane's story finally ends happily.

1963: CHARLOTTE BINGHAM AND *CORONET AMONG THE WEEDS*

Charlotte Bingham was born into the heart of the British establishment, in several different respects. Her father, John Bingham, was to succeed to the title of 7th Baron Clanmorris in 1960 and among Charlotte's earliest memories is a trip with her nanny to visit her grandparents at their home, the grand Bangor Castle in Northern Ireland.

But Clanmorris was not a wealthy title and the money that remained to the family was tied up in a trust that owned their house, so her father also worked for MI5, the government office concerned with intelligence. Both her parents were also writers and their work contributed significantly to the family income. Her father's novel, *My Name is Michael Sibley,* appeared in 1952 to great acclaim and he went on to write sixteen more espionage and crime thrillers. Her mother, Madeleine Bingham, was a playwright who later also became a biographer, writing about great theatrical figures

Herbert Beerbohm Tree and Henry Irving, as well as Mary Queen of Scots. When Madeleine visited theatres in London to persuade the managers to stage her plays, she sometimes took Charlotte with her, so from an early age she understood something of the reality of a writer's life. It was clear, however, that her mother was not the senior author in the house. 'My father had an office, of course, but I remember my mother at her desk. Although she was very successful, she never had her own office'.[25]

When their daughter, the Honourable Charlotte Mary Therese, was born in 1942, his family were unaware of the precise nature of John Bingham's wartime work, which was later revealed to be in counter intelligence and political infiltration. John Le Carré, a junior MI5 colleague and author of many acclaimed thrillers, notably *Tinker, Tailor Soldier, Spy,* revealed many years later that he had in part based the central character, the spymaster George Smiley, on John Bingham. (It was in fact Bingham who introduced Le Carré to his literary agent, but his own literary career was to decline as Le Carré's gathered strength).[26]

Charlotte wrote her own thriller, entitled *Death's Ticket*, when she was ten and a pupil at a Catholic boarding school in Sussex. 'My parents though this was a very good effort for a 10-year-old'. She continued to write and voraciously read as a young teenager, scribbling under her desk in lessons and hiding forbidden historical romances by Jean Plaidy and Georgette Heyer under her mattress at school. At sixteen, at the time Françoise Sagan was at the height of her success in France, Charlotte was sent to Paris to live with an aristocratic family and perfect her French. She returned to London and was enrolled in a smart secretarial college, where most of the students, like her, were also doing the debutante season. A typist's job in the War Office, arranged by her father, soon followed.

By then the traditional ceremony of presenting debutantes to the Queen at Buckingham Palace had ceased but the season, fuelled by the enthusiasm of newly-rich families for instant social standing, continued regardless – a terrifying marriage-market into which young women were dispatched to take their chances at cocktail parties, dinners and balls with young man who were mostly wealthy, well-born and drunk. Emerging from a year of relentless sexual harassment and ruthless social climbing, Charlotte began what she intended to be a novel.

I took a firm decision. I said, 'Right, from now on, no going out for six months: no boyfriends, no social life, nothing.' It was almost like entering a convent, sort of now-or-never. I had to have some sort of achievement before I was twenty, you see, something recognisable to myself, anyway, because twenty seemed so awfully old. I panicked. I was writing the book at night ... Black clothes were de rigueur. I would come home, go straight upstairs, change, then I'd write from eight o'clock until one or two in the morning and at weekends. I used to play opera records all the time and I would just sit there, you know, until something came along. I used to work in my lunch-hour as well. I'd go down to the lower Ritz bar and they would give me orange juice and peanuts for two shillings and sixpence and I could be quiet for an hour'.

It is worth noting that her face must have been familiar to the staff at the Ritz, as at that time an unaccompanied woman in the bar of a West End hotel was usually assumed to be a prostitute and invited to leave.

It was the first full-length book I'd written and I honestly didn't think I'd sell it, but I thought I might — you know that funny feeling you get? Half-way through, my father read it and said, 'Keep it up, you might make a hundred pounds.'

Then I was walking down Bond Street on a beautiful evening in early April and it was finished. I thought that this was one of the most wonderful nights of my life, nothing would ever beat it, I would remember every single thing about it. I would remember

passing Asprey and the colour of the sky... I could see the Ritz
ahead of me so I went down there and ordered a Scotch and I said
to Laurie, the barman, 'This is a celebration because the novel's
finished at last.'

And suddenly, by my shoulder, my father's agent appeared and
said, 'Do let me read it'. I said no. I just felt it was too much:
your father's agent, he'd just be kind. But finally he said, 'Look,
I'm going away for the bank holiday weekend. If you leave it in
my office I'll let you know what it's like.' He rang me up later and
said, 'can sell this anywhere'. Then a few days after that he said,
'Oh, I've sold it'.[27]

As Helen Fielding was to do twenty years later with Bridget Jones's
Diary, Charlotte had chosen to write about an adorable airhead
in search of a man to love. *Coronet Among the Weeds* is a breathless
comedy narrated in the first person and a stream-of-consciousness
style, teeming with colloquialisms, some of which were then
fashionable and others the author's inventions. 'My mother kept
hoping I'd be intelligent,' says the un-named narrator, 'but I was a
disappointment'.

The 'weeds' of the book's title are the unattractive young men she
has encountered. The book opens with the reflection: 'I must have
been out with nearly three hundred men and I still haven't found a
superman. I don't know what a superman is, but there must be one
somewhere'. There is no real narrative, but a flow of events that
closely mirrored Charlotte's own life: moving from convent school
dancing classes at thirteen to Paris at sixteen; the tea parties and
hunt balls of the debutante season; with passing crushes, innocent
romances, predatory suitors, desultory jobs and girlish meditations
on life along the way.

Charlotte intended the book to be a novel but, once the serial
rights had been sold to *People*, a downmarket tabloid newspaper,
Coronet Among the Weeds was promoted as the scandalous tell-all
autobiography of Lord Clanmorris's daughter. An instant bestseller

in Britain, it was sold in ten countries around the world, leading to a
year-long promotional tour as well as photoshoots for *Life* magazine
and *Paris-Match*. Back in the UK, Bingham was nominated, with the
iconic fashion designer Mary Quant, as a Woman of the Year. She too
was catapulted into instant celebrity. Unlike Shelagh Delaney and
Edna O'Brien, her upbringing as an upper-class English girl had to
some extent trained her for public life, but the experience was no
less traumatic for that.

1963: NELL DUNN, *UP THE JUNCTION* AND *POOR COW*

Nell Dunn had the most privileged background of all the writers in
this group although the unsmiling expression in her portrait taken
by the great society photographer Cecil Beaton in 1954 suggests she
was not comfortable with her inherited status. She was her parent's
second daughter, born in 1936. Her mother, born Lady Mary Sybil
St-Clair Erskine, was the daughter of the 5th Earl of Rosslyn, whose
forebears include King Charles II and Nell Gwynn. Her father was
Sir Philip Gordon Dunn, who was to inherit more than £20 million
from his Canadian steel magnate father. Nell and her older sister
Selina were evacuated to America during the war, while her father
joined the army and her mother drove tractors, managed a team
of Land Girls and sheltered evacuees and Civil Defence workers
at their estate in Hertfordshire. In 1944 her parents divorced and
her mother married the artist and Arts Council director Robin
Campbell, although the Dunns then remarried in 1969.[28]

Dunn's father did not believe that his daughters needed any
qualifications and as a result she only learnt to read at nine years
old and, 'whenever my father saw my appalling spelling, he would
laugh. But it wasn't an unkind laugh. In his laugh there was the
message, "You are a completely original person, and everything you
do has your own mark on it". He wanted us all to be unique'.[29]

Rather than achievement, her father valued enjoyment. 'You
dressed for pleasure, you ate for pleasure. What has stayed with me

is the knowledge that pleasure exists and that it is absolutely the thing to aim for'. Dunn wrote her first play at the age of thirteen, while she was at a convent school. 'I remember the feeling of excitement and I wanted to be a writer. I still find writing the most interesting thing to do'.[30] Her English teacher encouraged her and made sure she read, 'the classics. So I was well read'. But her parents saw no value in education and so the next year, aged fourteen, she left school.

Three years later she met her husband, Jeremy Sandford, whose father was the owner of a historic fine publishing house, the Golden Cockerel Press, and a founder of the Folio Society. Sandhurst, Eton and Oxford- educated, Sandford was a surrealist and a writer who was forging a career writing documentaries and working for the BBC. His interests, he told the *Daily Mail*'s gossip column, included a dancing robot and training singing birds.[31] Dunn was twenty when they married, with a wedding reception for 500 guests at the Ritz, which they planned to leave by hot-air balloon.

Their first home was a flat owned by her father on the grandest of all Chelsea's streets, Cheyne Walk, but Dunn cites the loneliness of these eighteenth-century mansions that overlook the Thames as the reason they made an extraordinary move from the height of privilege in Chelsea to the area that faces it on the south bank of the Thames. Battersea at that time was still largely a slum. The steep, grimy streets huddled around a few small factories with a pub on every corner, overhung by a miasma of smoke and steam from the eponymous power station and the smell of malt from Young's Brewery in nearby Wandsworth. The homes were mostly nineteenth-century workers' cottages and, tiny as these are, they were mostly in multiple occupation. Although it would remain a deprived area for some decades, regeneration had begun there and Battersea had some gaiety, with its park – developed for the Festival of Britain in 1951 – where a permanent funfair, with its screams of delight, glittering lights and raucous music, tempted revellers across the Thames every night.

Dunn doesn't remember the move as consciously political. 'It was no big experimental business, you know. It didn't have that charge, I liked [Battersea] and I moved in'. In her newly-adopted home she discovered friendship and community. 'I had the only bath in the street so there was always a queue for it because my friends opposite had to fill a plastic bowl with water from the kitchen tap and then take it up to the tiny back bedroom they shared to wash'.[32] She sent her sons to the local school and in the mornings watched the other young women who lived on the street who 'would go singing down the road to work, stopping at the bakers to buy fresh rolls to eat as they walked along'. She joined them and got a job in a sweet factory wrapping liqueur chocolates for 2s 7d an hour – slightly less than the average price of a pound (400g) of butter at that time.

Dunn was inspired by the area, listening intently to the everyday chatter of the working-class women in her neighbourhood and developing the acute ear for dialogue which distinguishes all her work. 'Whatever small talent I had was that if I'd heard somebody speak for a few days, I could almost speak in their voice. It just happened that I could do it and I enjoyed doing it'.[33] She began to write short stories about the people around her and sent them to various London magazines, at first with no success. Finally, the left-wing political periodical the *New Statesman* began to publish them and she credits the then editor, Karl Miller, for teaching her how to edit her writing.[34] After four had appeared, MacGibbon & Kee, the publishing house cofounded by Robert Kee, a protégé of the historian A.J.P. Taylor and friend of George Orwell, and then at the start of a distinguished career as a broadcast journalist, wrote to her proposing to publish the stories as a collection. *Up the Junction* published in 1963 to critical acclaim and a storm of controversy. Dunn was awarded the John Llewellyn Rhys prize in 1964, the first woman to receive this award, which was made to writers under the age of thirty-five, for ten years. In the *Guardian*, the critic John Gross described it as 'a dozen or so sketches, none of them very long,' but allowed that it was, 'a highly accomplished book, truthful and likeable'.[35] Other critics, as we will see later, criticised the lack of narrative and voiced middle-class horror at the desperate lives portrayed, expressing revulsion to everything from the swearing to the wide range of illegal activities, from grand theft to betting, that the characters considered normal.

The junction of the title refers to Clapham Junction, the area around a major railway station south of Battersea. The sixteen stories are about young working-class women, written in sparkling vernacular interspersed with pop-song lyrics. The stories describe the girls, with their beehive hairdos and winkle-picker shoes, as they racket about from the factory to the pubs and dance-halls in search of fun and excitement, seeking a, 'handsome fella,' hoping for romance, sex or, at the very least, a motorbike ride. They talk wherever they are: on the production line, at the launderette, loitering outside the rock-bottom pawn-brokers they call 'rag shops'. The mood of the stories slowly hardens but buoyant comedy ultimately carries them through. Two stories tell of abortions, illegal but commonplace. Some of the girls make extra money as hostesses at the 'clip-joint', a halfway house to prostitution; some go to court to see a boyfriend sentenced for theft; others visit their lovers in prison or try to avoid to the petty extortions of the rent-collector. Death, in a graphically-described motorbike crash or in toothless old-age, finally darkens the picture.

Dunn moved on very quickly to a novel in the same vein, but focused on a single character. I am considering the two books together here as companions in territory and topic. Three years later, when *Poor Cow* was published, *Up The Junction* had sold 500,000 copies. *Poor Cow* is written in the same realist style but focuses on one character, Joy, the name of an actual friend upon whose life Dunn based the novel and explores more deeply the protagonist's sense self and of motherhood.

Joy walks home from the maternity hospital, puts her newborn baby on a café bench and asks, 'what did I go and get landed with him for, I used to be a smart girl?' A few days later her husband, Tom, comes home with a bag stuffed with money, filling her life briefly with comfort and security before he is convicted of theft and she is left destitute. She falls in love with her husband's friend, Dave, but he too is sent to prison, so Joy moves into a bedsit with her aunt and scrapes a living as a barmaid and 'model', another portal to sex work. Tom is released and they are reunited but he reverts to crime and becomes violent. As the story ends Joy realises that love for her child is, 'all that really matters'.

In a full-length work Dunn was able to experiment, using both first and third person and, as well as the sentimental song lyrics which characterise *Poor Cow*, punctuating the story with advertising slogans, thus contrasting the commercial dream with reality. 'Above her head an ad with a lot of golden girls in bathing suits read, COME ALIVE, YOU'RE IN THE PEPSI GENERATION. "Fuck that," she said, as the snow fluttered thoughtlessly against the window pane'.

In the public's perception these two books were almost immediately conflated with their screen interpretations, which followed very soon after publication. One of Dunn's friends, the poet Christopher Logue, had written a play for Ken Loach, at the time a young producer contributing to a new anthology drama series, *The Wednesday Play*, at the BBC. He gave Loach a copy of *Up the Junction*, which Dunn and Loach together turned into a script for a television play that was screened in 1965, when they were both 29-years-old. The cast were little-known working-class actors, including Carol White, who was to star in the feature film of *Poor Cow*, Loach's 'debut masterpiece', two years later. In the interim Loach he also directed *Cathy Come Home*, a script written by Dunn's husband, Jeremy Sandford, also a *Wednesday Play*, again starring Carol White, and telling a similar but more politically dynamic story of a homeless and abandoned young mother who sees her children taken into care.

1964: VIRGINIA IRONSIDE AND *CHELSEA BIRD*

> For the first three days of my life, during the mini-Blitz of
> London in February 1944, I was put, for safe-keeping, under a
> large mahogany sideboard in the ground-floor dining room of a
> private nursing home…
>
> One hundred and twenty linoleum-covered stairs above, my
> unhappy mother lay on a bed in a tiny room that contained a
> Victorian hand-basin, a pitcher and a small coal fire. She had
> given birth to me to the noise of shrapnel pattering on the roof
> and to the shuddering thumps of nearby bombs.[36]

Virginia Ironside's parents, Christopher and Janey Ironside. met
when they were both students at the Central School of Arts and
Crafts (later the Central School of Art and Design) in London. After
the war the small family lived modestly in Neville Street, just north
of the Fulham Road. By coincidence, Lord and Lady Clanmorris
and their daughter, Charlotte Bingham, lived a short distance away,
although their parents moved in different social circles and the
girls met only occasionally and by chance. The stucco-fronted early
nineteenth-century houses of this area are now home to millionaires
but were then little more than run-down terraces ending ended
in a bomb site where Ironside was not allowed to play with the
'common' neighbourhood children. 'Money was extremely tight',
and her mother was 'working her fingers to the bone and looking
after a fractious child in a wretched grey city that looked like one
huge bomb site'.[37] It would be some years before her father became
a successful artist, designer and a teacher at the Royal College of Art
and her mother a fashion designer, later – in the same institution –
mentoring a generation of iconic names in her newly established
and still controversial role as Professor of Fashion Design.

During World War II Christopher Ironside had worked in a
camouflage design unit. His colleagues there had now become
the leading lights of artistic life in London. Her mother loved to

entertain despite their limited means, and Christopher's success as an artist further drew a 'grand bohemian' set around them. While 'there had never been any question of my going to university', Ironside was taken to art galleries by her father and to France by her mother, sat for great photographers and heard artists and writers talking over her head every day. School was a tiny establishment run by her great-aunt a few streets from her home

Nurturing her only child was more difficult for Janey than blazing a trail in the new artistic discipline of fashion design. When her mother was drunk, as she increasingly was, Ironside felt that she was trying to 'suck every drop of youth, femininity and life out of me'. As a young child, she was shy and suffered frequent, severe headaches. She slowly became aware that there were tensions between her parents. One night when Virginia was fourteen, her father came home alone, explaining, 'you know Janey. I'm afraid when we go out, she gets drunk, and then she flirts with men, and the usual happened last night, and I said that either she came home with me or she needn't come home at all'. 'So has she gone for ever?' Virginia asked, and he replied, 'Well, I don't know, but it rather looks like it'.[38]

The next day her mother came home only to collect her belongings and leave. She was later to cite the pressure of her career and sexual incompatibility, rather than her alcoholism, as the reasons for the failure of their marriage.

Once the young Ironside's feelings of shock had passed, she 'didn't miss [her] mother at all. Apart from the weekends when [she] came round, I was totally happy, alone with Christopher, having him all to myself'.[39]

With the depression that was to follow her all her life already stalking her, she left school at fifteen and passed miserably through a finishing school in Paris, a secretarial college in Oxford, the crisis-ridden Chelsea College of Art and then on into desultory jobs, which included assisting the radical politician, Shirley Williams. Her first date was with one of the most fashionable actors of the day; her first love affair was an obsession with a fellow language student in Paris and largely a fantasy.

Her father had fallen in love and married again when Ironside was seventeen. While the newlyweds 'were downstairs, basking in all the pleasures brought by a new-found relationship, I lurked in my two upstairs rooms like a malevolent insect, a lone sniper, writing a book'.[40] She had already been so struck by the absurdities of fashionable London life that she had taken to excusing herself on dates and rushing to the cloakroom to write down her companion's most ridiculous lines.

Helped by an old schoolfriend, she joined the copywriting department of Vogue magazine, where a team of writers devised witty headlines and captions for fashion photographs. 'I was drifting ever closer to journalism,' she recalled. She wrote a 'short, funny and cruel'[41] monologue in the voice of one of her dates, which was published by *About Town*, a men's style magazine where the features editor was Michael Parkinson, later the successful chat show host.

'I was amazed. I had no idea that getting into print was so easy… I got a letter from a company called Secker & Warburg asking if I had ever thought of writing a book'. She was aware of the success of her neighbour, Charlotte Bingham, with *Coronet Among the Weeds* – indeed, this book was such a sensation that Bingham had become a household name in London. The two young women now had occasional conversations on the street, and Ironside felt encouraged by her example. She was not aware that publishers were actively looking for a follow-up, and she knew nothing more about the publishing industry. By sheer chance, her uncle Robin, an artist who was also a writer, was visiting when the letter arrived and was able to explain that Secker & Warburg were a distinguished publishing house. She had by then finished her novel and replied to Secker & Warburg by sending the manuscript. They immediately wrote back, offered her a contract and proposed the title, *Chelsea Bird*. 'Bird,' which was supplanted by 'chick' in cool conversations a few years later, was slang for a young woman.

The protagonist of *Chelsea Bird* is Harriet Bennett, an 18-year-old student at the fictional Pimlico Art School, where she is frequently absent and appalled at the ease with which she can manipulate her tutors. At this time, art schools were becoming a nursery of creativity in all media, shaping the minds of both artists and musicians. Each of the leading bands of the sixties had at least art school graduate in the line-up, including John Lennon in the Beatles, Keith Richards in the Rolling Stones and Pete Townshend in The Who. In portraying the vapid pretension of this imaginary institution, Ironside was questioning the roots of the new culture itself.

Harriet's voice drifts between existential alienation and sharp satire as she floats from King's Road cafés to cool new clubs in Chelsea and a succession of Saturday night parties, where she observes the photographers, models (male and female), actors, artists, reporters, advertising executives and fellow students who make up London's *jeunesse doree* – exactly the social circle in which Ironside herself had moved. Beyond the normal depths of teen angst, Harriet is burdened by an intelligence and sophistication that sets her apart from the crowd. She is quick to see through their struggles to be fashionable, which involve faking working-class accents and manners and trading cultural references they barely understand. She is joylessly promiscuous, is momentarily attracted to Nick, a bad-boy photographer, but feels more comfortable with her fatally uncool friend, Tom. Finally, when a routine pot-smoking party moves on to injectable drugs, she rejects the group entirely, goes back to art school to finish her course but then turns her back on the arts, taking an office job and noting the tragic lives of many of her old friends.

Ironside was nineteen when *Chelsea Bird* was published. It was widely reviewed and immediately established her as the symbol of her generation. Her publisher, Fredric Warburg, then sixty-six and a legend in London literary life, threw a party in his own home that was studded with famous writers but, with fashionable London at her feet, Ironside felt insulated by her depression and had no sense of pride or excitement. The book sold well enough, but she had to buy her own flat as her father now had young children and his new family had moved into a smaller home that did not have a bedroom for her. She had enough money to go on a solitary tour of America, 'more on automatic pilot than with a sense of adventure',[42] but the more feted she was, the more alienated she felt. Success had, 'absolutely no effect on the low opinion I had of myself'.

Back in London she was offered one of the most sought-after roles in journalism and Paul McCartney had her home telephone number, but the people closest to her, her parents, were emotionally unavailable. Her mother was fighting discrimination at work both as a woman and as the standard-bearer of a new popular culture. Janey was also sinking further into alcoholism while Virginia's father seemed distant, wrapped up in his work and his new family. Ironside had no protective relationship in her life at all and had begun a lifelong struggle against depression.

1965: MARGARET FORSTER AND *GEORGY GIRL*

Carlisle, where Margaret Forster was born on 25 May 1938, is so close to Scotland that it is often called a border town. Her family's, 'cramped, shabby'[43] home was on a council estate[44] and they lived, as many stable working-class families did at that time, a fiercely restrained life that was finely balanced on the edge of extreme poverty. In the days before socialised medicine and a fully-functioning welfare state, any change in their circumstances, an illness, injury or unexpected pregnancy, threatened destitution. Her father, Arthur, was an engineering worker, who was 39-years-old when World War II broke out and was employed at Skelton power station, ten miles away, during the conflict. Having only light industries, Carlisle suffered little physical damage in the war, although there were food shortages, its young men were conscripted and evacuees from cities vulnerable to bombing were billeted with local families.

When Forster was nearly five, her mother, a devout Christian, asked the advice of her vicar in finding the best education for her daughter, who could already read well enough to tackle the parish magazine. She went early to a good school and remembered herself as, 'bright-faced, eager, absolutely desperate to please',[45] rushing to the library when a teacher mentioned a writer called Dickens and she hadn't heard of him.

Forster's mother, like many of her generation, had given up a white-collar job as a clerk in the office of a senior official in the local government, the Medical Officer of Health, to become a full-time housewife. She had no choice in this matter as the government did not employ married women and her husband would not allow her to work anyway. With three children and increasingly poor health, she nevertheless worked tirelessly to keep the home clean and the family fed. From a young age, however, Margaret 'wouldn't accept that my role as a female was to serve on the domestic front'[46], and her mother's disapproval and father's assaults with a leather strap did nothing to persuade her otherwise. She had set her heart on going to the Carlisle and County High School for Girls and achieved the grades she needed a year early, at the age of ten. Once safe at this publicly-funded institution, her next goal was to go to university and leave home. She took holiday and weekend jobs wherever she could: in Marks & Spencer, in a laundry and delivering Christmas post.

Her parents had long been expressing reservations that her educational ambition would make her arrogant and unfeminine. Discussing books they considered showing-off. Social mobility was a frightening concept to them and the fact that university education was now available free with maintenance grants to students from poorer families only scared them more. Her mother was also afraid that her daughter's education would create a gulf between them. Both parents started arguments about her reading. 'My reading was seen as a weapon I used against my family, a way of absenting myself from their company. 'All she does is that damned reading,' my father complained, and it was true. It made me strange to them. I even took to going to bed at six o'clock to have peace to read [...] My family, especially my father, hated my retreat'. By now she was longing to leave home.

In December 1956, Forster interviewed at both Oxford and Cambridge, telling the dons that she wanted to write biographies after she graduated. She was offered a scholarship by Oxford, where the Principal of Somerville College, Dame Janet Vaughan, who had interviewed her, was already something of a heroine on the word of her school history teacher. Cambridge offered only an exhibition, so she chose Oxford and Somerville, the women's college that would later welcome the future prime minister, Margaret Thatcher, as a student. It proved to be a disappointment. The work bored her and the quaint regulations enraged her, although she made good friends there and met inspirational women academics.

It has been said of Margaret Forster that she and the Queen were the only women in the country to have fallen in love as teenagers and stayed faithful to one man for the rest of their lives. Forster met – and initially ignored – her future husband, Hunter Davies, in Carlisle, when she was seventeen. They continued 'courting' while he went to university in Durham and she endured her three years in the dreary ivory tower of Oxford. She and Davies married on 11 June 1960, the day after she finished her final university exam, with friends as witnesses but without any of her family.

Hunter Davies, recalled in his memoir[47] that Forster had by now abandoned her childhood ambitions to be a missionary or an MP, and now, at the age of twenty-one, wanted to be a writer'. They moved to London and into a rented flat in Hampstead and, while he began work as a journalist with The Sunday Times, then Britain's leading quality Sunday newspaper, she spent three months writing her first novel, Green Dust for Dreams. With no training in keyboard skills, she wrote in longhand, in pen and ink, then took another three months to produce a typescript on her husband's portable typewriter.

Davies's job was as an assistant writer on the Atticus column in *The Sunday Times*. The column was devoted to gossip from the publishing industry and at one time had been edited by Ian Fleming. The need to be acutely aware of every aspect of publishing would have made him an ideal source of information for a debut author. Forster sent her novel to a young agent, Michael Sissons, who was then at the start of a stellar career which later won him the title of 'godfather of the industry'.[48] He wrote back suggesting revisions but asked her to meet him. Forster took this, which Sissons intended to be encouraging, as a rejection, so the industry insight she had gained through her husband was effectively negated by her unworldly sensitivity. She abandoned the book, took a job as a supply teacher and a few months later, at the age of twenty-five, began another novel, *Dames' Delight*, subtitled *An Oxford Romp*. It won her one of the leading literary agents of the day: Graham Watson, managing director of Curtis Brown, whose authors included prime ministers and the aristocracy as well a stable of gifted new writers.

Watson sold the novel, a heavily autobiographical campus comedy, to the most dynamic editor of the day, Tom Maschler at Jonathan Cape, who was pre-eminent in the industry as an impresario of new talent, particularly the Angry Young Men. Since 1961 he had published Edna O'Brien's second and subsequent novels, and taken considerable pains to protect them both from legal action for defamation by people who believed they had been portrayed in her books. It is surprising that he did not at first recognise the same danger in Forster's novel. Eventually the text was read for libel when it was already in production. The lawyers advised substantial revisions, pointing out that many of the academic staff would be identifiable, as would some of the author's friends, one of whom was described as having had an inappropriate relationship with a teacher as a schoolgirl. The book was withdrawn, revised after lengthy

correspondence and reprinted. The cost of £95.10s borne by
Forster, a normal contractual obligation for an author. *The Observer's*
reviewer condemned it as, 'vulgar and silly', although some noted
the author's promise. Forster found the experience so bruising that
she disowned the book, later saying of it, 'pseudo-Salinger – I'd
give anything not to have published it'.[49] Almost immediately, she
decided to take a different creative direction with her writing and,
in later years, was to refuse all attempts to reprint *Dames' Delight*

Forster was pregnant with her first child and presiding over
the restoration of what would become the family home when she
began her next novel, but remained determined to achieve both
commercial success and critical acclaim for her work. She wrote a
novel that was Davies describes as 'totally fictional' although some
characters clearly related to people she had met while teaching at
Barnsbury School for Girls in Islington. Watson sold this to another
gifted publisher of the new generation, Tom Rosenthal at Secker &
Warburg, the house that had also published Virginia Ironside. The
novel was *Georgy Girl*.

Being tall, heavy, freckled and bespectacled, the heroine of this
social comedy considers herself excluded from normal life because
she is so ugly. Even her androgynous name, Georgy, suggests that
she barely qualifies as female.and in the text the author sometimes
calls her simply George. At twenty-seven she is a virgin and calls
herself 'desperate' for a man. At the start of the novel, a disastrous
visit to the hairdresser further confirms her belief that she is unfit
to receive the traditional 'rewards' of a young woman such as love,
a husband and a family. She seeks escape into innocent make-believe
by teaching dance classes to children.

The novel opens with Georgy's father, Ted, laying out a suit for
James, the wealthy man who employs both her parents as servants
in his Knightsbridge mansion. Trapped in a disastrous marriage to a
beautiful woman James wants Georgy to be his mistress, believing
that – although unattractive – she was, 'intelligent and knew how
to enjoy herself; those were the things that mattered'. Although

Georgy finds him attractive, she turns down his proposition and returns to the flat in Battersea that she shares with Meredith, a beautiful violinist and, frequently, Meredith's boyfriend, Jos.

Meredith discovers that she is pregnant. Jos and Georgy bond in their delight and excitement about the baby's birth and subsequently fall in love. When the baby is born and rejected by Meredith, Jos and Georgy initially live happily as a couple with the child but soon Jos starts to feel that Georgy's devotion to the infant is part of her 'talent for martyrdom' and leaves. Georgy visits her parents at James's palatial home and discovers that his wife has died and he is now determined to make her his. She agrees to marry him, on the condition that they adopt the baby and that James 'pensions off' her parents.

The novel was an amazing commercial success, although reviews were mixed and Forster fretted, 'how much longer am I going to be thought of as just "promising?"' Offers for the film rights came in even before publication and, as with Banks's *The L-Shaped Room,* the film adaptation of *Georgy Girl* gave the novel access to an audience outside literary London – for whom it had great resonance. After the film's release, sales of the book soared but Forster felt embarrassed by the novel itself, did little to identify herself with it publicly and started to explore different directions in her writing.

2

A MAN'S WORLD: SEXISM

The young female characters created by the young female writers in this book are captured in the process of becoming women, which immediately leads the authors to ask what being a woman means. The composite picture of womanhood created by these works captures women of that time in the process of asserting themselves and in doing so rejecting the definitions imposed on them by their society. The writers wrote about a life passage, a transition to adulthood, which they themselves were undergoing and it was painful at times – both Edna O'Brien and Charlotte Bingham recall crying constantly as they wrote.

The protagonists, from 15-year-old Jo in *A Taste of Honey* to 28-eight-year-old Jane in *The L-Shaped Room*, are finding out who they are and who they want to become. In *The Country Girls,* Edna O'Brien begins Caithleen's story in childhood and traces her whole path from child to adult, while others, such as Delaney, Bingham, Forster and Ironside, choose shorter timespans and describe only the key scenes in their heroines' lives. Because the stories that our women wrote are about young adults, reflections of themselves or their experience, they can be viewed as coming-of-age novels that illuminate the steps that the characters make towards adult identities.

In literary theory, this is the territory of the *bildungsroman*, the coming-of-age novel that focuses on life-lessons learned by young protagonists. The form has its roots in folk tales such as Jack and the Beanstalk or Aladdin, in which a youth disregards the anxieties of his parents, behaves foolishly but overcomes the consequences of his folly with courage and daring. It began to emerge in Western literature late in the eighteenth century and *Wilhelm Meister's Apprenticeship* by Goethe added philosophical dimensions to the picaresque template shaped by *The Life And Opinions of Tristram Shandy* by Laurence Sterne and Henry Fielding's *The Adventures of Tom Jones, a Foundling*. Novels such as *David Copperfield* and *Great Expectations* by Charles Dickens and *The Adventures of Tom Sawyer* and *Huckleberry Finn* developed the form, with young heroes transcending disadvantage with the help of guides, benefactors, their own courage and the innocence of youth.

The novels of Charlotte Brontë and Jane Austen show young women protagonists in a parallel but distinctly different struggle. Jane Eyre in particular has to break free not only from poverty and misfortune but from the limitations placed on her as a woman. Unlike the boys of the male *bildungsroman*, girl characters contend with the restrictions imposed on them by society on account of their gender. Physical escape and adventure are not possible for them so they find their paths to maturity by negotiating with the people who seek to define them. Added to courage and innocence is a purity of intent. Even though they are uncertain of their own identities, they pursue self-determination and live by their personal principles in the face of the hypocrisy of those who seek to control them.

In 1951 in America the coming-of-age novel was transformed again, this time by J.D. Salinger's *Catcher in the Rye*, which portrayed the adolescent male in an agony of self-absorption, alienated, lonely and depressed, rejecting in his own turn a world that seemed only hypocritical and materialistic. Holden Caulfield, the narrator-protagonist, had no real opponent. He is in conflict with himself and his own bleak worldview, not with any external disadvantage or oppressor.

For young women, however, the fight for freedom had only just begun in the 1950s. The works in this study portray them struggling to establish their identities, adjusting to social mobility and rejecting the experience of their parents' generation. They rush out into the world, challenge the expectations and limitations of the past and start to build a sense of self from their experiences. They observe their parents but cannot accept them as models for their own lives. Instead they set out into the unknown future with friends and mentors appearing to share the journey.

For some, like Jane in *The L Shaped Room*, the quest for self-discovery becomes ever more acute as her twenties pass without bringing her any positive sense of who she is. Her experience, as she views it, is only of failure but while she has already tried independent living, she is still looking for a love relationship to make her feel complete. In contrast the younger characters in these works are only beginning to explore the world and collect the experiences through which they will define themselves. While it is remarkable that the protagonists in these works fight the same fights whatever their social class or level of wealth. It is also very clear that the middle-class heroines have more agency as a result of their ability to earn money, while the working-class characters are often shown as completely helpless.

The young women in these novels emerge into a world that is completely dominated by men. Economically, men are the only employers. As partners, men are the only means of support for mothers and children. As friends or lovers, they are barely possible unless they are marginalised characters like Geof in *A Taste of Honey* and or John in *The L Shaped Room,* whose disadvantages given them equivalent social standing to the young single mothers in these novels. It is only with marginalised male characters that they can achieve any sense of equality. The characters of men as fathers are either absent or brutally cruel. As strangers, men are often casually abusive and believe that this is amusing and makes them more desirable. In these works, the men who are positive figures are largely, like the heroines, viewed as inferior by the dominant male characters.

These works show young women confronting a world in which their own needs are denied. However privileged or deprived the society being portrayed, the needs of the men are the only ones recognised. Sexual harassment and violence are commonplace. At an everyday level, women are treated as inferior beings. In Edna O'Brien's *The Country Girls,* Caithleen's Dublin landlady, a character partly based on O'Brien's mother-in-law, gives her male lodgers better food. Jo's mother, in *A Taste of Honey*, asks her daughter's gay friend about her boyfriend and when her daughter speaks up for herself retorts, 'When I'm talking to the organ grinder, I don't expect the monkey to answer'.

The mothers in these books are often portrayed negatively and vary from monstrous to absent, with the exception of Edna O'Brien's mother figure in *The Country Girls* who is not judged by her daughter for colluding in her abusive marriage but viewed with tenderness throughout the novels. In general, the mothers of these characters do not provide offer them with a model for their own lives. In *Coronet Among the Weeds,* Charlotte Bingham portrays her narrator's mother as distant and uncomprehending, separated by a generational gulf from her daughter. In contrast, Helen, the mother in *A Taste of Honey*, is selfish, domineering and proud of it: 'Have I ever laid claim to being a proper mother?'

In many of these books, it is the girls' female friends who are the most important companions on their journeys. In *The Country Girls* trilogy, Caithleen and Baba are inseparable until different experiences in marriage begin to pull them apart. Similarly, in *Coronet Among the Weeds* there is Migo to share the narrator's adventures. Older single women, such as Jane's aunt, Addy, in *The L-Shaped Room* or Joy's Aunt Emm, a retired prostitute, in *Poor Cow* offer support or sanctuary but cannot provide the young heroines with a viable pattern for their own lives.

PURPOSE AND AGENCY

The women in these novels are universally struggling to find a bearable existence in a society that largely negates their identity.

Typically, those with caring parents, such as Caithleen in *The Country Girls* or the narrator of *Coronet Among The Weeds*, follow the path mapped out for them according to the needs of the family, although they know it is not what they would choose for themselves. Those with parents who don't care for them, like Jo in *A Taste of Honey* or Nell Dunn's characters, are left to determine their own destiny, to let their lives be shaped by accident or chance. Either way, the young women are reactive, rather than active, protagonists. However appealing some are as narrators, they express no sense of self-determination. Instead they respond to the actions of others – their families, lovers or partners – or to random events, but struggle to know what they themselves want. Often, they feel their lives are chaotic and so they appear as such to other characters as well.

There is a telling exchange in *A Taste of Honey* after Geof, the gay man who becomes a companion to Jo, finds some of her drawings.

Geof: Are these yours?
Jo: No, why. Put them down, Geof.
Geof: Obviously they are. They're exactly like you.
Jo: How do you mean?
Geof: Well, there's no design, rhythm or purpose.

In another conversation, later in the same act, Jo articulates her feelings about life.

Jo: Oh, Geof, the bulbs I brought with me! …They never grew…They're dead. It makes you think, doesn't it?
Geof: What does?
Jo: You know, some people like to take out an insurance policy, don't they?
Geof: I'm a bit young for you to take out one on me.
Jo: No, you know, they like to pray to the Almighty just in case he turns out to exist when they snuff it.

Geof: Well, I never think about it. You come, you go, it's simple.

Jo: It's not, it's chaotic – a bit of love, a bit of lust and there you are. We don't ask for life, we have it thrust upon us.

At the other end of the social spectrum, Charlotte Bingham's un-named narrator in *Coronet Among The Weeds* expresses the same sense of directionless drift in her year as a debutante.

Being a deb tailed off really. I went on being one officially till the end of that year. But I didn't feel like one much. I didn't feel like anything much. I just felt like someone who has been a beatnik and a deb, and rather bad at both. I didn't know what to be or anything. I didn't want to go on being a deb because I wasn't much good. And I didn't want to be a secretary. So I just kept going to all these parties to stop thinking about anything at all.

Harriet, the art student in Virginia Ironside's *Chelsea Bird*, is almost smothered in despair. 'Art school was awful. All my friends were awful. My room was awful. My dimples were awful. I had a vague feeling that I should be doing something, like writing a book or going to visit old ladies'.

BLAMING HERSELF

Emerging from this sense of powerlessness is the belief that when a bad thing happens to a woman, she is responsible and therefore guilty. *The L-Shaped Room* can be read as a novel entirely about self-blame and in its first pages Jane remembers an event which is a microcosm of the spiral of self-destruction that follows later. A drama school graduate, Jane has defied her father's predictions of failure and got a job in a stage repertory company. On a provincial tour she becomes attracted to one of the actors. Another member of the company, in love with the same man, finds them kissing and attacks Jane, inflicting cuts on her face that leave permanent scars.

Although they push away the attacker, the actor does not try to protect or defend Jane. In fact, nobody does, even though the facts of the event are soon widely known. Jane runs away from the scene and vomits from the shock. Her immediate reaction is to leave the company, throwing in her dream job and the salary that goes with it. She never considers complaining about the assault.

When her attacker comes to apologise and, in an emotional scene, begs her to stay with the company, Jane feels overwhelmingly guilty. 'I could imagine how, in a day or so, I would relive this scene and wish I had petted him and comforted him and forgiven him and agreed to stay, making it all his fault. But at this moment I knew it was my fault'. And so, she gives up the job and with it her fragile and tentative ambitions.

Jane's relationship with the actor fails and she finds herself broke with nowhere to live, too proud to go home. The idea of simply looking for another job in the theatre never seems to occur to her. Determined to punish herself, she gets a backbreaking job in a cheap cafe where the owner exploits her local notoriety and finds it amusing to threaten not to pay her at all. After she loses her temper and yells at him they establish a kind of bantering relationship, a connection that is based on her willingness to accept verbal abuse with good humour. After two months of drudgery she returns to London with £15 in savings and a very temporary belief that, 'I can do anything'.

Jane's sense of self-worth is short-lived, however. With no mother (her mother died some time before the story begins) she returns to the family home, which she shares only with her father, to the steady downpour of his denigration.

For months on end you've kept me, and every day of those months I've been aware of it. I felt you were wondering if I had no self-respect; not that you grudged the cost exactly, but I knew you were asking yourself what sort of person could live on her father when she was over twenty-one, rather than give up calling herself an actress… And when at last I gave in and started going to

secretarial school, do you think I wasn't conscious all the time
that this was the second career you'd paid to train me for. The day
I took my first secretarial job you told me I'd never stick it, that
any girl who could be content to sit behind a typewriter all day
must be a cretin... What do you want of me, Father? I thought
fiercely. What have you ever wanted?

When Jane realises she is pregnant with the actor's child she is too
afraid of her father to tell him for several weeks; when she does,
she feels responsible for upsetting him. He calls her 'no better than
a street-woman' and orders her to 'clear out'. Although she can
afford better, Jane chooses an infested room in the 'ugly, degraded'
district of Fulham (as it then was), describing herself as at 'rock-
bottom'. As the novel continues, Jane's room eventually begins to
supply her with a sense of identity, which she builds from the most
basic level of confronting the landlady about the bed-bugs.

This trajectory is the greatest illustration of the propensity many of
the women in these works display to blame themselves for bad things
that are not their fault. Several psychological studies have established
the links between depression, self-blame and low-self-esteem,
suggesting that the one is frequently associated with the others[1] and
the link between self-blame and low self-esteem is particularly strong.
Thus these authors depicted young women suffering a degree of
depression simply because they placed so little value on themselves.

SUPERMAN

The protagonist of a *bildungsroman* is defined as male, while a coming-
of-age novel about a girl who becomes a woman is called a *fraueroman*
by literary theorists. The essential difference is that the *fraueroman* is a
love story, in which the heroine's relationship defines her, whereas for
the hero of a *bildungsroman* a relationship of the male protagonist with
a woman is either absent or insignificant. If we are to consider *Jane
Eyre* or *Pride and Prejudice* as female *bildungsromans* it must be noted

that the relationship between the female protagonist and the most significant male character, while still central in the story, functions differently in allowing the female protagonist to discover her true needs. So it is even more remarkable that, in the works in this study, while some of the female characters do fall in love, the relationship is not their defining element, the focus of their quest nor the axis of the narrative. This was a revolutionary development in women's writing and one which prefigured the rethinking of primary relationships that was sparked by second-wave feminism at the end of the sixties.

At opposite poles of privilege, Joy in *Poor Cow* and the unnamed narrator of *Coronet Among the Weeds*, are the only ones in search of 'happy ever after' in the sense of a relationship that will shape their lives. From the novel's opening sentence, the narrator of *Coronet Among the Weeds* declares that she is on a quest for a superman. 'I don't know what a superman is. But I know there must be one somewhere'.

She searches diligently but unsuccessfully throughout the novel and in the last chapter concludes, 'I think you can class most men. Supermen, weed, drip, lech'. She continues to describe an encounter with one man who does not fit her classification system, whom she calls a 'vagabond' because of his desire for personal freedom. She also remembers being seized by the same instinct as a child, when running away from school, an act that provoked anger from her mother and punishment from the convent's matron, who carried a rosary and told her she would 'burn in hell'.

This unnamed vagabond becomes a catalyst to her own self-determination, reviving her instinct to break free from the expectations of her family and class and validating her independent spirit. After meeting the man by chance as they are walking along a country road, she spends a day at his large house nearby, in conversation. 'All the things you believe in your heart but you're not quite sure you're not a nit believing in them. He made you sure. When he told you about things. Suddenly you knew you were right to believe in the'. Although they talk about their experiences of love, the encounter isn't sexual. But it gives the narrator confidence in herself, for the first time in her life.

> He made you so certain you were right you could burst. You just thought you must have been mad before not to have been sure. And you were never going to not be sure again... He made you not mind about being you. Not someone who cared about corny old abortions. Not mind about having big hips or a pretty funny face. Or anything. Nothing mattered because here was someone who believed in magic and enchantment.

Physical well-being isn't an issue for Charlotte Bingham's narrator, living as she does among the wealthiest families in Britain. At the other end of the wealth spectrum, in *Poor Cow*, Joy lives in poverty but, as with Bingham's narrator, freedom is offered in the form of a man – in Joy's case, a lover who will save her from a perilous life that swings from prostitution to welfare. Dave and Joy spend only a few months together, but at the end of the novel he is behind bars, serving a twelve-year prison sentence. When Joy's deadbeat husband returns from prison, he arbitrarily moves her and their son to a new area, where she is friendless and isolated. He imposes control over every aspect of her life, even the way she styles her hair and finally becomes violent. Joy runs out of their flat in terror, goes to a friend's home and gets drunk, then tries to make sense of her emotions. She cannot reconcile the role of a subservient wife with her need to express herself, even if that expression is only in enjoying small pleasures.

> I want so many things – I don't know what I want, I'm so mixed up I don't know what I do want. If only I could find something worthwhile in life. Now Dave, he made it worthwhile – everything we done together he made it all a treat. Even going up the launderette was a laugh. But Tom, if you so much as mention a man at the buses stop engaged you in conversation, he'll say, 'You're always after men, I 'spose you were looking at

him'. ...If only I had a car – I'd be able to get away – drive off and find somewhere where there weren't no bleeding women with prams, where there weren't no television to sit in front of night after night and no bleeding husband to clamp down on every little whim that might come my way...I suppose my life is over – you only get one chance – it's not that I'm even suffering. I don't really care now I've lost Dave.

EVERYDAY SEXISM IN 1958

In their encounters with men, the female protagonists in these novels almost always accept an astonishing level of misogyny. In *The L-Shaped Room*, Jane recalls her first day in her job.

James, on my first morning, in response to some mistake I made, took occasion to inform me at the top of his voice that I was a silly stupid ignorant cow and that all women of my stamp should be lined on against a wall and mown down with a flame-thrower. He went on to say that while this was going on he would be laughing and dancing with glee and warming his hands at the merry blaze.

In spite of this, Jane finds this a 'pleasant change' from other employers, and replies with a witticism which amuses him. They swiftly develop a good relationship and he offers her a permanent job.

Among the art students of *Chelsea Bird*, Harriet has a brother-sister relationship with Tom. When they go on a date he orders her meal for her without asking her what she wants to eat or drink. She tells the reader that she finds his pomposity endearing, but later rages, 'Damn God for making me a girl expected to simper when a man makes fatuous remarks'.

THE PROSTITUTE

The figure of the prostitute appears in all these works, personifying an identity that threatens every heroine. The prostitute haunts the pages like a warning ghost and, at some point, all but one of the central characters asks herself, 'how am I different?' Her presence underscores the transactional nature of the women's relationships and the fragility of their sense of self-worth. Every heroine gets the there-but-for-the-grace-of-God feeling when a prostitute appears. The economic dependence on men to which most women had been condemned for centuries no doubt prompts this comparison, but women were not the only people to question the moral implications of living on a man's earning power. Nell Dunn's first husband, Jeremy Sandford, responded to a question from a journalist about their marriage by saying, 'I fell for a rich girl because I think money in girls is sexy and glamorous. They can do what they want. They're not scheming. Middle-class girls are just whores, selling themselves for security'.[2]

For some of these writers, the prostitute is more concept than reality, a shameful shadow that calls the integrity of their lives into question, but for others she is a close companion, showing them their likely fate if they do not resolve their need for security and intimacy. Even the narrator of *Coronet Among the Weeds*, drifting through a privileged world of debutante parties and desultory jobs, makes the comparison with prostitution several times, asking herself where the distinction lies between being a 'tart' and having promiscuous sex at a beatnik party or marketing herself to an agency recruiter. '...they usually say they only take on nice girls. So you try and look madly nice and know you're going to loathe all the other nice girls. Sometimes I think I'd rather be a tart than go to another interview. Still I suppose even if you're a tart you have to be interviewed by a pimp'.

To Harriet in *Chelsea Bird,* acutely uncomfortable with the anarchic social experiments of her art student friends, a prostitute is an aggressive and frightening intrusion from the real world. Like Charlotte Bingham's narrator, she struggles to resolve the casual promiscuity that is fashionable in her circle with the traditional view that 'nice girls' don't have sex. Out on a date with Tom, Harriet passes the traditional sex-workers of the time – prostitutes in Soho looking out for customers from their doorways. Frightened that one of the women will abuse them, she tries to hurry past, but Tom is keen to show off his liberal values.

'You mustn't be so shy, Harriet. Tarts are just as much human beings as you or I.'

One leant out of a doorway, and he winked at her, and she winked back. (Now I was afraid that they might start a long conversation, both trying to find out how the other half lived, and I would be left to catch a taxi home. Why was Tom driven to be so chummy with those people? A nice, frightened person would be scurrying along the streets, squeaking with fear and embarrassment.)

'What a super swinging birdie,' announced Tom.

Jane in *The L Shaped Room* chooses to live in a building where the basement is occupied by two prostitutes. She does not meet them until she has started a relationship with another lodger, Toby, to the distress of a third, John. Living in the room below Jane's, John has heard them making love and, unable to reconcile his jealousy, suggests that Toby has gone, 'downstairs with the other whores'. As if to define her difference, Jane knocks on the basement door. One of the women answers the door in a dressing gown with rollers in her hair. 'I stood staring at her. She was a good twelve years older than me, but allowing for that, I'd seen myself look not much better some mornings in the past few months'.

They have tea, and a chat, and the prostitute recounts her life story as she puts on her makeup and gets ready to go out to work. As they leave, she says:

'You go ahead, dear, and I'll follow you after a minute or two. You don't want to be seen with me.'. And before I could protest, she went on: 'I hope you found out what you wanted to know… What a lousy night! I hate this bloody mist, it gets into everything and makes your hair straight'. It was the first time she'd sworn… My language was considerably worse than hers... Looking after her, I saw her reach up and tuck a strand of hair into place before the dark mist swallowed her up. I suddenly remembered her name was Jane.

In *Georgy Girl* it is the heroine's mother who raises the question, after refusing to look after the baby that Georgy has adopted. Her argument, extracted in a bitter conversation with a parent she hates, is that Georgy will be considered an immoral woman and the child also stigmatised, because she is not married.

Doris set her lips, grimly. She wasn't going to be got round. 'They'll ask questions at any nursery', she warned, 'and then you'll cop it. They'll soon find out you're not fit to bring up a child'. 'What do you mean – "fit"', shouted George, 'I'm sick of hearing you say it. I'm not a crook, or blind or anything. I don't go around drinking or swearing or gambling. You'd think I was a prostitute the way you're talking. I'm perfectly fit'. 'It's no good shouting', said Doris. 'You're not married'.

It is the female working-class characters in these books, however, who feel closest to prostitution, as the reality of their economic dependence becomes clear. In *A Taste of Honey*, Jo's mother, Helen, is introduced as 'a semi-whore' in the second line of the play and Jo describes them as, 'living off her immoral earnings', a description borrowed word-for-word from the legal definition of pimping. Helen appears to be unemployed and relying on her fiancé for money and, as the play unfolds, she several times makes assumptions about Jo's financial circumstances, unable to understand that her daughter took several unskilled jobs in the early days of her pregnancy and has managed to save money.

Prostitution is almost normalised in *Poor Cow*. It becomes a possibility that confronts Joy as soon as her husband is sent to prison and she has to now provide for herself. She avoids it by moving in with her Aunt Emm, who lives on welfare, and is haunted by memories of her younger days as a streetwalker. Joy dreams of finding, 'a man of position' but gets a job in a pub and makes a friend in Beryl, another barmaid, who tells her how she once worked as a prostitute's maid, 'and then I figured I might as well have the two quid as well as her.'

Beryl offers Joy some pearls of wisdom: 'If you ever have any blokes, don't let them have it for nothing. You must charge 'em. I know you, you're soft. You must say, "Here, I'm a bit hard up", or something like that or, "Could you let me have a few bob?" You've got to get something out of them or they'll just use you – just use yer body – then go back to their wives and children.'

Joy enjoys sex for its own sake and doesn't ask the men she finds attractive for money. She doesn't see all sexual relationships as something to be monetised but is soon supplementing her meagre pay by asking the men she doesn't like for money. 'It makes you feel sick but the money comes in handy', Beryl says. The two women also earn money glamour modelling, effectively an organised soft-porn business in which men pay to photograph them in their underwear. They get £2 an hour for it, when their weekly wage might be only £3. Joy enjoys modelling and it gives her some personal confidence. 'When stripped before the cameras she was a queen… "Well, I love flaunting in the nude put it that way. Tom [husband] used to say no one would have me, you know, 'I don't know what's lovely about you,' but now I know there is something about me."'

When Joy is laid off by the pub, sex-work is the only employment she can get and she is poised to follow her aunt into full-time prostitution. Shortly afterwards, her husband comes out of prison and, although she no longer loves him and has begun divorce proceedings, she agrees to go back to him, reasoning, 'I haven't got a lot to give up'.

ACCEPTANCE
The writers are unsparing in portraying the injustices and inequalities which women suffered, yet they are very rarely angry – either with

the men in their lives or with men in general. They may despise some of the men they meet – even Charlotte Bingham's heroine, determinedly optimistic as she is, condemns the majority of them as 'weeds' – but they seldom judge them. Sometimes the protagonists ridicule men who make themselves ridiculous, as Joy does with some of her pub's customers. Individual men who behave contemptibly, like the doctor who tries to persuade Lynne Reid Banks's heroine to have an abortion, are condemned for their behaviour, but men in general are not blamed for the overall inequity of the women's lives. Edna O'Brien's Caithleen, in *The Country Girls* feels a kind of enchantment for Mr Gentleman, never questioning his motives in giving her rides home from school and gradually sexualising their relationship. Her deeply romantic nature means that she is an easy victim for a sexual predator.

In contrast to many novels of the second-wave feminism era, the women in these works are surprisingly free of rage or bitterness. They are often conscious that their position is disadvantaged and would like the world to be different but – perhaps because they are so young – the wider picture of inequality is not clear to them Nell Dunn, the writer who had the most potential to weave political argument into her stories chose not to do so. Instead, the writers relied on the authenticity of their stories, putting the truth before their readers and inviting them to make up their own minds.

3

FORBIDDEN KISSES: CLASS

Social class is a British obsession. It is an informal, unwritten and all-pervasive system of division by which people define themselves and others. Class is a complex consensus, constantly evolving and forever developing new layers of nuance, but in all of British history the most dramatic transformation of the class system took place in the time of these writers. The changes were so profound that it seemed as if the old order was swept away overnight, bringing in a new dawn of egalitarian values and boundless aspiration. Within the space of just a few years ruling elites were dispossessed and the citadels of power captured by the former underclasses. The mood was summed up during a Beatles show at the Royal Variety Performance in 1963, when John Lennon, inviting the audience to join in on the last song, said, 'The people in the cheaper seats, clap your hands,' then smiled at the Queen Mother in the royal box and added, 'And the rest of you, if you'd just rattle your jewellery'. The Queen Mother waved, the audience laughed and the revolution seemed complete. The following year the Labour leader Harold Wilson, grammar-school educated and with a distinct Yorkshire accent, defeated the right-wing Conservatives and became the youngest prime minister for seventy years. He was forty-seven. In 1965 all four Beatles were awarded the MBE in the Queen's Birthday Honours.

While the change seemed sudden, the drivers of it had in fact been gathering strength for decades. From 1918 free education for children up to the age of fourteen had created a population that was 91 per cent literate by 1961[1]. Added to mainstream education were many schemes that gave for adults from poor backgrounds access to arts and culture. For some decades, working-class people had been able to develop the skills to understand their world and take part in shaping it. The trade union movement, in supporting the Labour party, had created real political power for working class people and broken up old systems of patronage.

Successive governments throughout the century had plundered the personal fortunes of the wealthiest in Britain, raising inheritance tax rates and lowering tax thresholds. Noel Coward's famous ditty, 'the stately homes of England, how beautiful they stand, to show the upper classes still have the upper hand', was sung satirically for the first time in 1937 and chronicles the impact of punishing taxation on those who had wealth to inherit, who are forced to sell their possessions and watch the ancestral homes they cannot afford to maintain decay before the next generation demolishes them and sells the land, a cycle to which Charlotte Bingham alluded in *Coronet Among the Weeds.*

Conscription in the two World Wars had forced together people of different backgrounds who might otherwise never have even spoken to each other and the result was a sudden awareness of privilege or deprivation, and a democratisation of taste in everyday life, the 'sergeant's world', as observed by Evelyn Waugh. The country's great centres of heavy industry and manufacturing were now in decline, with output reducing from 40 per cent of the economy in 1946 to 10 per cent today, meaning that millions of young people left the ghetto-like working-class slums of industrial centres and found white-collar jobs in the growing service sector, thus expanding the middle class. But there were still deep divisions between the classes which the writers in this study capture in crystalline detail in their works.

The desperate poverty of Nell Dunn's Battersea is casually but unsparingly portrayed. In *Up The Junction* local women wait at the rag shop for the 'totters', the rag and bone men who walked the streets with carts collecting old clothes and reusable rubbish. Under a sign that reads HIGHEST PRICES PAID FOR GOLD, SILVER AND ARTIFICIAL TEETH, the women wait to get first pick of the old clothes when the totters pass by with their barrows. Joy in *Poor Cow*, living in one room with her baby son, boils water in a bucket for his bath because the house has no hot water system.

The gulf between the poorest members of society and those in the middle classes seem unbridgeable in these works. Almost none of the characters meet or mix with those of a different status. Occasionally the divide was bridged such as when Joy, as a barmaid, serves men in white-collar occupations: salesmen, engineers, small time entrepreneurs, though, 'they might have been from Mars for all the communication she could have with them'. She thinks of, 'taking elocution lessons and becoming select' but has no concept of what being 'select' might mean, other than the 'decent' or 'respectable' attribute of not having sex. Her letters to her lover when he is in prison make it clear that she is barely literate, but her focus is on sounding or looking good, rather than on education.

The divide between the classes is uncomfortably illustrated when Joy decides to divorce her husband and visits a lawyer. At the poorly-appointed office the receptionist and typist act disdainfully towards her and she struggles to understand the man's questions.

Joy sat in the chair and looked at the solicitor. He had a smooth face and a grey suit. 'How can I ever get through to him', she wondered.

'No, he didn't have a job – he gave me what he earned'.

'You mean illicitly'.

'What does that mean?'

The man shifted in his chair and wrote on a large sheet of paper, with 'Steadman' on the top right hand corner.

'I'm working at this pub but I can't go every day because of my little boy. I have a fiver a week and I make it do.'

'So really, you exist, you live, on five pounds a week?' the solicitor looked at her amazed.

Class difference, from Joy's perspective, is about small gradations of wealth, so she takes pride in finding the money for her son to have the same toys and amusements as richer kids in the neighbourhood in order to maintain his status. She and her friends also see social mobility as having to give up pleasures and accept unwelcome restraints for the sake of appearing superior. Deferring gratification, as she understands it, is a hypocritical process, only about demonstrating social status, not about giving up momentary fun for lasting later benefits. Later, in the pub, she tells her friend about the encounter in the lawyer's office.

'Do you think them sort of people ever really know trouble?' she asked Beryl.

'In the upper classes you can get around, that's the best thing about the upper classes. But there are a lot of people that have got plenty of money and would like to be like us – go out, have a good time, but they can't – they have to be careful over the people they mix with'.

'I've heard it said there's as many abortions among that sort of person as there is among us – thought they don't use the same methods'.

Peter, the car salesman who is the lover of Jo's mother in *A Taste of Honey*, also correlates poverty, immorality and inferiority – all conditions he despises. He complains about the cockroaches in Jo's bathroom and demands her mother leave the apartment, saying, 'I don't like the smell of unwashed bodies, woman. I dragged you out of the gutter once. you want to go back there it's all the same to me ... it's your own bloody level'.

Georgy Girl is a novel which is substantially situated on a fault-line in the class structure, since Georgy, the heroine, has been brought up as the daughter of two living-in servants and is courted by and eventually marries James, the wealthy man who employs them. Her inferiority as a woman is underscored by the fact that her parents are his servants and further highlighted by the fact that there is a real companionship between master and manservant. The novel begins with Ted, her father, getting one of his employer's suits ready to wear, pressing and brushing it, enjoying the exclusive bespoke tailoring but disliking the garments' sober style.

> James was a lot taller and a lot fatter, which maybe explained why he picked what Ted thought very quiet suits. They had no go in them at all, not like their owner. James was all go and always had been, which was why he went on being rich. But Ted and he were very alike in other ways, suits apart. They both liked football, cars, television and the music hall as it used to be.
>
> James picked Ted up at a music hall … Ted noticed James, which wasn't surprising as James was very imposing looking, and James noticed Ted, which was surprising because Ted was very ordinary. He was small, seedy and at that time thin because it was 1935 and he was out of work. James wore a beautiful fur coat and a rakish hat tilted over one eye. Ted didn't have a coat of any sort.

Ted follows 'the toff' into the street after the show, hoping to see his car as, 'he looked rich enough and dashing enough to be a car man'. When he admires James's Rover, they strike up a conversation, the beginning of the companionship that Ted values as much as the comfortable life and economic security which comes with the job James offers him. James effectively rescues Ted and his wife, Doris, from a life of unrelieved poverty and in return Ted gives him faithful service, lifelong gratitude and, when he and Doris have a child, a surrogate daughter.

> Sometimes Ted forgot Georgy was his daughter and not James's. She was his gift to James in a way, his living sacrifice on the altar of gratitude he'd erected. When she'd been born Ted had been bitterly disappointed. It would have been so much more

impressive to make over a son … luckily, he discovered that James had two other names – George and Charles – and so he called his daughter Georgy Caroline and been very satisfied.

Both Georgy and Doris feel that being a servant is an emasculating role for Ted and occasionally try to persuade him to find an independent job, which leads to family arguments. Their own social inferiority does not trouble them until, at the beginning of the story, James asks Georgy to become his mistress. She rejects him but does not tell anyone about the proposition. The anger she suppresses surfaces as increased contempt for her father, which she begins to voice at lunch with her parents.

'The trouble with you', said Ted, cutting his meat viciously, 'is that you don't realise how lucky you are, and you never have done. Living rent free in this beautiful house, everything you could possibly want and nothing to worry about. You'd have known about it if I'd gone on being a two pound a week mechanic'.

'Mechanics are quite well paid these days,' said George suddenly.

'You be quiet. You're a fine one to talk – you've had everything money could buy from Mr James'.

'Is there anything he couldn't buy from you?' said George suddenly.

'No, and I'm proud to say it. There isn't anything I wouldn't give a fine gentleman like Mr James. Not that there's a thing he wants. He's clever enough have seen to that'.

'Would you give him me?' pressed George. 'If he asked you to, and gave you £100, would you have me chopped into small pieces and presented to him?'

Ted thumped the table and rose to his feet.

'By God, I won't have you mocking Mr James. I'll thrash you if you talk like that again'.

At the end of the novel, when James proposes marriage and Georgy accepts, pragmatically, for the sake of her adopted daughter, she has only one condition – that he fire her parents.

> 'One thing,' said George. 'My mother and father. I don't want them around when we are married. You can sack them'.
> 'Ted?' said James, perturbed. 'What would he do?'
> 'That's something he should have found out for himself a long time ago,' said George.
> 'I'll pension him off, handsomely,' said James.
> 'You can do what you like, as long as he isn't here to kow-tow to you when we get back,' said George firmly.

Georgy's relationship with her parents, never warm or supportive, deteriorates over the course of the novel, so that the reader can imagine that her hostility to them is as much about their harsh treatment of her as their presence as markers of her social mobility. She also wants to take her father's role as James's friend and companion. While Ted meekly accepts his dismissal, Doris cannot process the implications of her daughter's new status and reflects that, 'It was disgusting of [James] to marry her. It made a mockery of all those past years'.

A few blocks away from James's home on a Knightsbridge square, Harriet, the protagonist in Virginia Ironside's *Chelsea Bird*, is enmeshed in the world of creative young London. To her fellow art students and the junior advertising executives she dates, social mobility is cool, exciting and the only game in town. Ironside encapsulates the hypocrisy of Harriet's social group with wonderful clarity in the way that they emulated the speech, tastes and values of the working-class (although, as middle-class intellectuals, their model of the working classes is gleaned only from social realist films). Repelled by the faux-egalitarian group-think of her peers, Harriet calls their pretensions, 'the smartness racket'.

Tom at that time was in the throes of the 'It's In to be cockney' rage. This fascinated me. Not only was it smart to be young, but a cockney or regional accent, particularly a northern one, could get one a lot of places. Frank Norman was a leader of the cult, the admen were after it hot foot, and *Saturday Night and Sunday Morning, This Sporting Life*, Albert Finney and Terence Stamp all contributed to the movement. It maddened me to hear directors discussing the reasons for making films about sordid life in Manchester suburbs, and saying that realism, stark and unaffected, was what people wanted because t hey were sick of false glamour and smarty ways. 'They now want to see real life, unvarnished, basic, and true'.

Maybe, but it was all part of the smartness racket. And as soon as people had seen the latest Tony Richardson movie, and read the latest Colin McInnes, their one idea was to get more lower class than anyone else. (In an upper-class way of course, in a smarty way). Black men became people to know, Teddy Boys were good people to be able to nod to in the street status-wise, and transport caffs were the only places to go for food, even if it meant cold greasy fried eggs and chips, which was called, however revolting, 'Super nosh'.

Another few blocks westward, in the seedy streets of Fulham, Lynne Reid Banks's heroine finds herself, as a middle-class woman, treated as a specimen of a dying species by the owner of a corner shop who feels threatened by the changing times.

'Bloody commies,' he said suddenly. 'Why couldn't they leave the middle classes alone? Never did no real harm as I could see. Live and let live, I say, all except the bobos, [black people] you have to keep them in their place. And the old faggots with their bleeding houses. Sorry, miss'.

I realised with surprise that he was apologising for saying bleeding. It was as if he were in the presence of a corpse – the corpse of the middle classes. He was looking at me as if I were its last twitch.

One of the features of British and also European societies which puzzles observers is that an aristocratic title does not imply wealth. A family may be able to trace its ancestry back to the Norman Conquest but will still include many younger sons and daughters who, thanks to the principle of primogeniture which preserved large estates, inherited little themselves. The rising rates of inheritance tax after World War I ensured that even heirs might have far less wealth than status and asset-rich, cash-poor was a common condition among the aristocracy. Charlotte Bingham's father was the heir to a baronetcy yet had to pawn his watch and cufflinks to take her mother on dates.[2]

Ditzy as she is, Charlotte Bingham's narrator contemplates the end of upper class privilege with clear eyes. The coroneted napkins and other details that adorn descriptions of the narrator's house, recall scenes from Charlotte's own London home, which was crammed with family possessions after the sale of her great-grandparents' estate, Bangor Castle.

> It's funny how quickly it goes. I mean one minute there are castles and footmen and coronets and all that, and the next there you are stomping about among lavatory brushes and coroneted napkins and that's all that's left. Because when you see all your castle sitting in your dining room you jolly well know that everything like that's finished now. And if you don't realise it's all finished now, you've had it. You get weeded out. No honestly you do. I know lots of people and they just can't cope because they don't want to realise it's finished. They won't let themselves realise it.

Coronet Among the Weeds has a double meaning that implies this decline. 'Weeds' is used by the novel's narrator in the sense of the public-school slang term for some who is weak or ineffectual, but it the title also suggests weeds as a symbol of decay and neglect and conjures the image of the coronet, the ceremonial token of nobility, lying abandoned on waste ground. The novel's narrator finds being a member of the aristocracy to be a disadvantage in the new age of social mobility, not least because of the expectations of her as a debutante in what was left of society, but also because it created a barrier between her and other people. She describes day-to-day relationships poisoned by inverted snobbery but enjoys the acceptance she finds with other 'ordinary' young women in the typing pool in a chemical company.

> All the girls were frightfully nice, and lent you things ... They didn't even mind when they found out that my father was a lord. A lot of people mind terribly. They become awfully peculiar with you, or the spend the whole time asking you if he eats or has a bath or if he's even been on a train. And when you say, he does have a bath, and he spends most of the morning there reading the Flutters, they don't believe you. Or they hate you. Yes, honestly. They hate you before you've even opened your mouth and they hate you doubly more than they hate anyone else.

4

ALL FALSE: LOVE

It was difficult to know what love was in 1950s Britain. Love during wartime, captured in hugely popular films such as *Casablanca* (1942) and *Brief Encounter* (1945), was poignantly idealised as an illicit relationship that awakened a couple's conscience and inspired personal sacrifice for a great cause, be that defeating the Germans or maintaining a marriage. A decade later, however, when the daily threat of death was something the earlier generation were trying to forget, there was no need for such heroism.

After the war, love as a life-changing passion threatened the consensual nostalgia for formalised, secure relationships. Fluffy romcoms were popular. The mass media and mass-market literature, such as paperback romance novels, portrayed love as an entertaining prelude to marriage, as in the films of Doris Day or Audrey Hepburn. The emphasis on the meet-cute, bringing together a woman and a man of different values or from different backgrounds, encouraged audiences to set aside personal differences and bond at all costs. The traditional conflicts of a love story were no longer the life-or-death moments of wartime romance but the trivial spats like those immortalised in the song, 'Let's Call the Whole Thing Off,' in which a couple disagree over the pronunciation of 'tomato' and 'potato.'[1]

Love is still an ideal for the women in these novels, although many are not sure what it might be. There is a clear division between Caithleen in *The Country Girls*, who has a soft-focus yearning for love and Baba, her friend, who has a strong idea of the adventures she wants. In their shared room in a boarding house in Dublin, they argue.

'Look, Caithleen, will you give up the nonsense? We're eighteen and we're bored to death'. She lit a cigarette and puffed vigorously. She went on: 'We want to live. Drink gin. Squeeze into the front of big cars and drive up outside big hotels. We want to go places. Not to sit in this damp dump'.

'Hear! Hear!' I said, and I clapped. She blew smoke straight into my face.

'But we want young men. Romance. Love and things,' I said despondently. I thought of standing under a streetlight in the rain with my hair falling crazily about, my lips poised for the miracle of a kiss. A kiss. Nothing more. My imagination did not go beyond that. It was afraid to… But kisses were beautiful. His kisses. On the mouth, on the eyelids, and on the neck when he lifted up the mane of hair.

'Young men have no bloody money. At least the gawks we meet. Smell o' hair oil. Up the Dublin mountains for air, a cup of damp tea in a damp hostel. Then out into the woods after tea and a damp hand fumbling under your skirt. No, sir. We've had all the bloody air we'll ever need. We want life'.

For Baba, the indistinct vision of love for which Caithleen yearns is blotted out by poverty and sexual revulsion and as the girls' story continues through *The Country Girls* trilogy she comes to look on love as a fatal delusion which she is thankful to have avoided. Two years after this conversation the girls find out how to crash promotional receptions at a big hotel. At one of these, a wine-tasting, they encounter a young PR executive whom they know, and with him is, 'a strange man with a sallow face', a film director named Eugene Galliard. Caithleen is immediately attracted to him. They meet again a few weeks later near a bookshop where she has gone for a 'free read' and he is sheltering from the rain. She has an instant physical response. 'My body became like jelly just from standing close to him, smelling his nice smell'.

He invites her for tea and she is overcome with a romantic, slightly desperate, sense of destiny. 'I forget what we talked about. I remember being speechless with happiness and feeling that God, or someone, had brought us together'.

Eugene is reluctant to begin a relationship as he is still married, although his wife has deserted him. Eventually, Caithleen writes to him to suggest a meeting and after that they see each other regularly over some months and she begins to visit him at his home, although the affair is unconsummated for a long time. When her father finds out that she is seeing a married man, he forces her to return home. She soon escapes back to Eugene and – jobless – moves in with him, becoming increasingly dependent upon him. He renames her Kate, demands she wears less makeup and begins the process of controlling her. Sexual attraction, Caithleen's yearning for independence and the fear of her father's threats are conflated into a bond that in her calm moments, she can see is fatally flawed.

> And even in loving him, I remembered our difficulties, the separated, different worlds that each came from; he controlled, full of bile and intolerance, knowing everyone, knowing everything – me swayed or frightened by every wind, light-headed, mad in one eye (as he said), bred in (as he said again) 'Stone Age ignorance and religious savagery'. I prayed to St Jude, patron of hopeless cases.

Here Caithleen clearly articulates the excitement she feels in her lover's contempt and even in the futile, doomed and tragic aspects of their affair. She seems to luxuriate in all the negative aspects of their relationship, to find pleasure in pain. Baba later describes her as 'prone to the old Via Dolorosa.' This compulsion will prove fatal. In the concluding book of *The Country Girls* trilogy, *Girls in their Married Bliss,* the hard-headed pleasure-seeking Baba has taken over the narration and 'Kate', divorced from Eugene who has custody of their child, is losing her mind and on the brink of suicide.

> I could see it coming. I knew there was some bloody man and that he was probably married and that she saw him once a fortnight or less, but of course saw him in street lamps, rain puddles, fire flames, and all that kind of Lord Byron lunacy. This was the real thing, it was different from all the rest, he and she were meant, Tristan and Iseult, soulmates, et cetera.

Kate eventually drowns in the swimming pool at a spa where she has gone to 'recoup', an ending that Baba suspects is suicide. 'Oh Kate, why did you let the bastards win?' she asks as she waits for the coffin to arrive on a train at Waterloo station. After the funeral, with Mozart and Van Morrison, and the cremation, she has planned to travel with Kate's son to Ireland to scatter the ashes, 'between the bogs and the bog lakes and the murmuring waters and every other fucking bit of the place and that (sic) imbued her with the old Dido desperado predilections. I hope she rises up nightly like the banshee and does battle with her progenitors.'² The clear implication is that her friend's faith in love has killed her, and that the conflation of romance with longing and tragedy is a legacy of her rural Irish heritage, something Kate had accepted but that Baba had instinctively rejected.

The only heroine in these works for whom love becomes a reality, rather than an ideal, is Joy in *Poor Cow*. She, too, begins with a tangle of half-recognised feelings. When her husband is sent to prison, she goes to live with her Aunt Emm, a former prostitute who survives on benefits. She is afraid of every possibility of her situation, afraid of domesticity, of Tom's neglect, of being destitute and unable to look after her son, of her need for sex and her own volatile emotions. She tries to decide what she really wants.

Into this fear and confusion comes Dave, who begins to court her with outings, shopping and flowers, until the day after he 'cracked it for a few hundred' she and her son move into his flat. What follows are months of bliss with a man who is affectionate and loving towards them both, happy to put up shelves, to cook, to share trips to the launderette, to make love often and to take the little family away on camping trips where the beauty of nature and the joy of being together leave Joy with the happiest memories of her life. She has a clear and healthy concept of love that embraces loyalty, kindness and care for a family as well as sex. Dave's love for her and her son, however, does not extend to finding legal work. He is more ambitious in crime than Tom, and gets a twelve year sentence, but Joy writes to him faithfully.

> Do you remember Norfolk, all our memories started there and you liked it so much and you was happy. I can imagine you and me sitting on the wall near where you stayed last year we cuddled. Oh it was so nice, Jonny picked me some Daisys, but we never took no photos. Still not to worrie we could lose our photos but not our memories we've got them for ever and ever.
>
> Oh my love please don't worrie, I thought of you so much today it realy hurt me to know way down deep inside of you you have really give up but Rember Davie I Love You. Oh Dave so much in facked the love for you is killing me every day I fill a big lump in my froat leaving you behind. Oh Darling what can we do. Stick-to-gether through thick and thin. That's your Joy, and she will but I need you and all your love.

At the end of the novel, with her husband Tom out of prison and back with her, Joy has nothing except a clear picture of love and the heart-breaking knowledge that it has been denied to her.

With the exception of Harriet, the art student narrator of Virginia Ironside's *Chelsea Bird*, the other heroines also dream of love without being able to say exactly what it is. In their different ways they are afraid of it, mistrust it and doubt that they are worthy of it. Jane, in *The L-Shaped Room,* finds Toby, her neighbour in their run-down boarding house, appealing, amusing and kind. When they make love, she feels a desire she has never known before. Afterwards, when he tells her he loves her, Jane panics. She is deeply immersed in feelings of shame and unworthiness, and a man's love, something she had previously sought for years, comes as a shock. She has felt a strong desire, but otherwise is afraid to define her feelings for him. When she recognises this she feels even more ashamed, wanting an emotional attachment to 'counter-balance' the physical desire but unable to decide what her feelings really are.

Hesitantly, in fits and starts and with painful conversations in which Toby expresses his horror that she has 'another man's child inside you' and his fear that his barely-established identity as a writer will be lost, they begin a warm and caring relationship and get ready to celebrate Christmas with the other lodgers in the house. Then, on Christmas day, Toby withdraws from her and eventually says simply, 'It's gone'.

Almost before she can feel pain, Jane's aunt Addy visits her and sweeps her away to her cottage in the country. Toby leaves the boarding house but visits Jane after her baby is born to tell her that he has finished a novel. There is a moment at which the possibility of renewing their relationship is there, but she decides to let it pass.

> I sensed his unease. I think he was afraid I'd make some demand on him which would lure him away from his new-found singleness of mind. I hesitated. If I answered 'Because I love you and need you and feel like half a person without you,' he would probably respond with the corresponding need in himself and the whole think would start again. I wanted it to, and in a way I think he did. But it would be a risk. Later, perhaps, when his new disciplines were more firmly established, it would be possible to add a full-time love relationship. As our hungry need for each other diminished, and we grew stronger as individuals, we'd have more to give.

For the youngest characters in this study, love is simply distant and unreal. In *A Taste of Honey*, 15-year-old Jo tells her boyfriend that she loves him after he proposes, but when he replies, 'how do you know?' she quickly deflects his interest by quoting Clarence Henry's song 'I Don't Know Why I Love You, But I Do' and they never talk about it again. Charlotte Bingham's narrator, passionate and despairing at the end of *Coronet Among the Weeds*, says, 'I believe in everything corny. I believe that there is a superman. Somewhere. I believe in love. My mother says I'll end up in a two-roomed flat in Hampstead because I do. She says it's the worst thing to believe in. I don't care. I do'. Harriet, in Virginia Ironside's *Chelsea Bird*, is so overwhelmed by the sexual demands of the men she meets that she gives no thought to love at all. And perhaps the saddest attitude of all is that of Georgy in *Georgy Girl*, who has an unshakeable belief that because she is not conventionally pretty, love is impossible for her. Repeatedly, throughout the book, she cites her lack of beauty as a reason why no man can love her. Even when Jos, her flatmate's boyfriend and the father of the baby she adopts, falls in love with her she focuses obsessively on the baby and withdraws from him. When James, her father's employer, asks for an answer to his proposal that she become his mistress, she expresses her feelings with brutal clarity.

'It's so absurd, it embarrasses me', she said.
   'What's absurd about it?' said James. 'I love you and want to live with you'.
   George clicked her tongue in exasperation.
   'Can't you see?' she said. 'Look at us in that mirror. A fat, middle-aged man and a tall, ugly girl. We don't know anything about love. It's a stupid word to use'.

5

'I WISH I HAD A CAREER':
ASPIRATION

A career is as vague an ideal as love to the young women in these works. It is something that some of them tentatively think about but, unlike love, work and the education that would provide the qualifications for a white-collar job is something that many of them are vigorously discouraged from acquiring. Their parents believe that no man will want an intelligent wife and their employers see them as capable only of menial work.

The school leaving age, for both boys and girls, was fifteen until 1972, when the government raised it to sixteen. As the British economy shifted away from work in manufacturing and production and towards jobs in the service industries, the government recognised that school-leavers needed higher levels of literacy and numeracy. Nevertheless, these developments had little impact on most young women of the time. All the women in these works leave school almost as soon as they can, none of them think of university and most are strongly discouraged from education entirely, either by parents, friends or partners. Charlotte Bingham's narrator, with a clear imperative to marry as soon as possible issued by her parents, is sent to Paris to learn the attributes of a young upper-class wife.

'I was nearly sixteen by this time. So, my mother said I should leave school. She doesn't believe in girls knowing a frightful lot or going to university. She just thinks girls should have a bit of culture, and know how to cook and keep things clean.'

The requisite bit of culture is acquired by going to a few lectures and cookery classes in Paris and a secretarial college and modelling school in London, at all of which she is a resounding failure. Her mother's opinion seems justified when, at her first dance, she is left partner-less by the manoeuvres of an older and more attractive girl who, 'used to take all these girls around with her to parties and introduce them to boys and say how clever they were to these boys, and of course these boys would never look at them again; they'd just swoon around her saying they were terribly glad she wasn't clever'.

In Edna O'Brien's *The Country Girl*, Caithleen is considered a good student at convent school. She expects to come first in tests in every subject and at the end of the first term is awarded a statue of St Jude – patron saint of hope as well as lost causes – for coming first in the examinations. Her academic aptitude, however, is overcome by horror of the oppressive discipline and terrible food and she goes along with her friend Baba, a dunce but ever impatient for the wider world, in a successful ploy to get expelled. Baba's influence leads her to give up on education and follow her friend to Dublin, where she gets a job in a grocery shop. Only Baba's father is perceptive enough to notice that she has thrown away her educational opportunities. In Dublin Caithleen feels nostalgic for books, pretends she is studying English and soon provokes Baba's anger when her liking for literature threatens a night out with two middle-aged businessmen who are buying them dinner.

'Will you do me a favour?' she asked. She was looking up earnestly into my face. I was much taller than she.

'Yes,' I said, and although I was no longer afraid of her, I had that sick feeling which I always have before someone says an unpleasant thing to me.

'Will you, for Chrissake, stop asking fellas if they've read James Joyce's Dubliners? They're not interested. They're out for a night. Eat and drink all you can and leave James Joyce to blow his own trumpet'.

'He's dead'.

'Well, for God's sake then, what are you worrying about?'

'I'm not worrying I just like him'.

'Oh, Caithleen! Why don't you get sense?'

When Caithleen meets the documentary director, Eugene, he embodies the intellectual life she wants. When he invites her for tea his first question to her is, 'Tell me, what do you read?' and she replies, 'Chekov and James Joyce and James Stephens and...' before stopping herself, worried that he would think she was showing off. Indeed, by the time she is living with him, Eugene mocks Caithleen for her malapropisms and tells her she must give up reading books. She accepts his derision, which chimes with her own sense of inferiority.

At the end of the second book in *The Country Girl* trilogy, Kate has left Eugene and moved to London with Baba, where is she studying English at university evening classes, but by the opening of the final book, *Girls in their Married Bliss*, she has contacted Eugene again, become pregnant and married him. After the wedding ceremony he calls her, 'nothing but a farmer's daughter reverting to type'.[1]

The working-class women in Nell Dunn's books read neither books nor magazines. The newspapers that come into their homes are brought in by men for the racing pages. School is only mentioned as the place where Joy, in *Poor Cow*, met her husband. The girls quote pop songs and advertising slogans and Nell Dunn uses these to contrast the idealised pictures of romance, home and family with the reality of tin baths, bed bugs and prostitution. Joy listens to pop songs on the radio and has a television in her flat (when her husband has made enough money to buy one) but seems unengaged with the medium. If she needs information, she asks her Aunt Emm, or more knowledgeable friend Beryl.

Similarly, Jo in *A Taste of Honey* quotes pop lyrics, recites nursery rhymes and proudly says she never reads newspapers. When Geof moves in and wants to take care of her, he buys her a book about pregnancy 'off a barrow' and the only sign that she might have once received an education is when she compares it to *Little Women*, for its twee and patronising tone. She is violently conflicted about her pregnancy, as about every aspect of her life. Geof, an art student, discovers that she has been drawing and suggests she go to a 'good school' but she deflects the issue, saying, 'I've never been to any school'. Earlier, when her mother makes the same suggestion, she implies that her unstable childhood has undermined her education, 'I've had enough of school. Too many different schools and too many different places'.

At this time it was relatively easy for a young woman to find work. The world economy was enjoying a boom and Britain had seen a dramatic rise in the standard of living, famously expressed by the Conservative Prime Minister Harold Macmillan saying 'most of our people have never had it so good' at a party rally in 1957. Fears of inflation even led to a wage freeze and other measures to curb rising inflation three years later. The working-class women in these works have no difficulty finding jobs, but need to work long hours to make enough money to survive or to save. Jo has a bar job lined up before she even leaves school. None of the women in Nell Dunn's books are out of work except Aunt Emm, the ageing former prostitute who prefers living on 'National Assistance' (benefits) to 'men or cleaning'.

Joy in *Poor Cow* realises that she needs to provide for her infant son and occasionally thinks of taking elocution lessons, like her friend Beryl, who, 'definitely [doesn't] want to stay in my own class, I want to go up in the world – I want a position – I'm going to classes on how to speak properly and how to approach people'. Beryl tried training to become a nurse, but left after a few days because she 'couldn't stick' the need for discipline. Her alternative plan is to become 'respectable' and marry.

It was so easy for a young woman to find an unskilled job that by the mid-sixties employers were grumbling about 'job-hopping dolly birds' who moved on quickly to more entertaining positions.

For most young women, however, the work available remained menial and poorly paid. Work at McCrindle's factory, packing liqueur chocolates, gives the girls in Nell Dunn's *Up The Junction* both wages and companionship, although their working conditions are squalid and degrading. The women wear clogs but even so their feet are black with dirt at the end of the day.

> My eyes began to ache in the cold electric light. There are no windows in the room where we have been sitting since eight in the morning earning our two-and-fivepences an hour – ten pence an hour for the under eighteens. The siren hoots. 'Tea's up. Go and get some sugar, Bent Sheil!'[2]
>
> 'I'll come with you'. Bent Sheila and I go up the broken staircase to the loft and turn on the light. Mice scuttle. She dips the chipped mug into an open sack… I thrust my cup under the urn and watch it fill with grey tea, then follow Rube and Lily into the cloakroom. There are no chairs. We sit on the concrete floor among the bicycles, leaning our heads against the coats that hang from the walls. Joyce, a girl with long auburn hair caught back with two pink slides, cuddles in a corner eating some cold chips out of a bit of newspaper.

Charlotte Bingham's narrator is eventually forced by her father to work as a typist in the office of a firm owned by one of his friends. It is a far more privileged environment than the factory girls have to endure in *Up The Junction* and the work, although skilled, is still menial with a sharp gender divide between the male executives who dictate and the women who type the letters. With no social connection to her co-workers, Bingham's narrator is miserably lonely and feels as alienated as if the other women were speaking a different language.

> None of these women liked me. I didn't really blame them. I don't think I'd have liked me if I'd been them either.

Harriet, in Virginia Ironside's *Chelsea Bird*, chooses the same fate. After leaving art school, she goes for the only other option – secretarial work. Most of her fellow art students are horrified.

> The rest of them despaired of me. 'Secretary,' they sneered. I couldn't explain that I was really catching the last train from the crumbling city. Most of my contemporaries left and ended up with part-time jobs in factories and painted in their spare time or even took secretarial courses.

The idea of a career, of working for a lifetime, developing skills and fulfilling personal potential, is completely absent from the lives of these women. In this the authors, most of whom had challenged the limitations imposed on their gender and had clear ambitions to be writers, were recording what they saw around them rather than using their own experience. Work is something done to survive financially, nothing more. Jane, in *The L-Shaped Room*, has tenuous ideas of being an actress, which she abandons at the first set-back and her next job, in the publicity department of a smart hotel, she regards as, 'a piece of incredible good luck and a source of constant satisfaction'. Promotion happens in spite of her senior manager telling her that he didn't 'approve of women in key positions' and only because her boss gets drunk. She resigns when she discovers she is pregnant, without telling her employer the reason. Statutory maternity leave was two decades in the future at this point and many employers routinely sacked women on pregnancy or marriage. Jane, herself, sees her pregnancy as the end of what little career she had. 'I would never have the courage to ask for my job back after my baby was born', she lamented.

The only other woman in these works to have a career is Meredith, the cruel beauty who is Georgy's best friend and flatmate in Margaret Forster's *Georgy Girl*. Meredith is a musician – the second violin in a well-known orchestra. As a character, she is distinguished by obsessive emotional detachment and unrelieved selfishness, which she can inflict on other people because she is beautiful and manipulative, although there is no suggestion that her heartlessness is either a cause or effect of her career. Meredith never discusses her work and Forster presents it only as the means by which she meets the large number of men she seduces and abandons.

The women in these novels have adopted and internalised such a sense of inferiority from their families, friends and employers that they never question the unspoken restrictions of education and work that are placed on them. If they have intelligence it must be hidden. If they have talents, they are not worth developing. If they get jobs, they are unskilled, low paid and unpleasant. If they begin a career it is down to luck, not judgement or planning and it will end when they marry or have children. They all share an overpowering sense of worthlessness, which in turn prevents them from making any move towards establishing an identity for themselves through their work. Their lives are such that they will never be financially independent and never know what it is to gain a sense of achievement in the workplace.

6

THE GREAT UNMENTIONABLE: SEX

Sex was something a young woman knew nothing about in 1958. A girl would typically begin menstruation without knowing what was happening in her body and a warning to 'keep away from t'lads'[1] might follow if her parents were caring and responsible. About a quarter of young people learned about reproduction in school biology lessons, but compulsory sex education in schools would not be legally required for almost forty years, when the 1995 Education Act was drafted in response to the AIDS epidemic.

A bride might have the advantage of a leaflet provided by her embarrassed mother – *Married Love* by Marie Stopes for the most enlightened, but more often just a vague tract suggesting that 'Divine blessing and peace'[2] would take care of everything on her wedding night. The shock and revulsion when a couple first have sex, depicted by Ian McEwan in *On Chesil Beach*, was a common experience.

Both screen and print media were, at the time, rigorously censored to exclude any sexual activity beyond a fully-clothed heterosexual kiss. The euphemistic treatment of gay characters in Terence Rattigan's plays, which prompted Shelagh Delaney to create a credible homosexual character, was a compromise with the extreme sensitivity of the Lord Chamberlain's office, responsible for theatre censorship. In 1958 John Trevelyan, the newly-appointed Secretary of the British Board of Film Censors, ordered the words 'lust' and 'bitch' to be cut from *Room At the Top,* a film based on a novel by John Braine, one of the Angry Young Men. Pornography was illegal and what today is called 'soft porn' was only available from shabby specialist shops whose customers were only male. Condoms could be bought but not advertised, and the only other form of contraception, the cap, was exclusive to married women on prescription from a doctor. Thus, both young men and young women arrived at sexual maturity in substantial ignorance and their peers were their main source of information.

The factory girls in Nell Dunn's *Up The Junction* talk about sex freely and often but when they start to have sex they know nothing about it. The final story in the collection, *The Children*, describes a 10-year-old girl boasting of having 'done it' in a game of mothers and fathers and another girl warns her, 'you can be sent to prison for doing that,' but at the same time a boy shows off his knowledge, saying, 'do you know what newly-weds do? Have a bit of a kiss and a cuddle. I know the facts of life, I do'. Another story, *Sunday Morning*, is set in a home for unmarried mothers, where most of the women got pregnant in total ignorance. 'I never once lay down with him. I used to meet him in a back alley off the Latchmere. I didn't really know what he was at – I never got no pleasure out of it. I didn't know I was carrying till I was five months'.

In Edna O'Brien's *The Country Girls* Caithleen, in her complete ignorance, is even more vulnerable to a predatory male. When she is about eight years old her alcoholic father sends her with a begging letter asking for money to call upon a man known as Mr Gentleman, a French-born Dublin solicitor with a weekend home in their village. He immediately starts to groom her with sips of wine, cigarettes, and rides in his car. Her mother dies when she is about fourteen. By the time she is boarding at convent school Mr Gentleman is taking her out in the holidays, kissing her hand and soon following up with a 'proper' kiss that awakens the desire that she will be unable to control. He makes declarations of love and promises of marriage, as does a local boy, a childhood friend whose wholesome affection she finds unattractive because of her obsessive attachment to Mr Gentleman.

Some years later, when Caithleen moves to Dublin, they start
dating until Mr Gentleman tries and fails to seduce her. He
then plans for them to leave together for England. At this point
Caithleen's father, who all-but prostituted his daughter as a child,
threatens Mr Gentleman who then breaks off the relationship. His
memory has become 'a shadow' by the time she meets her future
husband two years later, although her addiction to unavailable
men has been established. Their relationship is unconsummated
until after she is kidnapped and Eugene beaten up by her father
and two other men from the village. It is only after this that he
begins divorce proceedings and then makes love to Caithleen. 'I
felt no pleasure, just some strange satisfaction that I had done
what I was born do to. My mind dwelt on foolish, incidental
things. I thought to myself, So this is it; the secret I dreaded and
had longed for'.[3]

In Britain this 'age of ignorance' slowly began to fade away in the
early sixties, with a loosening of general attitudes towards sex. In
1960 a pivotal moment arrived when Penguin Books was acquitted
of the charge of publishing obscene material in its edition of
D.H. Lawrence's Lady Chatterley's Lover – a book in which the word
'fuck' appeared eight times on one page. In the words of Geofrey
Robertson QC, one of Britain's leading liberal lawyers, 'No other
jury verdict has had such a profound social impact'.[4] A few months
later, in 1961, the contraceptive pill, which was almost 100 percent
effective, became available for the first time through the National
Health Service, but only to married women, although a very small
number of specialist clinics accepted patients without asking about
their marital status. By 1964 half a million women in Britain were
using oral contraception and it was made legally available to all
women from 1967, although the provision was not widespread and
restricted to special clinics for some years afterwards.

The entire culture of courtship and love was dramatically altered by
these changes. Philip Larkin's often-quoted poem, 'Annus Mirabilis',
records the process and it is worth giving attention to the second

verse, much less hackneyed, describing a man's view of relationships before the new age:

> Sexual intercourse began
> In nineteen sixty-three
> (which was rather late for me) -
> Between the end of the 'Chatterley' ban
> And the Beatles' first LP.
>
> Up to then there'd only been
> A sort of bargaining,
> A wrangle for the ring,
> A shame that started at sixteen
> And spread to everything.

The 'wrangle for the ring' is something that the female characters in this study would not recognise. The women in Nell Dunn's stories go out to bars and cafés to meet young men, looking for the handsome, sexy ones they fancy, ready to set off in a pack on the boys' motorbikes down to Clapham Common or around London's peripheral highway, the North Circular Road, where the thrill of speed adds to the fun. They stay together for protection.

> 'Hear about Tom?' says Rube. 'He walked Pat home the other night. She wouldn't let him in the bedroom so he nearly kicked the door in'.
>
> 'Any bloke'll try and get in the bedroom if her mum's out. It's only natural, ain't it?'
>
> 'It's not like Pat to shut a bloke out of the bedroom. [...] Any boy you go out with, nine times out of ten you end up talking about sex'. [...]
>
> 'Met a gorgeous bloke last night – the sort of bloke when you see him you want to grab hold of him...'
>
> '...He kept pressin' himself against me, then his hands began to wanter. "You ain't half hot blooded," he says. I kept takin' them

away, then he'd put them back again. "I can't help being sexy,"
I says. […] He drove me out to London Airport for a snoggin'
session. We sat in the front and June and his mate, Ron, were
in the back. June says she'll have it with Ron if he goes steady
with her first because she's bin let down that way once or twice
before'.

Other women prefer the variety of 'one-night fellas' to what they
see as the boredom of going steady. Most marry soon after leaving
school, but the relationships are unstable, not least because many
of the men are professional criminals. Joy in *Poor Cow* marries
her childhood sweetheart, with whom she doesn't really enjoy
sex, but she revels in the playful love-making she later enjoys
with her lover, Dave. When Dave, too, is sent to prison Joy is
destitute, lonely and misses making love. She begins to see her
sexuality as both a blessing and a curse, bringing pleasure even
without love but also causing dependence and vulnerability. At the
pub where she works the customers are mostly men and sexual
opportunities abound.

> Gradually Joy got good at enjoying her men. She began to get
> really involved in sex – she could shut out who they were and
> what they looked like, and become a femme fatale for that night,
> geared up in her lacy underwear and false pony tail.
> … Proper lusty I was getting – it used to be love but it's all
> lust now – it's so terrific with different blokes. Sometimes you
> fancy it all soft and other times you want them to fuck the life
> out of you. Well you can't get that from the same bloke can you.

Before long, Joy has a stable of regular lovers. Some give her money,
'I touched him for a fiver,' and others presents, like the baker's
delivery driver who brings her fresh bread. And some, much to her
friend Beryl's disapproval, make love to her and give her nothing
but pleasure.

For the younger characters created only four or five years later, sex does not hold the promise of pleasure, rather a constant fear of assault and harassment. They found themselves precipitously thrown into circumstances in which the restraints on sexual behaviour and the arguments against having sex which protected their mothers' generation were no longer relevant. In their place was the expectation that they would have sex anytime with anyone. Even the most casual exchange between a man and woman could be sexualised. For the art students and their circle in *Chelsea Bird*, sexual propositions were part of everyday conversations.

'Got a cigarette?'

I pushed a Woodbine in his direction. He was so attractive he really deserved it.

'Thanks, baby. I'd like to sleep with you one day'.

The remaining vestiges of the old morality were still seen in the language of courtship, in which rape and seduction became telling euphemisms. 'Seduce' is used lovingly in *Poor Cow*. 'It's your turn to seduce me today,' said Joy, and very gently he took off her stockings.' In Virginia Ironside's *Chelsea Bird*, Ann, a girl who embarrasses the narrator with her innocence, confides that she has been on a date with a man who tried to have sex with her afterwards, but she doesn't know if he succeeded or not. A few moments later the man himself appears in the same café and tries to hide from Ann.

'What do you want to bring her in here for?' he whispered. 'Oh, God, what a night!'

'You behaved horribly to her, she's all cut up. You really are nasty,' I said coyly, adjusting my slick *Jules et Jim* hat over my eyes.

'She feels cut up! What do you think I feel? I plug her with gins and she won't even be raped! Some people. They don't know when they've got the chance of a lifetime'.

The word rape is used jokingly here but underscores a fact that was seldom expressed in the turbulent process of redefining acceptable sexual behaviour: the fact that a woman might not want to have sex. In this case, Ann was so inexperienced that she was only clear that the man's actions were unwanted. Similarly, Charlotte Bingham uses the word in *Coronet Among the Weeds* when her narrator refers to the sexual harassment that she discovers is an accepted part of the debutante season. Young men and women who were going to country house balls were typically hosted by local families, who arranged dinners before the balls, at which many of the men got drunk, but were nevertheless expected to drive the young women guests to the events.

> It was nerve-racking if you got taken to the dance alone in a car … you can't tell some old hostess you don't want to go with someone because he's a sex maniac, and being raped by a weed would be no joke. I'm not exaggerating: some of those weeds there was nothing they wouldn't stop at … My mother used to get very cross. About these types asking if they could rape you all the time … so I asked her what I should do about these rapey sorts of weeds … She made me keep this pepper-pot in my evening bag. So if a weed really leaped on me with a low growl all I had to do was open my evening bag, get out the pepper-pot, unscrew the lid and chuck the pepper in his eyes, in one easy movement.

In spite of this, Bingham's narrator does not have sex at all in the novel, or meet anyone she would like to have sex with. In contrast, Harriet in *Chelsea Bird* endures a succession of sexual encounters with many men she doesn't find attractive, because she feels it is expected of her. One man she does like is Nick, whom she finds attractive in spite of, 'his beastliness and cool'. By this time, however, she has had unwanted sex so many times without pleasure that she cannot imagine that sex with someone she wants will be any better. She thinks,

> 'You're going to be seduced whatever face you put on so you might as well be honest and admit you wouldn't mind staying the night with him.⁵ … I screwed myself up and shut my eyes as tight as I could. I felt I wasn't going to enjoy this, so I nerved myself to the ordeal. I hoped he wasn't going to be a two-hour character.
>
>   'Have a cigarette?' he said, when it was all over. 'Sorry about that'.
>
>   'Sorry about what?'
>
>   'Oh hell. I mean … never mind. Have you got a light?' When we had lit up, I started up on my own special bed clichés. 'You look like a Georges de la Tour picture in the light of your cigarette,' I said, looking at him.

The spend the night together, struggling to keep hold of the blankets in his single bed. ' Single beds cause more rows than almost anything. I felt quite terrible the next morning. Nick had woken me up at about seven-thirty wanting a repeat performance and eventually I had to give up pretending to be asleep. It's extraordinary the way men go on so. And at seven-thirty. How anyone could feel like sex at that time after a sleepless night with no pyjamas is beyond me.'

Reflecting on this time in her own life, Virginia Ironside recalls:

> 'There was so much sex around it almost became boring. In the sixties, feminism hadn't yet reared its head, and it was almost a matter of good manners to have sex with anyone who picked up the bill after a meal. It wasn't always nice or fun. In fact, most of the sex that I had in the sixties was grim. For women, the phrase "No means no" had not yet come into existence, but the pill was easily accessible and sex seemed the "thing to do".'

The concept of sexual consent would not become properly established for another half-century. Young women in the sixties were caught between male expectation and centuries of social conditioning that made it hard for them to simply refuse a man's request or tell him they did not find him attractive. The sense of a woman's agency, her right to determine what should happen to her own body, was almost non-existent but at the same time, the most powerful traditional argument against having sex – the likelihood of pregnancy – had been, ironically, undermined by the pill.

Most of the women characters in this study do enjoy sex when it is with men they like and find attractive. For some, like Joy in *Poor Cow*, their sexuality is an Achilles heel that makes it impossible for them to maintain a balance of power in a relationship with a man. Because sex is meant to be traded, for money, food, or even a driving licence, 'giving it away' devalues the woman. When Joy stops desiring her husband once he starts to ignore her and later abuse her, she interprets this loss of attraction as related to her need to feel independent and have a sense of identity and so she concludes that the 'respectable' status of a stable marriage is something to which she cannot aspire.

> How can I go back to all this – I'm not the same any more. I can't stick this sort of security. I can't stick all these women and their kids… You go in the shops it's bleeding women, you go to the park, it's bleeding women, all so sure, so full of themselves and sex – sex. I can't stand it anymore, when he tried to have it this morning I felt quite dizzy – I screamed at him 'Let me go – let me go you dirty bastard'. I can't bear him to touch me – it's the four walls, the kitchenette, each day the same, I think I'm going round the bend. I'm not like that anymore, he wants to make me an old granny pushing a pram – why shouldn't I be a mum and a glamour girl too.
>
> I just want to be something. I can't be nothing all my life.

Because Georgy in *Georgy Girl* is described as essentially unattractive, the strong sexual desire that she feels comes across as inappropriate and pathetic. When Georgy has sex with Jos, he tells her he loves her and makes love to her. The story is told at this point from Jos's point of view, as if the author cannot bear to imagine an ugly woman's sexual feelings.

> It should all have been so right. She was relaxed and wanting him, every nerve quivered with eagerness, but as he penetrated her, gasping with haste, he could feel her flinch and contract. He felt it but could do nothing about it, he was too preoccupied with his own climax. He wanted to reassure her, to stop, to do more slowly, but he couldn't contain himself and he had to go on, leaving her suffering behind him.
>
> She lay and wept. Exhausted, he wanted to turn over and go to sleep. He needed to gather strength to soothe and silence her.

Almost the same age as Georgy, Jane in *The L-Shaped Room* has never felt desire very strongly until she and her boarding-house neighbour, Toby, get drunk together and her conflicted feelings make her cry.

> And then he's was taking the tears with his lips, he was kissing them away; he was kissing my eyes and my mouth and our arms were round each other and somehow my crying changed, I wasn't crying in despaired and wretchedness any more, but with a kind of luxury. My tears weren't coming out of pain now, but out of a new feeling, a feeling his lips were rousing and his hands, and there was no part of my mind or body that wished to resist it, or had the strength to; without reasoning or doubting, all of me wanted what he wanted. [...] And the thought that wasn't really a thought fled before the pleasure I didn't deserve, but which came anyway, swelling and overtaking, in a generous wild exploding splendour that I had thought I would never know.

7

DROWNING IN DELIGHT:
MOTHERHOOD

'A bit of love, a bit of lust and there you are. We don't ask for life, we have it thrust upon us'.

For Jo in *A Taste of Honey*, as for the other female characters in this study, it was easy to get pregnant in 1950s Britain, but harder to match up to society's ideal vision of a wife and mother. Of the seven protagonists considered in this study, four become single mothers. The central characters of *A Taste of Honey* (Jo), *The L-Shaped Room* (Jane), *Georgy Girl* (Georgy) and *Poor Cow* (Joy) are all single mothers, a provocative choice by the authors at a time when the 'unmarried mother' was a pariah figure.

This chapter additionally considers Dame Margaret Drabble's third novel, *The Millstone*, published in 1965 when the author was twenty-six, which also imagines the experience of single motherhood. Drabble, had taken the traditional route to literary success, graduating from Newnham College, Cambridge with a starred first in English Literature. She is considered, perhaps unfairly, to be a leading exponent of the so-called 'Hampstead novel' as her early stories describe adventures among the intellectual elite. Her highly distinguished literary career, while similar in some ways was achieved without the sense of rebellion that characterises the Rebel Writers. *The Millstone* takes its title from the Gospel of Matthew, chapter 18, verse 6: 'Whoso shall offend one of these little ones who believe in me, it were better that a millstone were hanged about his neck and that he were drowned in the depth of the sea'. Thus from the title itself it argues the paramount duty of adults to a child, something which the characters in this study readily accept, no matter how difficult their circumstances. The narrator, Rosamund, working on her PhD thesis at the British Library and living comfortably in the central London apartment belonging to her parents, who are conveniently travelling abroad, couldn't be further from the female characters in this study, yet her experiences, feelings and actions are remarkably similar, as this chapter will show.

A MOTHERLESS GENERATION

Motherhood is not a joyful experience for all the women in these works. While a substantial proportion of the characters considered here are happy and devoted mothers, Nell Dunn's women in *Up The Junction*, for whom flirting and kissing are all part of a good night out, accept pregnancy as one of life's inevitable hazards, but they do not aspire to motherhood, which is viewed as something between an irritation and a tragedy. *Sunday Morning*, one of the stories in *Up The Junction*, is set in a home for unmarried mothers-to-be and features several girls who got pregnant by accident. The sense that pregnancy was mysterious, a random act of nature, something on which you had to take a chance, is shared by most of them. None of them plans to conceive, nor do they take any action to prevent it, and neither to their lovers.

In spite of their inexperience and naivety, when the young women in the works of this study think of motherhood, they are reminded of the often difficult relationships with their own mothers and vow to do better. Their mothers are invariably portrayed as either absent or as negative forces in their lives. The most monstrous is undoubtedly Helen in *A Taste of Honey*, who neglects, demeans and insults her daughter, Jo, viciously throughout the play and then, in the final scene, invades her home, wrecks her fragile independence and drives away Geof, her caring companion. The clear threat is that she will extend the cycle of her alcoholic abuse to the child that Jo is expecting.

Georgy in *Georgy Girl* despises her own mother across a gulf created by class division. While her mother, Doris, is uneducated and dependent on her husband and employer, Georgy has had a middle-class education, a self-employed job and a home of her own. She does not acknowledge that her elevated position depends entirely on the support of her parents' employer.

The period of this study saw an unprecedented gulf develop between generations, which undoubtedly explains the complicated relationships that are portrayed between the novels' mothers and daughters. Contemporary terms like 'youthquake' or 'sexual revolution' expressed the profound changes that medical advances, prosperity and peace brought about in everyday lives. The unique experience of those who had been adults during World War II distanced that generation from their own children, whose reality was entirely different. The economic power of the baby-boom generation, born from 1945 onwards, exacerbated the generation gap as advertisers, retailers and industries found it profitable to target the youth market. As a result, the bond between parents and children and between grandparents and grandchildren was strained to breaking point. Mothers and daughters were particularly alienated from each other because the new realities of life in the sixties were felt first and foremost by young women. Suddenly able to control their own fertility, have children almost when they wanted (potentially without pain) and even rely on modern inventions such as washing machines and dishwashers, the women of the sixties had, in many ways, easier lives than their mothers. As a result, these young women were a motherless generation who could not share the same experience of womanhood with the women who gave birth to them.

All protagonists in the works in this book are distanced from their mothers in one way or another. In *The L Shaped Room* and *The Country Girls*, the protagonists' mother dies. In *Poor Cow* and *Chelsea Bird*, Joy and Harriet's mothers might as well be dead as they are never mentioned. The only protagonist who has a vaguely-functioning relationship with her mother is the narrator of Charlotte Bingham's *Coronet Among the Weeds*, whose mother dispenses well-meaning but useless advice and designs her daughter's education to maximise her marriage potential.

Marriage and sex are sometimes seen as the price a woman must pay in order to have a family and, more than an idealised longing or love for children, the desire to be a different kind of mother is paramount. Love for their babies and delight in motherhood come later, as wonderful surprises, sometimes after what was an initial revulsion. Jo, in *A Taste of Honey*, insists, 'I hate motherhood', in a conversation about breastfeeding. *The Country Girl's* Caithleen, admits that she 'dreaded babies'[1] and when she has her son, she never expresses feelings for him beyond a vague: 'children are nice'. Joy asks herself, 'What did I go and get landed with him for? I used to be a smart girl'. Each in her different style is expressing the fear of the great unknown that will begin with childbirth, when their status as women will change forever.

STRONG AND EMOTIONAL

Margaret Forster wrote *Georgy Girl* when she was pregnant with her own first child and the novel can be viewed as an essay on motherhood. As a 'big, strong girl', Georgy considers herself unworthy of love or marriage, but takes delight in the children in her dancing class. She is thrilled when Meredith, her cold and selfish flatmate, reveals her pregnancy and demands that her boyfriend, Jos, marry her. The moment that Georgy falls in love with Jos is when he buys a cot for the baby. After the little girl is born her love for the child is almost obsessive, the only love an 'ugly' woman can reasonably express. Georgy devotes herself to the baby, making Jos feel so rejected that he leaves.

> Really, she hadn't guessed how she would react [to the baby] either, even though she had thought so much about her. She had never imagined love for a baby, especially a baby that wasn't yours, could be so strong and emotional. When she'd held her for the first time, there was a physical sensation not unlike one of desire. The same weak feeling in her stomach, the same breathless anticipation... At the back of her mind, without knowing the exact day, she'd been vaguely conscious that she'd lost interest in Jos. He was an interruption in her relationship with Sara, a figure who came and went and didn't share in anything. She'd probably wanted him to go for some time.

Becoming a mother also offers these young women new identities. The sense of a new self, of purpose and independence, is something that they all articulate. Jo, in *A Taste of Honey*, tells her mother, 'Do you know, for the first time in my life I feel really important. I feel as though I could take care of the whole world. I even feel as though I could take care of you'. For Joy, the protagonist of *Poor Cow*, this new self is so fragile that it seems to disappear when her baby sleeps. While he is awake and she is busy cooking up his tiny meals, ironing his playsuits and brushing his sparse black hair, she is all right, but when he falls asleep she is overcome with desolation.

Rosamund, the narrator of Drabble's *The Millstone*, a Cambridge PhD student with the use of her parents' comfortable London flat, has mixed feelings about her pregnancy. For her it signals an end to the independence she has cherished. 'I felt threatened. I felt my independence threatened: I did not see how I was going to get by on my own'. But the reality is that she revels in motherhood and its unexpected blessings – the immediate love she feels for her baby, the love her baby has for her. In her mannered, academic voice, she muses:

> I was continually amazed by the way in which I could watch for hours nothing but the small movements of her hands and the fleeting expressions of her face... As she grew older she began to favour me, and nothing gave me more delight than her evident preference... I certainly had not anticipated such wreathing, dazzling gaiety of affection from her whenever I happened to catch her eye... Indeed, it must have been in expectation of this love that I had insisted upon having her. [2]

Earlier in the novel, one of Rosamund's boyfriends, unaware that she is pregnant, calls her 'a very unwomanly woman,' but once she is a mother she feels that her femaleness, even her own humanity, has been confirmed as she begins to connect with other people rather than hiding away in her research.

NO BETTER THAN A STREET WOMAN

The obverse of the picture of ideal motherhood in the fifties was the condemnation of unmarried mothers, on medical as well as moral grounds. Even in supposedly liberal and enlightened circles, the casual condemnation of a single mother was commonplace. Thus, the distinguished critic Philip Hope-Wallace, writing in the left-wing *Manchester Guardian*, described Jo in *A Taste of Honey* as 'a pregnant slut,' even though the text makes it clear that she has had sex with her boyfriend only once. [3]

Of the works in this book, *The L-Shaped Room* pursues this attitude in most depth, although allusions to it appear in all of them When Jane, the protagonist of *The L-Shaped Room*, suspects she is pregnant she makes an appointment to see a doctor picked at random from the phone book. Without examining her, the doctor tells her that she is pregnant. After hearing that the child's father is absent and following the initial mutterings of dismay, he assumes she will want an abortion and names his fees. When Jane tells him she wants to continue with her pregnancy, he responds, 'I wonder how much thought you've given to the child. A lot of the women who come to me aren't just panic-stricken cowards trying to escape their just deserts, you know. They have the sense to realise they're incapable of being mother and father, breadwinner and nursemaid, all at once. A lot of them have thought what the alternative means, of handing the child over to strangers who may or may not love it. And don't make the mistake of imagining the word bastard doesn't carry a sting anymore. There aren't many illegitimate children in this world who haven't. some time or other, thought unkindly of their mothers'.

Jane leaves the consulting room in anger but, as the weeks pass and she begins to suffer morning sickness she realises she will have to make plans. She lives at home with her widowed father and breaks the news to him, asking, 'What's the worst thing I could do to you?' Shocked and angry, he tells her to leave their home, saying she is, 'no better than a street-woman'. Jane's actions after this express her own guilt and shame. It is her sense of guilt that leads her to find a place to live in a bad neighbourhood. Although she could afford her own flat in a good area, she rents the room of the book's title in the run-down area of Fulham, where the landlady immediately looks at her belly to see if she is pregnant.

Jane is almost paralysed by shame and tells no one that she is expecting a baby, but one by one the other tenants tell her they have guessed her secret. One of them, a retired wardrobe mistress, offers her the traditional home-abortion kit of gin and pills. She wants to end the pregnancy but can't bring herself to do it. She avoids her friends, rebuffs her new neighbours and provokes her employers into firing her. Her spiral of self-blame is only broken when, after an Indian meal – then an exotic novelty – she gets violent indigestion, faints and thinks she is having a miscarriage. A week in hospital follows and she leaves feeling, 'a tremor that was partly apprehension and partly excitement. Still in there, safe and growing!'

The doctor's brutal assertion that single motherhood would be a stupid and unworkable choice reflected the medical orthodoxy of the time, for which one man was principally responsible. John Bowlby, the son of a baronet whose nursemaid brought him to see his mother for an hour a day during his early childhood, was a psychiatrist whose highly influential attachment theory was based on his work with child thieves and refugee children in London. At the end of World War II, he was commissioned to write the World Health Organization's report on the mental health of homeless children in post-war Europe. His book, *Maternal Care and Mental Health*, appeared in 1951 and identified 'maternal deprivation' as a primary cause of neurosis and criminality. This theory resonated strongly with people's nostalgia for family security and anxiety about social change. Although Bowlby later expanded it to suggest that continuity of care, rather than the specific attention of a mother, was the key factor in healthy child development, his theory was soon reduced to the principle that mothers should not work and the child of a single mother should be adopted into a two-parent family.

This simplistic corruption of Bowlby's ideas was extraordinarily pervasive and something that the Rebel Writers questioned instinctively. Even in the frothy, privileged world of *Coronet Among The Weeds,* the narrator argues against the conventional view that a single woman could not bring up a child successfully. 'And they say all those corny things like it would only grow up to be miserable. How do they know it would be miserable? It might grow up to be ecstatically happy'.

Rosamund, in *The Millstone*, breaks the news of her out-of-wedlock pregnancy to her sister (whose own Oxford economics degree had resulted not in a career, but in full-time motherhood as the wife of a scientist). She expects, 'goodwill and sympathy by return of post,' but instead receives a long passionately critical letter advising,

> ... this is the most dreadful mistake and would be frightful for both you and the child. Just think, if you had it adopted you could forget about the whole business and carry on exactly where you left off... It would be bad enough for you but it would be far, far worse for the child. Through no fault of its own it would have to have the slur of illegitimacy all its life... I know that ideally, in a decent society, no child ought to suffer because of this kind of handicap, but this isn't a decent society, and I can't bear the thought of what your baby would have to go through, and what you would have to go through on its account.[4]

Social attitudes were more easily brushed off than government policy, which clearly discriminated against the one-parent family. Housing policy denied public housing to single parents and in family law the opportunity to humanise the process of divorce offered by the Royal Commission of 1956 was not taken. The Commission, a rarely convened way of reviewing legislation, was set up because many different agencies agreed that divorce law was outdated and disadvantaged both women and children at the end of a marriage. It deliberated for five years but did not recommend any significant modernisation of the law, nor did it create the 'no-fault' principle which later allowed a couple simply to acknowledge that their marriage was no longer viable. As a result, divorce remained painful, expensive and weighted in favour of the husband. The law actually protected fathers, both married and unmarried, from the obligation to support their children, so a single mother in early twentieth-century Britain, whether divorced or never married, struggled to survive with her family (unless she hailed from a wealthy background). 'She'd have to go on the National Assistance and starve', as a character in *Up The Junction* describes it.

Rosamund is clear that, with her qualifications, well-paid job, independent mind (and a home courtesy of her parents), she is well placed to become a single mother. The reality for most women was that the combination of Victorian morality, British family law and Bowlby's theories of child development worked at a disadvantage to any unmarried women who became pregnant. She was likely not only to be shamed in her community and family, and shunned by employers, but also condemned by the medical profession. Many young women were sent away to mother and baby homes like that portrayed in *Up The Junction*. From these institutions, some of which were hardly less brutal than the Irish homes depicted in the films *Philomena* and *The Magdalen Girls,* the new-born babies were taken away and placed with adoptive families, at best and at worst fatally neglected. Despite her privileges, Rosamund's world was as hostile to pregnant young women as the rest of the more disadvantaged women in the works of the Rebel Writers, if not more so. A pregnant or divorced woman could expect to lose her job, as well as her family and friends. If she was one of the very small number of women undergraduates at Oxford or Cambridge, she would be sent down, while the child's father was left free to continue his studies.

As positive as the portrayal of single motherhood is in these works, the authors were careful to have their characters achieve that state accidentally. Jo, in *A Taste of Honey*, had a proposal of marriage and a ring to prove it before she conceived. Georgy becomes a mother only by adopting her friend's child. *The L-Shaped Room* Jane loses her virginity to her first love in a misguided attempt to test the strength of their attraction. Rosamund, in *The Millstone,* also has sex for the first and only time in emotional confusion with no pleasure. 'Before I knew where I was I found myself thinking that I couldn't stop him if I really wanted to, because I liked him so much, and if I stopped him he would believe that I didn't'. Joy, in *Poor Cow*, finds herself alone as a single mother after both her husband and lover are sent to prison.

GETTING RID OF IT

The language used by the young women characters in this study reflects the prevailing prejudices of the day, as well as their social positions. For working-class girls, being pregnant is often described as being 'in trouble'. Caithleen's friend, Baba, in *The Lonely Girl* (the second of Edna O'Brien's *Country Girls* trilogy), warns her friend:

> 'Brace yourself'. She said, touching my glass with hers. 'I have bad news…'.
> 'I'm in trouble,' she said.
> 'What kind?' said I, hopelessly.
> 'Jesus, there is only one kind'.
> 'Oh no,' I said, drawing back from her as if she had just insulted me. 'How could you?'

Similarly, Georgy observes, when speaking of her friend and flatmate, 'it was Meredith got herself into trouble'.

The shadow of abortion falls over the lives of every woman portrayed by these authors. At the most insouciant level, Charlotte Bingham's narrator makes friends with an actress who tells her of her pregnancy, '…just like that. For heaven's sake, like you'd say: "have an olive". She was going to a psychiatrist and he'd prove her unfit to have a baby then she'd have an abortion… It was dead simple'.

This path, open to confident or protected middle-class women who could find an amenable doctor, was the only legal means of terminating a pregnancy in Britain at the time. It exploited a narrow loophole in the law. While the governing legislation, the Offences Against the Person Act of 186, ruled all abortion to be illegal, a precedent was set in 1938 when a physician, Dr Alex Bourne was acquitted after he performed an abortion on a suicidal 14-year-old rape victim. After this, the law deemed that a pregnancy could be terminated only if two doctors agreed, 'on reasonable grounds and with adequate knowledge of the probable consequences', that continuing the pregnancy would cause the woman serious physical or mental harm. This decision applied to mainland Britain only and the most restrictive law on abortion in Europe still applied until recently in Northern Ireland and Eire. Edna O'Brien's Caithleen, when living in Dublin hearing that her friend, Baba, is pregnant, says she will, 'have to go to England'.

Women with the means and inclination were able to exploit this loophole. Thus Meredith, the biological mother of the child in *Georgy Girl,* tells her boyfriend, Jos, that she is pregnant and wants to marry him. When he is not immediately enthusiastic, she says:

'I just feel like a change. But I've told you – you don't have to. I can easily get rid of the baby. I've no tender feelings about it'.

'I have,' said Jos, gloomily. 'I always knew I would have. I couldn't let you destroy it'.

'Don't be stupid,' said Meredith, tartly. 'I've destroyed two of yours already'.

Jos stared at her. 'When?'

'I've forgotten. You made me pregnant twice and I've got rid of them, that's all'.

Women for whom a legal abortion was unattainable tried home remedies, such as the gin and 'pills' offered by a concerned neighbour in *The L-Shaped Room,* or the castor-oil drunk in a hot bath by Baba in *Girls In Their Married Bliss.* Quinine is suggested, without much conviction, by a character in *Bang on the Common*, a story in *Up The Junction* about Rube, a 17-year-old factory worker who realises she is pregnant and is taken by a friend to an abortionist who has clearly done so well that she has bought herself a 'big place' in the genteel outer suburb of Wimbledon. She agrees to perform the procedure for four pounds, plus ten shillings for a quarter-bottle of whisky and her method involves inserting a syringe into the uterus.

It is not effective and Rube has to go back to the abortionist seven times before anything happens. A terrible pain seizes her one Sunday morning. The abortionist refuses to help and Rube, screaming and semi-delirious, at first refuses to have a doctor called in case, 'they might try and save the baby'.

> The baby was born alive, five months old. It moved, it breathed, its heart beat.
>
> Rube lay back, white and relieved, across the bed. Sylvie and her mum lifted the eiderdown and peered at the tiny baby still joined by the cord. 'You can see it breathing, look!'
>
> Rube smiled. 'It's nothing – I've had a look meself'.
>
> 'I reckon she had some pluck going seven times,' said her mum.
>
> Finally the ambulance arrived. They took Rube away but they left behind the baby, which had now grown cold. Later Sylvie took him, wrapped in the *Daily Mirror*, and threw him down the toilet.

In 1962, 14,600 women in England and Wales were treated in hospital after illegal abortions and unofficial estimates put the number of back-street abortions carried out annually at over 100,000. Four years after *Up The Junction* was published and after mass demonstrations in London, the Abortion Act of 1967 legalised the termination of a pregnancy by a qualified doctor, up to twenty-four weeks of gestation, in circumstances in which – broadly speaking – the mother would be more at risk if the pregnancy continued.

The proportion of children born in England and Wales to women who were not married – whether single, divorced or widowed – doubled between 1955 and 1970, but remained very low, at just over 2 per cent. Under the influence of researchers such as the social reformer, Margaret Wynn, who published her study *Fatherless Families* in 1964, welfare agencies began to consider the problems of single parent households to be the result chiefly of poverty rather than maternal deprivation, although it would be many decades before paternal abandonment was also identified as a contributing factor. The dominance of Bowlby's theories was slowly eroded. In 1967 housing law was modified to allow single parents to apply for public housing but it wasn't until twenty years later that the Family Law Reform Act of 1987 finally legislated against discrimination towards single parents and their children.

It is impossible, of course, to show a causal link between the works in this study, popular and influential as they were, and these advances, which many agencies across the board supported. However, the Report of the National Council for the Unmarried Mother and Her Child (now known as Gingerbread), the leading charity in the field, noted in 1969 'welcome signs of a trend towards tolerance. Some credit must go to the press, television and radio for their sympathetic presentation'.[5]

8

A ROTTEN BARGAIN: MARRIAGE

The wedding industry was born in the fifties. After half a century of war and depression, people were desperate for something to celebrate and what better symbol of hope than a wedding? The publication that encapsulated this whole new industry — *Brides & Setting up Home* magazine — was first published by Conde Nast in 1955 and edited by a 23-year-old rising star in journalism, Penelope Gilliatt — who was herself a newlywed. The launch cover featured a smiling bride carrying a posy of daisies in her white gloved hands and receiving a respectful, if faintly patronising, kiss on the forehead from her groom. The following year, Hollywood film star Grace Kelly married Prince Rainier of Monaco in front of the world's news media, in antique Brussels lace and 400 yards of ivory silk faille, the gift of MGM, the studio to which she was contracted. The image of the pure, beautiful young bride was seared into the collective consciousness.

The role of wife was fetishised across the social and community spectrum. Both families and schools trained young women to be worthy of their calling — which was, ultimately, that of wife and mother. 'Be a good girl/Lead a good life/Meet a good husband/And make a good wife,' was a rhyme mothers wrote in their daughters' autograph books.[1] At school, girls learned how to make clothes, to cook and to clean a home. Class differences were clear; at secondary modern schools the emphasis was on sweeping, polishing and washing up, while grammar school girls, with a higher academic ability, were taught to launder the embroidered cloth for the tea tray, 'in case a duchess came to tea'.

Marriage was considered to be a woman's entire life work. A study of school leavers in 1962 found that 89 per cent of secondary modern school girls and 76 per cent of grammar school girls expected to marry between the ages of twenty and twenty-five.[2] One girl's ambition was quoted verbatim: 'what she wanted *have* was a wedding ring, what she wanted to *do* was to get married, what she wanted to *be* was a wife and mother'.[3]

MARRIAGE IN REAL LIFE

This vision of the virginal bride embarking on a blissful future of child-rearing and domestic work is entirely absent from the works of the Rebel Writers. The first model of marriage that a child has is usually that of their parents, but four of the Rebel Writers, Lynne Reid Banks, Charlotte Bingham, Virginia Ironside and Nell Dunn, find various ways to keep the parental relationship out of their work and for those who chose to portray the family life of their heroine, such as Edna O'Brien and Shelagh Delaney, the picture is a horrifying one. The clear implication is that their mothers' way of living is not a model these writers would choose for their own lives.

In *A Taste of Honey* there is a sharp contrast between the mundane brutality of a marriage proposal made to Jo's mother Helen and the child-like romance between Jo and her boyfriend. At the beginning of the play Helen and Jo are moving into a new room and the implication is that Helen is trying to get away from Peter, the man who has been paying her for sex. Peter tracks her down to her poor new home, tells her to 'get rid' of her daughter and then starts fumbling with her clothes. When she resists, he says,

> PETER: Well, put your hat on, let's go for a drink. Come on
>   down to the church and I'll make an honest woman of you.
> HELEN: [She goes to put her coat on, then changes her mind.]
>   No, I don't fancy it.
> PETER: I'm offering to marry you, dear.

HELEN: You what?

PETER: Come on, let's go for a drink.

HELEN: I told you I don't fancy it.

PETER: You won't find anything better.

HELEN: Listen, love, I'm old enough to be your mother.

PETER: [petting her] Now you know I like this mother and son relationship.

HELEN: Stop it!

PETER: [sings] 'Walter, Walter, lead me to the altar!'

HELEN: Some hopes.

PETER: Helen, you don't seem to realise what an opportunity I'm giving you. The world is littered with women I've rejected, women still anxious to indulge my little vices and excuse my less seemly virtues. Marry me, Helen. I'm young, good-looking and well set up. I may never ask you again.

HELEN: You're drunk.

This, in reality, is Larkin's 'wrangle for the ring'. Peter, described as a 'brash car salesman' of about thirty, throws in the idea of marriage as a way of persuading Helen to have sex with him again. He follows up with chocolates, flowers and a meal in a restaurant and tells her he's found a house. Helen buys a wedding outfit, but it is not clear that they ever marry and by the second act he has deserted her for another woman.

In contrast, when Jo's boyfriend, Jimmie, meets her at the school gate and asks her to marry him the marriage seems to be a game of playing house for them both, a place where he can escape naval discipline and she can start to build an identity away from her emotionally abusive mother. Although Jo responds to the proposal with some defensive joking, their exchanges are loving and he gives her an engagement ring that she wears on a string around her neck because it is too big for her. When Helen sees it and Jo tells her she's going to get married, her mother replies, 'You stupid little devil!

What sort of a wife do you think you'd make? You're useless. It takes you all your time to look after yourself. I suppose you think you're in love. Anybody can fall in love, do you know that? But what do you know about the rest of it?'

When Jo's boyfriend returns to naval duty a few days after he proposes to her, she never writes to him or makes sure he will know where to find her when he returns. For Jo, marriage – indeed, happiness – is hardly more than a mirage. She thinks of Jimmie as 'only a dream I had' and, with her mother's life as a 'semi-whore' as an example, she cannot believe that she is worthy of love, or that a man will really want to marry her. Although she does not play on her youth in the text, it also seems likely that, as a schoolgirl in her mid-teens, she sees marriage as a far-off, adult undertaking. When her mother asks if she has tried to trace Jimmie, she answers, 'I wouldn't do that, it's degrading'.

In the play's second act, when Jo's flatmate, Geof asks her to marry him, her ideas of what a marriage might be are as contradictory as her feelings about motherhood.

GEOF: Do you remember when I asked you to marry me?
JO: Yes
GEOF: You just went and lay on the bed.
JO: And you didn't go and follow me, did you?
GEOF: No
JO: You see, it's not marrying love between us, thank God.
GEOF: You mean you just like having me around till you next prince comes along?
[…]
JO: It's a bit daft talking about getting married, isn't it? We're already married. We've been married for a thousand years.

Edna O'Brien paints an even darker picture of a marriage in *The Country Girls*. In the house surrounded by fields in the west of Ireland, Caithleen often wakes in terror because her father is once again missing from home. At breakfast she looks at her shy, gentle mother and imagines what lies behind her silence. 'She was thinking. Thinking, where was he? Would he come home in an ambulance, or a hackney car, hired in Belfast three days ago and not paid for? Would he stumble up the stone steps at the back door waving a bottle of whiskey? Would he shout, struggle, kill her, or apologise? ...All this had happened to us so many times it was foolish to expect him to come home sober'.

Caithleen's mother drowns in a nearby lake shortly afterwards but a few years later her daughter starts to replicate her supine suffering in her own marriage. At the opening of *Girls in Their Married Bliss*, the third novel in the trilogy, Caithleen's friend Baba observes, 'Not long ago Kate [Caithleen] Brady and I were having a few gloomy gin fizzes up London, bemoaning the fact that nothing would ever improve, that we'd die the way we were – enough to eat, married, dissatisfied'. The 'wrangle,' in the case of these women, was for meals in restaurants. Marriage is discussed, but for Kate (Baba has anglicised her name, Caithleen) as for so many young women it only becomes a reality after she is pregnant.

Although Kate/Caithleen's husband Eugene is not an alcoholic like her father, he is a bully, manipulative and controlling. Their married life is devoid of affection and Kate's status in the household is not far from that of their live-in servant, with whom Eugene is also having sex. He sleeps until noon, when Kate brings him his morning tea on a prettily arranged tray, and obsessively writes notes and journal entries. When Kate becomes drawn into a flirtation with another man, she vows to, 'expiate all by sinking into domesticity', but to no avail – Eugene finds out and the marriage ends, bleakly, with him threatening to take her son away.

Baba, in contrast, agrees to marry the uneducated but wealthy Irish builder, Frank, whose construction business in London has made him rich despite his social 'limitations'. He has had sex with prostitutes but has no idea how to have sex with his wife. Their marriage is eventually consummated but Baba is not physically

Never having it so good; the advertisers' fantasy of 1950s family life.

Meet the Robinsons...

At home to that good meal they need!

Could be your family is like the Robinsons. There's young Jimmy, who's developing into a demon fast bowler; sister Angela who's a fully fledged librarian; Father is 'something in the city' and Mother describes herself as 'something in the kitchen'. They have their ups and downs, of course. For instance, take Father tonight. Came in, plumped himself down behind a paper, said his new assistant was a pain in the neck, and that he was too tired for anything

but a snack. Not that anyone took any notice of that! "It's roast beef and potatoes for you just as I planned" said Mother firmly. "Don't forget the Batchelors Peas" cried young Jimmy. Mother didn't. See how soon this good meal is putting Father into a good temper again!

Batchelors Peas go with practically everything. They turn good meals into wonderful meals. They are the nicest, plumpest peas sold in Britain. Lay in a stock today!

Batchelors PEAS

make a good meal WONDERFUL

4 out of 6 women know how to make a good meal wonderful

A nation-wide survey showed that of all women who named their favourite brand of peas, 4 out of 6 named Batchelors.

The reality; a woman with her children pictured in South London in 1971.

Françoise Sagan, pictured by Bert Hardy in Paris, the year after *Bonjour Tristesse* was published.

Shelagh Delaney in 1958.

Angela Lansbury and Joan Plowright in the 1960 Broadway production of *A Taste of Honey*.

Edna O'Brien pictured
with her husband,
Ernest Gébler.

Edna O'Brien in 1970,
free to write at last.

Lynne Reid Banks;
one writer who
managed to be
photographed at
her desk.

Charlotte Bingham with her
mother, Madeleine Bingham
(Lady Clanmorris) at lunch
to celebrate the publication
of *Coronet Among the Weeds*.

Nell Dunn in 1965;
a portrait for *London
Life Magazine*.

Virginia Ironside, reluctant
teenybopper novelist.

Paul Danquah and Rita Tushingham as Jimmie and Jo in Tony Richardson's 1961 film adaption of *A Taste of Honey*.

Margaret Forster pictured at home with her husband, Hunter Davies, and one of their children.

Suzy Kendall, in the white mini-skirt, cast as the posh girl who moves to Battersea in the 1968 film adaption of *Up The Junction*.

attracted to her husband and knows he is still visiting prostitutes. She starts an affair with another man, who disappears, leaving her pregnant. Her husband is angry but she knows that he will not want a divorce because much of his business is with Catholic customers. She leaves him for a few hours until they agree to stay married. 'Among other things I did not relish going out into the world to sell buns or be a shorthand typist'. The marriage thereafter endures for decades and Baba consoles herself with casual affairs until Frank is half-paralysed by a stroke and she is content to be his caring companion.

NO SORT OF COMPLIMENT
For Charlotte Bingham and Virginia Ironside, two of the youngest authors in this study the concept of marriage – either their parents' or their own possible future – simply does not feature in their works despite the fact that Charlotte Bingham's narrator is dispatched to the debutante season, London's upper-class marriage market; her focus is on her ideal partner, the 'superman,' rather than marriage itself. For Ironside's Harriet the whole concept is impossibly unfashionable.

Marriage is portrayed as the concomitant of pregnancy by Margaret Forster and Lynne Reid Banks. Terry, the father of Jane's baby in *The L-Shaped Room*, does what he feels is expected of him and feebly proposes marriage. Jane turns him down immediately. When she tells him that she and her father are reconciled, so she has financial support, he is, 'giddy with relief' and she reflects that, 'his proposal wasn't any sort of compliment, when you came right down to it; it was simply an attempt at expiation. I was fond of him, but I didn't respect him and more than he did me. Which wasn't much, whatever he might say. To him I was irretrievably that sort of girl for ever.'

For Nell Dunn's women in *Up The Junction*, marriage is expected of them at a young age, and is also often a consequence of pregnancy.

These teenage marriages are flimsy connections that break apart under pressures of poverty and new attractions. Sylvie, a character in the story *Wedding Anniversary,* remembers:

> I was the youngest bride in Battersea, married at fifteen, had Mike when I was fifteen-and-a-half. Ten minutes after he was born I was sittin' up in bed suckin' a stick of rock... [He] Expected me to live in a furnished room in Brixton. What could I do in one room all day! If you've got two, at least you can go from one to the others. Didn't even like me going early-morning cleaning with me mum, so then he starts going to the dogs every Wednesday night and I meet up with this Fred, handsome fella! Every Wednesday in his ten-ton truck, waitin' on the corner. Cor...

Sylvie reminisces on the day that Princess Margaret, the Queen's sister, is married – with all the pomp and extravagance of a royal wedding – in Westminster Abbey. The pubs in Battersea stayed open all day in celebration, a sharp juxtaposition by Dunn of the bleak reality of working-class marriage with the idealised media picture of a royal wedding. She also uses advertising tropes and pop song lyrics throughout her books to underscore the irreconcilable gulf between the consumerist dreams of the time and the reality of life for working-class people.

The order and cleanliness as portrayed in such advertisements are impossible aspirations for the teenage wives of Battersea. Their homes constitute of one or two rooms in houses occupied by dozens of others, with a shared bathroom down the stairs and meagre shared cooking facilities. Many are in debt to small-time loan sharks who sell them poor quality blankets or clothes for their children at exorbitant prices, knowing to visit them on the days that their welfare benefits are paid and threatening to tell their husbands or take them to court if they don't cough up the crippling instalments to which they were forced to agree. Hot water and indoor plumbing were by no means universal; Joy in *Poor Cow* has to carry cold water up to her room from the bathroom and heat it on her stove to give her baby a bath. The new labour-saving devices of the time – a fridge, freezer, washing machine, tumble dryer or a dishwasher – are unknown to them and worth more than their annual wages. The only household innovation that is often mentioned is a television, which could be rented for only a few shillings a month. Without refrigeration, the women shop for food every day and keep milk fresh in the winter by putting the bottle on the windowsill. They wash baby clothes by hand and take dirty adult clothes down to the launderette a few streets away, where is put in the machines by an elderly woman who had worked in a 'bagwash' all her life, since long before laundry was mechanised. A wife is expected to undertake this relentless struggle to maintain basic living standards as well as earning whatever money she can by working.

When Joy thinks about marriage, it isn't only this drudgery that repels her but the fact that she doesn't enjoy sex with her husband, which on closer reading implies that she has no sense of intimacy or of affection. Tom, her husband, prevents her from doing anything that gives her a sense of pleasure or independence. Towards the end of *Poor Cow*, when Tom is released from prison and has become violent, she suddenly realises how little she can do to make her life bearable. ' I suppose my life is over [...] I'm frightened of being on my own [...] it would be one room and National Assistance and Jonny in a day nursery'.

Joy is already reliant on National Assistance because Tom, a professional burglar since childhood, is struggling to steal enough to provide for the family because the associates needed to plan and execute profitable robberies are still in prison. The welfare system at this time was structured to support marriages by assuming that the husband was the head of the household and paying benefits to him. Housing benefit was also paid on the assumption that the family in need of a home was headed by a man, so a mother's access to all benefits was restricted and could be controlled by her husband.

This meant that a woman without a well-paid job, and probably also the support of friends or family for childcare, could not leave her husband no matter how bad the marriage.

The extent to which single mothers were invisible to the welfare system was extraordinary. At the time that Nell Dunn was writing *Poor Cow* a commission of civil servants, all male, was assessing the National Assistance payments. They concluded, in 1965, that welfare payments were too low and did not take account to changing norms, such as the shift from coal as a primary household fuel, or the introduction of labour-saving devices. Apart from one reference to 'a young, active widow with growing children to look after,' there is no mention of a single mother, whether divorced or unsupported, and no account taken of the unstable family structures that are the norm among Nell Dunn's characters.

9

GOOD OLD JOHN: RACE

THE AGE OF THE LONELY LONDONERS

This study begins in 1958, the year which saw the first race riots in London in which groups of white people, inspired and organised by British fascist organisations, attacked black people in Notting Hill, an area of the city which had a substantial community of immigrants from the Caribbean. The riots were triggered after passers-by tried to intervene between a wife and husband who were arguing. Majbritt Morrison was white, from Sweden, and her husband, Raymond, was black, an artist from Jamaica. The following day a group of white men attacked Majbritt and threatened to kill her. When police arrived to protect her the men began a violent rampage through the streets and were soon joined by gangs organised by fascist organisations such as the White Defence League, a precursor of the British National Party.[1] The riots lasted for five days with mobs several hundred strong in the streets of Notting Hill Gate, chanting 'We will kill all black bastards – why don't you send them home?' The weapons seized by the police included knives, clubs, razors, broken bottles and petrol bombs. Thus the women in this study were writing at a time when racial tension was intensifying in Britain and the population was becoming polarised between liberal and fascist factions.

As the eminent historian Mary Beard, among others, has established, people of African origin had been living in Britain since Roman times, at least.[2] A diverse population will develop in any small island that is much invaded and always dependent on trade. In the

colonial era, statesmen, industrialists and diplomats from Africa
and Asia were frequent arrivals in London and, as authors including
Paul Scott in *The Raj Quartet* and Hari Kunzru in *The Impressionist*
recorded, their children studied at British public schools.[3]

So a small degree of diversity was nothing new among the elite.
What was different in the post-war era was the mass migration
of blue-collar workers from the countries of the former British
Empire, notably countries in the Caribbean region, which was
promoted by the government to provide the labour force necessary
to rebuild the country after the conflict. Many of the young men
who came to Britain to find work had had fought in the war as
servicemen. They are now known as the Windrush generation, after
the name of the government-owned troopship that brought the first
500 immigrants to London from Jamaica in 1948, the same years as
the British Nationalities Act gave all Commonwealth citizens British
citizenship.[4]

The Rebel Writers observed racial tensions in the communities
they portrayed. The attitudes and language some their characters
display towards people from ethnic minorities are clearly racist
and often ignorant. They seem crude and offensive to a modern
reader, although they were an authentic depiction of Britain in
the late fifties and sixties. While people of colour were a familiar
sight in some parts of the country's cities, many British people had
never seen, met or spoken to a person of another race at that time.
The choices made by Shelagh Delaney and Lynne Reid Banks in
particular, whose work included Jimmie, Jo's fiancé in *A Taste of
Honey*, and John, who becomes a pivotal character as the story of
Jane and Toby's relationship unfolds in *The L-Shaped Room*, were
ground-breaking in this respect. By the late Sixties attitudes had
changed in liberal London, and, as Virginia Ironside observed, it
was fashionable to be part of a multi-cultural friendship group.

Quirks of the capital's geography had concentrated West Indian
immigrants in two central areas. Those who were looking for
work were housed temporarily in an old air-raid shelter in the

region of Clapham, just south of Battersea, and some stayed in the area, settling in the even more deprived area of Brixton nearby. A substantial proportion also followed the much larger influx of workers from Ireland, who settled in the run-down multi-occupancy houses in another notoriously poor area in the inner north-west, Notting Hill.

The new arrivals found work in factories, hospitals, offices and transport industries. By 1971 Britain's total population of just 56 million included 3 million immigrants; 171,000 of Jamaican origin, 313,000 from India and 676,000 from Ireland. Unlike the much larger number of immigrants from Ireland, like the farm worker Hickey in *The Country Girls,* or the wartime refugees from Europe, the West Indians and Asians were instantly identifiable by their skin colour. Racism against all immigrants was ingrained and overt, expressed in job advertisements and room-for-rent signs reading 'No Irish, No Blacks, No Dogs'.

The Trinidadian writer Sam Selvon portrayed the experience of West Indian immigrants, male in the majority, in his 1956 novel *The Lonely Londoners* and the London-born author Colin MacInnes followed the next year with *City of Spades,* with a Nigerian protagonist, the first of a trilogy set in Notting Hill. They paint a picture of a cold, unwelcoming place to live, in which people are isolated and marginalised. Within the multi-ethnic areas of deprivation, immigrant communities are beginning to form and develop their own culture, defending themselves against the hostile city. The writers in this study, however, focused on inter-racial relationships, depicting racist hostility as well as love and friendship between their white and black characters.

Shelagh Delaney and Lynne Reid Banks created substantial black characters with essential narrative roles, and most of the writers in this study note the everyday racism of their time. The ignorance on which racist attitudes are founded, unsparingly written, would be funny if it were not set against the real-life backdrop of violence. In *Poor Cow*, Joy's rooming house neighbour warns her, 'A man broke in and done (robbed) our meter last night. The police says, "I pity you white women in this house with all these coloureds down the street". They could tell he was coloured from the fingerprints.'

Dunn's community is almost completely monocultural, and, while bombed buildings still stand as a reminder of more turbulent times, a stable, unchanging life, however hard, offers a form of security, She writes of people who have lived all their lives within an area bounded by a few streets, and families that have been established in the same neighbourhood for generations. Battersea, situated to the west of Brixton, has some West Indian or Asian people; her characters refer in passing to an 'Indian gink'. There is a black woman among the women in the hostel for unmarried mothers, who is told by the matron, 'You coloured girls should be grateful to be here at all with what goes on out in Africa'. Black women as well as white visit their menfolk in prison: 'Look at the state of their tarts'. The tally man, selling cheap clothes door-to-door, reports from Brixton that 'Sixty per cent of me calls are black – I'm like the white hunter, at the end of the street you can practically hear the Tom Tom going 'Sandy's back again'.'

The Tally Man is a short story in Up the Junction which the author steps into the foreground as narrator. Another of the salesmen invites her to come with him,

'Come on, I'm selling a suit to a darkie'.

He banged on the door and a gentle-faced Negro let us in. 'Hello, sah'. [...] He lived in one bow-faced room and I looked the other way while he tried (the suit). In one corner was a neat cot and a sleeping baby, black face snudged against the white sheet. The cooker was under the window next to a shiny walnut radiogram and beyond a double bed. On the other wall was a dressing-table with a small mirror above it in which the Negro bent up to see himself in his new suit. [The Tally Man persuades him to buy the suit although it is too small for him.]

The baby woke and started to whimper so he picked her up in his great arms and put a record on the gramophone. 'She likes music,' he says, smiling.

Outside Barney bent himself in half. 'They just make me roll up...'

We drove back towards home. 'You see the blacks have only got half the brain cells to what we've got. They never had a civilisation, they never even invented the wheel – what jerks to go through life without inventing the wheel'.

The organised racism that led to the Notting Hill riots has no purchase on the lives of Nell Dunn's characters, although the British fascist movement had been active in Battersea since the 1930s. Dunn's characters pass racist graffiti: BLACKS OUT FOR A WHITE CHRISTMAS, so are aware of racial tensions, but while they express ignorant beliefs, their racism is largely unconscious and they accept their black neighbours as just another minor change to a way of life that would always endure. There is a sense that their black neighbours, as the poorest of the poor and without the support of a long-established community, have a natural right to sympathy.

Over the river, in Fulham, Lynne Reid Bank's heroine in *The L-Shaped Room*, Jane, has just moved into the room of the novel's title. Seeing that the partition wall that creates the room's odd shape is very thin, she taps it to test its strength. Immediately she is answered by knocking from the room next door and, intrigued, knocks back to communicate.

> I felt a shiver of nervousness as the clear, hollow sound emphasized the thinness of the barrier. Suddenly the knocking changed. It was on glass this time, near the ceiling. I looked up and saw, in the little window, a huge black face.
>
> I gasped with fright and ran back round the angle (of the wall) again where I couldn't be seen. I felt my heart slamming and caught sight of my own face in the mirror, as deathly white as

the other had been black. I blundered about for a few seconds
in a blind panic, and then my knees buckled and I flopped on to
the cold lino by the bed with a thump. [...] I took a deep breath
and forced myself to relax. After all, why in God's name should
a black face be more alarming than a white one? So, I was next
door to a negro. [...] I didn't know what atavistic terror had
caused me to behave so stupidly.

The noise of her collapse alerts the man who lives below her, Toby,
with whom she is already friendly. He comes up to see if she's all
right, helps her light the gas and open and bottle of wine and then
tells her about her black neighbour, John. 'He wouldn't hurt a fly,
old John. He's got those great brutal-looking hands that you'd think
could snap your backbone like a twig, and then, when he shakes
hands with you and you feel them, damn me, they're like a baby's
bottom'. He goes on to tell her that John is a fine cook and also does
needlework. They have a conversation through the wall. Next day,
John, who proves to be a guitarist, comes to the door of Jane's room
with a cup of tea.

Jane, Toby and John swiftly become friends, going out to the pub
as a threesome and forming the basis of the urban family which is
such a feature of this writing. When Toby and Jane becomes lovers,
still in the room next to John, he is shocked and can't easily resolve
his feelings, but once Toby leaves the house John becomes her
devoted protector and, in secret, makes a crib for her baby.

In *A Taste of Honey*, Jo's boyfriend and the father of her child, is
described as 'a coloured naval rating'. After he proposes marriage
and gives her a ring, he says:

BOY: What will your mother say?
JO: She'll probably laugh.
BOY: Doesn't she care who her daughter marries?
JO: She's not marrying you, I am. It's got nothing to do with
     her.

BOY: She hasn't seen me.

JO: And when she does?

BOY: She'll see a coloured boy.

JO: No, whatever else she might be, she isn't prejudiced against colour.

Delaney does not suggest that Jo has chosen Jimmie (as she gives his name later) to confront her mother and assert her identity, nor does she imply that she has done so from a sexual motive. The audience could believe that Jo has had sex only once, and did not particularly enjoy it. She does regard Jimmie as exotic, however.

JO: Sometimes you look three thousand years old. Did your ancestors come from Africa?

BOY: No, Cardiff. Disappointed? Were you hoping to marry a man whose father beat the tom-tom all night?

JO: I don't care where you were born. There's still a bit of jungle in you somewhere.

Much later, in conversation with Geof, she sings a few lines from a traditional American folk song recorded by the bluegrass singer, Leadbelly, switching the words from 'black girl' to 'black boy': 'Black boy, black boy, don't you lie to me...' Momentarily, she romanticises Jimmie as an African prince.

Despite claiming that her mother is not racist, she eventually tries to defend herself against her mother's control of her life by telling her, 'My baby may be black'. Helen's response is a paroxysm of shock.

HELEN: You mean to say that ... that sailor was a black man? ... Oh my God! Nothing else can happen to me now. Can you see me wheeling a pram with a ... Oh my God. I'll have to have a drink.

JO: What are you going to do?

HELEN: I don't know. Drown it. Who knows about it. [...]
And what about the nurse? She's going to get a bit of a
shock, isn't she?
JO: Well, she's black too.

In this text a relationship between a white woman and a black man
is portrayed as shocking only to the ignorant and ill-intentioned.
Jimmie is conscious that he may meet racist attitudes but does
not seem to have internalised a sense of exclusion. Jo, equally,
responds to him as different and from a world outside the confines
of her unhappy life. She is a habitually provocative character, and
enjoys Jimmie's 'otherness' but only tries to exploit her mother's
racism when she is desperate to defend herself and has nothing
else in her armoury. The play's ending implies that, after a drink,
Helen will get over her alarm and persist in moving in on her
daughter.

While London's first settlers from the West Indies seemed
resigned to the racism they encountered, the people who made the
journey in the early sixties, such as the activist and politician Darcus
Howe, were determined to push back, supported by liberal whites
and inspired by the Civil Rights movement in America. They founded
the Campaign Against Racial Discrimination in 1964 and Howe
edited one of several news magazines aimed at the black community.
Martin Luther King visited London three times between 1961 and
1964, when he preached to a standing-room-only congregation at St
Paul's Cathedral, the capital's largest Anglican place of worship. Black
Panther leaders Malcolm X and Stokely Carmichael followed, and
the British Black Panther movement was set up in 1968. However,
there were significant differences between the British and American
black power movements, as the activist Selma James explained in
an article in the *Guardian* commemorating King's sermon: 'In the
US, you cannot say black people are not American, but here people
did question the Britishness of black people. There were questions

about the extent to which the UK was like the US, but it was different because we didn't have the whole weight of slavery and lynching. But there was the common thread of persecution and how to confront it'.[5]

The common causes made between civil rights groups and the adoption of radical liberalism as almost an intellectual fashion statement led to the phenomenon lampooned by Tom Wolfe in his decade-defining New Yorker essay, *Radical Chic: That Party at Lennie's*. This portrait of the senior officers of the Black Panther party as guests of honour at a soiree given by composer Leonard Bernstein captured the awkwardness of privileged liberals seeking to demonstrate their beliefs by entertaining the leaders of the most extreme black power groups.

Radical chic also had its days in London, as Virginia Ironside and Edna O'Brien observed. Black guests were sought-after and sometimes lionised by the intellectual elite which was not always to their advantage. In The Slashers, nightclub preferred by the models, writers and art students of *Chelsea Bird*, Harriet tries to escape to the toilets for some respite from her date's relentless pretentiousness and encounters a group of white men determined to get their black friend drunk.

> I pushed my way through all the 'In' people up the stairs, past a drunk black guy who yelled, 'Kiss me, kiss me,' after me and heard the murmurs of appreciation of this remark between his friends ('Great GREAT guy! Fabulous man!') as they picked him up and rushed him downstairs to buy him another drink.
>
> Who was patronising who? I wondered, as I entered the Ladies.

And in *Girls in their Married Bless* Kate is asked to a spontaneous party by an acquaintance, a photographer who she liked because she had casually confided that she too had a violent husband. The

Thames-side house, lit with candles in bottles, is crammed with
people but in her fragile mental state Kate thinks:

> Possibly everyone in the room had had a catastrophe, so why
> should hers be condonable?
>
> 'Darling, just make yourself known to everyone,' the hostess
> said. Kate looked around. Two West Indians were arguing.
> Sophistication. She thought of telling them of a sign she'd seen
> in the Underground which said NIGS GET OFF OUR WOMEN,
> but they might not laugh. They might just tell her to hoof off'.

10

BEFORE THE URBAN FAMILY: FRIENDSHIP

The Rebel Writers portrayed friendship as the most important relationship for the new generation of women. If family links were exploitative and love a chimera at best, friendship was the great sustaining force for the young women in these stories. It might be a casually contracted relationship seemingly based on being in the same place at the same time, like the close bond that springs up between Jane, Toby and John in *The L-Shaped Room* or a lifelong one-to-one connection based on shared heritage and experience, a traditional pairing of complementary characters, like the hard-headed, adventurous Baba leading on the sensitive Kate in Edna O'Brien's stories, but it was genuine.

Friendship between woman is such a common phenomenon that the parents of a girl who does not seem to have a close friend would worry, yet it is strangely absent in literature before the second half of the twentieth century.

In the Old Testament of the Christian Bible, and in the Ketuvim of the Hebrew scriptures, *The Book of Ruth,* tentatively dated in the 6th Century BC, is almost unique in ancient writing offering a picture of a close, loving and supportive relationship between two women, Ruth and her mother-in-law, Naomi. The world's great myth cycles tend to depict goddesses as consorts, or as rivals for male approval as in the legend of the judgment of Paris. Literature, as it developed, concerned men. And women were only considered in relation to men. Even in the nineteenth century, when women writers at last created female protagonists, none of them had good girlfriends. There is a deep connection between Jane Eyre and the saintly Helen Burns, but it is cut short when Helen dies of tuberculosis before Jane has even left her orphanage. It is tempting to speculate that things might have turned out very differently for Jane Eyre or Catherine Earnshaw if either had had a decent girlfriend to talk sense into them, as Baba frequently does to Kate in *The Country Girls* trilogy.

Margaret Atwood, in her *New York Times* essay, 'That Certain Thing Called the Girlfriend', noted the extraordinary absence of this most widespread bond between women in both literature and in factual records, quoting Professor Carroll Smith-Rosenberg: 'the long-lived, intimate, loving friendship between two women, is an excellent example of the type of historical phenomena that most historians know something about, few have thought much about and virtually no one has written about'.

The generational attachment between women was the subject of Mary McCarthy's novel *The Group,* published in 1963, and very much a companion to the works in this study because the women's friendship is predicated on their shared experiences after leaving college, where they too find themselves in a world in which their mothers' life experience is no help to them. It is a thousand pities that Edna O'Brien turned down the opportunity to write the screen adaptation of this novel. In the period following this study the feminist novels of the early 1970s, notably *Down Among The Women* by Fay Weldon and *The Women's Room* by Marilyn French, relationships between women are finally at the centre of the story, but between the lone harbinger of *The Group* and the post-feminist cohorts, however, come these novels by young women in which friendship is a life-shaping force.

GIRLFRIENDS

The first two novels of *The Country Girls* trilogy, narrated from Caithleen's viewpoint, feature Baba as the bolder, richer girl who

Caithleen, living in fear of her alcoholic father, also envies because she is glamorous and seems to have a normal, loving family. 'We were walking in the middle of the road and from behind came the impudent ring of a bicycle bell. It was Baba, looking glorious on her new puce bicycle. She passed with her head in the air and one hand in her pocket. Her black hair was plaited that day and tied at the tips with blue ribbons that matched her ankle socks exactly. I notice with envy that her legs were delicately tanned'.

Caithleen has picked lilac from her mother's garden to give to her teacher but Baba 'Grabbed the lilac out of my arms and said, 'I'll carry that for you'. She laid it into the basket on the front of her bicycle and rode off, singing, 'I will and I must get married,' out loud to herself. She would give Miss Moriarty the lilac and get all the praise for bringing it.

Caithleen says, 'she shouldn't have taken it. She's a bully,' and wavers between envying Baba her prettiness, her elegant free-spending mother and her affectionate father, and despising her for her stupidity. Baba ridicules Caithleen for her run-down home and her drunken father, plays cruel pranks on her and shamelessly boasts about her family's relative wealth. When they go to convent school, Caithleen is on a scholarship which Baba denigrates because, 'it's nicer to pay', it is Baba who gets them expelled, and Baba who resolves to go and find work in Dublin. 'Poor Caithleen, you've always been Baba's tool,' says her friend's gentle father.

Caithleen is more academic than Baba, but as her friend despises school work and the approval of teachers, this cannot give her a real sense of superiority. The only area in which she can compete is with the predatory Mr Gentleman, the Dublin lawyer who cuts something of a figure in the village. When Baba's mother takes the girls to a performance by a touring theatre company, Baba demands to sit next to Mr Gentleman but her mother firmly says she will take that place herself. Baba replies, 'Anyhow, he has some dame in Dublin. A chorus girl,' making it clear that her interest is precociously sexual. Mr Gentleman picks Caithleen for his attentions, probably because she is a near-orphan and so more vulnerable, with no savvy mother to protect her and a father who can be bought off. Caithleen can get an edge in their rivalry by confiding details of their developing relationship to Baba, with much exaggeration. Becoming the victim of a sexual predator is the only thing that gives her leverage in this unequal friendship.

The girls move to Dublin and enter 'that phase of our lives as the giddy country girls brazening the big city'. The cruelties of childhood are behind them, replaced by a deep affection. 'We were young, and, we thought, pretty. Baba was small and thin, with her hair cut short like a boy's and little tempting curls falling on to her forehead [...] But I was tall and gawky, with a bewildered look, and a mass of bewildered auburn hair'. They are lonely in the city, indeed the title of the second novel in the trilogy is *The Lonely Girl* and their friendship comforts them so that Caithleen finds their boarding house room 'cheerless and empty' if Baba leaves it even for a few minutes.

In Dublin, however, the girls start down the different paths in life that eventually separate them. Baba, looking only for restaurant meals and good times, drags Caithleen to bars to pick up men, but Caithleen is by now obsessively attached to Mr Gentleman and the end of their unconsummated affair marks the end of the first novel in the series. In *The Lonely Girl* she falls in love with Eugene. His casual disparagement of every aspect of her life mirrors Baba's schoolgirl superiority, although whereas Baba was no more than accurate in noting that Caithleen's father was a drunk and her home poor and dirty, Eugene has no grounds whatever to call the grocery store where Caithleen works a 'huckster shop'. At the end of this novel Eugene has broken off the relationship, Caithleen is distraught and Baba has got enough money to move to London. She sees Caithleen through four days of despair with the help of pills and whisky, and then they embark for England.

Caithleen gets a job in a delicatessen and takes evening classes in English Literature. 'Even Baba notice that I'm changing, and she says that if I don't give up this learning at night, I'll end up a right drip, wearing flat shoes and glasses'.

Baba, as ever, is right. In the final novel in the trilogy, ironically entitled *Girls in their Married Bliss*. Baba takes over as first-person narrator and the episodes in Kate's life are written from the close third-person point of view. Baba is the bridesmaid when the pregnant Caithleen, now Kate, marries Eugene. Love of any kind is something Baba despises; she marries a rich Irish builder and enjoys a few affairs. It is to Baba that Kate runs when Eugene orders her to leave their home.

At the end of the novel in its original form Kate has loved and been rejected again, Eugene has kidnapped their son and she has paid for a private sterilisation operation. Baba visits her at the clinic when she is recovering and finds her reading a newspaper report about a group of women isolated in a cave as part of a scientific experiment. 'Doctors ... continue to be astonished at the physical resilience and lively spirits of the women, who were unknown to each other before the vigil began'.

Baba brings the news that her husband has suggested Kate move in with them. 'She was glad at being able to make the offer [...] They would have each other, chats, moments of recklessness, they could moon over plans they'd stopped believing in, long ago'.

The first edition of the novel ended there, with the promise that the lifelong friendship would be sustained. When the trilogy was reissued in 1986, however, O'Brien wrote a tragic epilogue to the story of Kate and Baba. Kate, 'prone to the old Via Dolorosa' has died from drowning like her mother, although she may well have ended her life deliberately. It falls to Baba to organise the funeral and to evade her son's questions 'because there are some things in this world you cannot ask, and oh, Agnus Dei, there are some things in this world you cannot answer'.

Edna O'Brien is the only author in this study to place the friendship between two women at the heart of her novels, but others make much of their heroine's friendships. In *Poor Cow*, Joy is almost mentored by the more experienced barmaid, Beryl, with her 'exuding ripe body,' her stories and her wisdom. Like Joy, Beryl enjoys sex, and she has also managed to get a prescription for contraception. She teaches Joy how to manage their predatory customers, and deplores the soft-hearted streak. 'Don't let them have it for nothing. You must charge 'em. I know you, you're soft.' She turns to Beryl for advice, shares her fears, talks about life and death. When her husband gets out of prison, stops her working and moves away, she is desolate.

Predictably, in *Georgy Girl,* the friend is someone even less physically acceptable than the heroine, an obese woman named Peg who lives in the same house, a shoulder to cry on, a playmate in childish fantasy games and ultimately a bridesmaid in whose point of view the last page of the novel are written. Charlotte Bingham's narrator, supposedly on the debutante's mission to add hundreds of new friends to her bulging address book, endures all the cooking classes and cocktail parties with her constant companion, Migo. Hardly half a paragraph into the novel she tells us: 'Migo's my girlfriend, she's a good thing. She's not soppy, but she agrees with me that somewhere there must be a superman'.

Harriet in *Chelsea Bird* has an interesting relationship with Ann, a fellow-student with whom she can enjoy an honest and unpretentious conversation, even if she despises her for being dull, conventional and badly dressed. With Ann, she doesn't have to play the 'smartness game'.

> Ann said how difficult it was for her to find a pair of shoes to fit her because she had such narrow feet, and I said I found it was difficult because my feet were so wide, and she said, 'Oh, not too wide at all', and I said, 'But not as nice as yours'. And then she said didn't men stink, and I said how right she was and they were

all bastards, and she said, 'They only want one thing ...' 'You're so right,' I replied. The conversation followed a pleasant formula. It was convenient having Ann around because I could release all these trite observations and moans without boring real friends with them. I was so glad that no one overheard our conversations, as they would have classed us both as being feminine nit-wits. Ann was, admittedly, but I wasn't, except with her.

Harriet, tortured by the twin terrors of seeming uncool and despising the fashionable kids who define cool itself, finds Ann's devotion cloying but is grateful to her for signing the art school register for her on days when she's absent. When the innocent Ann describes the aftermath of a date to Harriet, asking if Harriet thinks she has actually had intercourse, Harriet is both flattered and embarrassed. At the end of the novel Ann follows Harriet in dropping out of art school, 'becoming less jumpy and more predictable', which implied that the friendship continues even if Harriet is reluctant to admit its importance.

MEN FRIENDS
One of the shockingly innovative aspects of *A Taste of Honey* is that Jo, the 15-year-old protagonist, lives with a gay man, Geof, an art student. The opening of the second act of the play is dedicated to exploring their relationship. It begins with them coming back from a fairground with balloons, like two children. In a taunting conversation Jo asks Geof if his landlady has thrown him out because she caught him with a man, and then tells him he can move in with her if he will 'tell me what you do'. When he is offended and gets up to leave, she apologises and he stays.

The tender and supportive relationship soon becomes the most positive force in both their lives, although they are both struggling to find ways to live. Geof assumes a maternal role in her life, helping her resolve her conflicted feelings about her pregnancy, cooking for her, cleaning their apartment, worrying about her, nagging her about pre-natal clinic visits and buying her a book about pregnancy. While she wavers from excitement at first feeling the baby move to anger and thoughts of suicide, he is thinking about baby clothes and getting someone to make a cradle for the newborn. 'You're just like a big sister to me,' she says.

In an extended scene they explore the nature of their relationship. To both it is a family connection of some kind, although they can't fit their reality into the form of any of the conventional family bonds. She puts her arms around him 'playfully' and says, 'Would you like to be the father of my baby, Geofrey?' to which he replies, 'Yes, I would'.

Geof then introduces the idea of a sexual relationship, saying 'What would you say if I started something?' which Jo dismisses jokingly. He does not drop the issue, but reveals that he has 'never kissed a girl' and then asks to kiss her. It's clear from the text that he is holding her at this point. She struggles, but he kisses her, saying:

GEOF: How was that for first time?
JO: Practise on somebody else.
GEOF: I didn't mean to hurt you.
JO: Look Geof, I like you, I like you very much, but I don't enjoy all this panting and grunting...
GEOF: Marry me, Jo.
JO: Don't breathe all over me like that, you sound like a horse. I'm not marrying anybody...
GEOF: I wouldn't ask you to do anything you didn't want to do.
JO: Yes, you would.

They eat some chocolate then Jo tells Geof that she doesn't think that living with her is doing him any good. He agrees, but he also says, 'I'd sooner be dead than away from you. [...] Before I met you I didn't care one way or the other – I didn't care if I lived or died'.

In his anxiety to do all the right things for a mother-to-be, Geof has tracked down Jo's mother and told her that her daughter is pregnant. In the second half of this act Helen crashes back into her daughter's life, trailing the drunken Peter after her. She abuses Geof, calling him a 'pansified little freak'. (Stronger insults, including 'pervert' were cut when the play was censored). Peter follows up with 'lily' and 'fruitcake parcel'.

On this visit Helen leaves, and in the following scene, some months later, Jo and Geof seem closer and more in harmony than ever and her baby is almost due. But Helen returns. Peter has left her and she announces that she is going to look after Jo. While her daughter is asleep she picks a fight with Geof, throws out the shopping he brings in, denigrates their preparations for the baby and finally tells him to leave. He protests that Jo 'said she wanted me with her when she had it because she said she wouldn't be frightened if I was with her,' but Helen adds protestations of disgust to her bullying and he leaves, saying, 'the one thing civilisation couldn't do anything about – women'. Delaney's original text of the play ended with the clear suggestion that Geof was going to commit suicide, but Joan Littlewood softened this, leaving the possibility that he might return.

In portraying a gay man, Shelagh Delaney was deliberately pushing the boundaries of the theatre. Homosexuality was illegal in Britain in 1958 and gay characters were a major concern for the theatre censorship body of the time, the Office of the Lord Chamberlain. All plays had to be submitted to the Office for review before being licenced for performance. As a result, gay characters were portrayed with a ridiculous armoury of euphemisms. It was the typically hypocritical depiction of a gay man by Terence Rattigan in his play *Variation on a Theme* that had provoked Delaney to write *A Taste of Honey* and this feature of the play was to have significant consequences.

It seems as if something of this motivation was clear to the reader at the Lord Chamberlain's Office who submitted a report on the play. 'It seems he is really quite a normal young man, only not very strongly sexed, and with a very real desire to marry and settle down and have a family,' he wrote, concluding, 'This is a surprisingly good play – thought God knows it is not to my personal taste'. He asks for speeches in which Geof is abused as a 'pervert' and 'castrated little clown' to be reconsidered and adds, 'The point I wish to make is that this play is balanced on a knife-edge: It is the perfect border-line case, since it is concerned with the forbidden subject in a way that no one, I believe, could take exception to. In my opinion, therefore, it is RECOMMENDED FOR LICENSE'. Second and third opinions were added to the report, one of which was, 'I think it's revolting, quite apart from the homosexual bits,' but the original judgment stood.

The single mothers portrayed by the works in this study gather around them a group of friends who are united in their care, support and affection for women at the most frightening time of their lives. There is a clear suggestion that children are raised by a community, not just by their biological parents, and that parental feelings are latent in many childless people. Every resident of the run-down house that includes *The L-Shaped Room* rallies round in their way to look after Jane, as do others beyond her blood family. John, the West Indian guitarist, is the first person to put a hand on her belly and feel the baby move, and stays at the hospital all night when she gives birth, sitting with her lover, Toby and her father. But the retired costume designer makes baby clothes and her former boss brings diapers while the obstetrician himself lends her a pram.

Georgy Girl depicts a similar swirl of concern around its protagonist, even though the baby is not hers, but born to her unfeeling flatmate Meredith. These relationships are more conflicted. It is Georgy who tries to bring traditional elements of celebration to the wedding of Meredith and Jos, buying Meredith a beautiful dress, and arranging flowers and a celebration. As Jos shows signs of fatherly care, getting a steady job and buying a cot, Georgy becomes more and more enchanted with him. However, the novel suggests that her loving and nurturing character cannot be fulfilled because she is too ugly to attract a lover. By the time Meredith's pregnancy becomes a catalyst in her life, she has internalised this failure to the extent that she cannot respond to Jos when he falls in love with her. She becomes obsessed with the baby even before it is born. Jos tries to argue that their own marriage will be unhappy if she adopts the child, and tells her she must choose between them. She argues that 'they're both the same thing,' but Jos, by now desperate for her commitment, suggests that the child may not be his. Their love affair does not survive long after this bitter argument and once Georgy has adopted his baby she tries to exclude Jos from her bond with the child. His tentative bid to be an active father is over and he follows Meredith in leaving.

These relationships are initially formed by geography – the people involved in them are most young, low-paid, and estranged from their families. They need places to live and have made homes side-by-side by accident, in a harsh urban environment. They are also lonely, and the multi-valent relationships that sustain them are a defence against the alienation of city life. They take the place of the stable and monocultural communities that once supported vulnerable people, which are still evident in Nell Dunn's work, in which women living in the same few streets keep each other company in every phase in life. Women in her Battersea terraces live in groups, from the teenagers who stick together to protect themselves from predatory men to the customers of the launderette who mourn the death of woman who worked there. Without a community around them, however, the new generation sets out to explore new ways of living, and find companionship on the journey.

In *A Taste of Honey*, *The L-Shaped Room* and *Georgy Girl*, the characters form transgressive friendships that provide more than company in adversity. These works demonstrate bonds forming between people who had been excluded from the traditional social hierarchy, so that a black musician, a struggling writer, a gay man and a single mother are all united in their sense of marginalisation. Finding the courage and determination to endure is the challenge they can share.

All these works suggest that the inherent goodness of human nature can be found in the most casual and disparate of connections, whatever the age, race, gender or sexual orientation of the people who are together. Experiences can be admitted by choice and discussed from positions of empathy, so that common values are established. The phenomenon of the 'urban family,' which was eventually celebrated in mainstream popular culture by the TV series *Friends* which ran from 1994 to 2004, is foreshadowed here.

PART TWO

OUT INTO THE WORLD

'WHERE IS YOUR BABY?'

A writer becomes a public figure at her peril. Twin monsters are waiting to savage her. The writing can be written off as autobiography, and the writer herself will be taken over by a celebrity identity that is shaped by society's needs. This chapter looks at the attempted transformation of the Rebel Writers after their initial success.

Perhaps particularly because they were women, the focus of attention was immediately on the author, rather than the work. Reviews were vastly out-numbered by lifestyle features in the press and the emphasis overall was on the author herself rather than her writing. In consequence, the value of the work itself was diminished and young women's writing became a short-lived media craze rather than a continuation of the tradition of maturational novels of Jane Austen and the Brontës.

A celebrity identity was imposed on each author. Françoise Sagan described the experience lucidly in her autobiography, *Reponses*, in 1974.

> I became a commodity, a thing, the Sagan myth, the Sagan phenomenon. I was ashamed of myself. I hung my head when I went into restaurants and I was terrified when people recognised me. I wanted to be thought of as a normal human being. […] It took me a long time to realise that I needed a mask, that I had to hide my face. I adopted the legend as my mask and it stopped bothering me.

In commercial terms, the Sagan effect had demonstrated to the publishing industry that there was a great market for confessional fiction by young women. In cultural terms, however, it meant that every young woman writer was fitted to the Sagan mould, even if her work was vastly different or even ideologically opposed to that of the French author. It is true, of course, that every debut writer is at first described in terms of those who have gone before. (I cherish the memory of the *Time* magazine writer who asked me if I was going to be 'the new Danielle Steele'). With the Rebel Writers, however, their individual positions on sexuality and gender relations were ignored and traduced by the media focus on sex, consumerism and the authors themselves.

The press instantly dubbed Shelagh Delaney the 'new Françoise Sagan'. She was also called an 'Angry Young Woman,' referring to the contemporary group of male writers called the Angry Young Men but this comparison was an isolated one. Although Delaney's early plays were immediately followed by the thematically similar works in this study, the critical press did not make the connection or suggest a literary movement was emerging. By the end of the decade of this study, some publishers were clearly looking at young women's novels as a new genre, but never used the term. In contrast, the history of the Angry Young Men shows the combined cultural industries creating a literary movement out of almost nothing, certainly not on the authors' work, much of which was in fact unrelated.

THE CHELSEA GIRL AND THE SIXTIES CHICK

In place of literary identity, these writers, and their characters, were immediately picked on as zeitgeist symbols, spirits of their age, the raw human material which the media attempted to use to tell its own story. Young women have long been selected as icons used to focus of public attention, taken up as secular saints, each with her specific area of patronage. Before mass media there were mythical figures embodying ideals or nations, like Marianne, Britannia or

Liberty. By the twentieth century, the process became more aggressive and popular culture in films, advertising, propaganda and television began to pick out a young woman to embody each decade or generation.

The literary editor of *The Sunday Times*, Leonard Russell, told Edna O'Brien that she was 'the Scott Fitzgerald of the sixties' after reading *August is a Wicked Month*.[1] Fitzgerald created the figure of the flapper, who symbolised the Jazz Age and was indivisibly (and willingly), blended with the identity of his wife, Zelda. After the Flapper came the It girl, devised by Elinor Glyn and portrayed on screen by Clara Bow in the late 1920s. When war broke out, Norman Rockwell's image of Rosie the Riveter was successfully slimmed-down and fixed-up by J Howard Miller to symbolise the millions of women working in factories and shipyards. While they personified new social philosophies, the real-life women on whom these figures were modelled were left to poverty, obscurity and mental illness.

By the fifties the culture was again searching for a sacrificial maiden, this time to embody the generational optimism and impatience with traditional values and restraints that finally signalled the end of post-war trauma and austerity. The harbingers of the new age, from the Royal Court Theatre to the first fashion boutiques, clustered around the inner London are of Chelsea and *Chelsea Bird* was itself one of the epithets tried out. Virginia Ironside's novel took its title from the street phenomenon and her narrator, Harriet, self-consciously ends her story by saying, 'And I ... well, I'm just a super birdie still'.

The consensus eventually fixed on the Chelsea Girl, an image that originated in London but became conflated in the US with the 1966 Andy Warhol-Paul Morrisey film based around the Chelsea Hotel in New York, while in Britain it later became the brand name of a new chain of high-street boutiques bringing edgy modern fashion to the provinces. Like the Flapper and the It girl, the Chelsea girl was characterised as very young, hedonistic and free-spirited, unshackled by traditional taboos, an androgynous, childlike rebel out for a good time. Her freedom to explore the world extended to sex, and by the second half of the decade, as Virginia Ironside noted, multiple sexual relationships were almost an obligation in liberal-intellectual circles.

This early-sixties figure was an image as well as literary concept, a fashion construct just right for the increasingly visual culture of the age. The studiedly-gawky young woman, wearing an op-art dress, Courreges-inspired knee high boots and a Breton hat that was remarkably like the standard item worn by schoolgirls at the time, was defined by the fashion designer Mary Quant who opened her legendary Bazaar boutique on Chelsea's King's Road in 1955. There was little point in resisting the pressure to be the iconic sixties 'chick,' as Virginia Ironside's experience demonstrated. 'They wanted to put a picture of me on the cover [of *Chelsea Bird*] and when I said no, they went out and found a model who looked like me and used her instead'.

WHERE IS YOUR BABY?

Lynne Reid Banks recalls her mother warning her that *The L-Shaped Room* would be assumed to be an autobiographical novel, and the prophecy being immediately fulfilled when reporters asked, 'Where is your baby?' even though at that time she had no children. Fitting the authors themselves, as well as their characters, into the developing mould of the generational icon was not only a stress on their own self-perception but also a denial of the significance of their writing. Their identities were ignored, all their writing was assumed to be autobiographical even when it clearly did not align with the known facts of the authors' lives, and external stereotypes, the Sagan mould and the Chelsea Girl model, were imposed, obscuring both the authenticity of the writing and the individuality of the author.

When a woman's work is called autobiographical the implication is that the female experiences portrayed have no meaning beyond the subjective perception of the creators, which, as they are female, is of no significance. As the male viewpoint is the norm, the female, being different, becomes an aberration. As Simone de Beauvoir wrote in *The Second Sex* in 1947, 'He is the Subject, he is the Absolute—she is the Other'.

Repeatedly critics dismissed these works as schoolgirlish, 'writing like a nitwit' or, as Noel Coward had it, 'written by an angry young lady of nineteen'. Interviewers tried to establish that the work was merely memoir, not really fiction. Feminist writers would subsequently assert the importance of the female experience. Given that our history, philosophy and literature had predominantly seen the world through male eyes, with male as the norm and female the aberration, women creators were later to treasure and celebrate women's subjective experiences, but at this time a personal narrative from a woman was discounted, while the same exercise written by a man was reverently received.

The automatic conflation of author and character diminished the former, suggesting that no creative effort was involved in the writing. This part of the process is endured by many writers, whatever their gender. Whether deliberate or merely unin-formed, there seems to be a denial reflex among the non-creative which blinds them to the way the imagination works. For Philip Roth, an exact contemporary of the women in this study, the characterisation of his work as 'autobiographical' or 'confessional' he took almost as an insult to his abilities as a writer, suggesting to the French writer Alain Finkielkraut that to do so was 'not only to falsify their suppositional nature but ... to slight what-ever artfulness leads some readers to think that they must be autobiographical'.[2]

Critical responses to Edna O'Brien's work, to which were added the vituperations of her ex-husband and his family, demonstrate clearly how a woman's autobiographical writing is presumed worthless, indeed, self-indulgent. Her novelistic engagement with her own past has also been criticised as a sign of artistic inadequacy or a parasitic dependence on her autobiography for the materials of her art: 'she has plundered somewhat recklessly

from her life', one interviewer writes, 'stirring in just enough
fantasy to hit the fiction shelves' (Honan). Gébler's nephew, Stan
Gébler Davies, synthesized these kinds of criticism to attack
stringently O'Brien's fictional portrayal of his uncle in *Time and
Tide*, writing that it was 'the sort of self-indulgent drivel written
by housewives seeking to escape Wimbledon'.[3] Ernest Gébler first
instructed her by 'running her diaries through the typewriter,'
as he put it. It is a technique well-known to all scribblers and,
while it may not often produce high literature, it is frequently
lucrative.[4]

Discussing the response to her early novels, Edna O'Brien said:

> If you write in a kind of personal tone, as I do, they assume
> without any shadow of doubt that everything in it happened to
> you. They don't understand that the soul of a book like *A Portrait
> of the Artist as a Young Man*, or even, to a lesser extent, *The Country
> Girls* springs from a fusion of fact, feeling and imagination. People
> are constantly asking, Is it autobiographical? I said, 'Well, I'd be a
> goner now if I did everything I wrote'.[5]

Even within the publishing industry, editors imposed a bias towards
autobiography, especially when there was profit involved, and
journalists focused on it to the exclusion of literary or social merit,
the writer's ambitions or almost any other aspect of the work. The
dismissal of a novel as mere memoir was most striking with *Coronet
Among the Weeds*, which Charlotte Bingham wrote as a novel, with
a comically ditzy protagonist closely related to Helen Fielding's
Bridget Jones.

Charlotte Bingham's original title for the novel was *My Search for
a Superman*. Her publishers began to exploit her family background
in marketing the book, and changed the title, trying out a number
of versions featuring the word 'coronet' — the small ceremonial
crown worn by English earls — before settling on *Coronet Among
the Weeds*. Her editor, Charles Pick wrote to her father to ask his

opinion of the new title, perhaps not entirely disingenuously as the author was legally minor and her father was an established author. Pick also asked the Earl for a cover quote. He wrote back to decline, courteously but disdainfully.

An early draft of a press release began 'the autobiography of a 20-year-old ex-deb' immediately prompting Charlotte Bingham to correct the error, writing a note headed 'WARNING' and continuing:

> This book must, I suppose, be classified as autobiographical – although it actually only deals with certain selected episodes – but I think I should point out that, for reasons of courtesy, some of the episodes are in fact an amalgam of several others.[...] I have changed the names and integrated the characters of many people I have met. If therefore, any reader hopes to recognise himself or herself in these pages, or any mutual acquaintances then either he or she will be disappointed or else must be suffering from an excess of vanity.[6]

If Bingham *père et fille* had been less reasonable and polite their views might have prevailed. The serial rights were sold to *The People*, a downmarket Sunday newspaper for the huge sum of £14,000 and the newspaper sensationalised it as the autobiography of Lord Clanmorris's daughter. While the publishers marketed is as a novel, and some critics approached it as such, the *Guardian*'s reviewer described the book as 'the purest piece of self-portraiture'. All missed the fact that this was a deliberate comic construction, which the author described as drawing on her own experience 'like being a stand-up comedian'. The year-long worldwide publicity tour on which she embarked was also predicated on the idea that this was the autobiography of an aristocrat's daughter.

Author and publisher eventually decided to follow the money. In her next book, a self-declared memoir, *Coronet Among The Grass*, Bingham looked back on the post-publication period a few years later. 'The money was lovely and in the end that was all I used to think about. Every time a journalist asked me whether I'd slept with royalty… I just used to close my eyes and see these lovely blue £5 notes floating by. It was just a sort of capitalists' yoga, if you get my meaning'.

Virginia Ironside was also legally a minor at the time *Chelsea Bird* was published and when her father, a distinguished artist and teacher at the Royal College of Art, learned that her publishers intended to put a photograph of his daughter on the cover of her book, he wrote to them forcefully:

> I gather from Virginia that there are differences of opinion as to whether her photograph should appear on the front of the jacket of *Chelsea Bird*.
>
> If her photograph appears on the front the implication of autobiography will be strong and this is something I wish to avoid.
>
> I feel sure you will appreciate my concern, which is shared, I understand, by her mother. In fact any implications from the publisher that the book is fictionalised autobiography or True Confessions stuff might be harmful to her mother or to me in the spheres in which we work.[7]

Virginia herself wrote shortly afterwards to stress that she did not see herself as Harriet, 'Heaven forbid, in fact'.[8]

In the absence of a first-person narrator or a character who could be passed off as the author, she might be inserted into the story by a third party. With *Up the Junction*, a work akin to documentary with no autobiographical content at all, the urge to implicate the author was evident in the film adaptation. Nell Dunn's short story collection was first dramatised, with the uncredited input of Ken Loach, for the BBC as a work of serious drama, and the fragmented structure of narrative, episodes linked by recurring characters left more or less intact.

After the success of the feature film of *Poor Cow*, however, *Up the Junction* was also filmed and traduced in the process. The director,

Peter Collinson, whose place in movie history was later assured by *The Italian Job*, had made only one feature before he was hired which starred the actress Suzy Kendall as a rape victim. The screenwriter, Roger Smith, had already collaborated with Ken Loach, with whom he later formed a long-standing association. The minutes of her publisher, MacGibbon & Kee, reveal that Nell Dunn withheld one story, *The Clip Joint*, from the sale of the rights, perhaps sensing Collinson's sensationalist tendencies. Collinson cast Kendall again in *Up The Junction,* as Polly Dean, a new central character who does not appear in the book and is clearly based on Dunn herself, an heiress who moves to working-class Battersea in search of a more authentic life. The scenario departs from Dunn's biography when Polly herself starts a morganatic relationship with a petty criminal (played by Denis Waterman). 'I was appalled,' Dunn recalls, 'and in fact I have never seen the film because I know I would be upset. In those days if you sold the film rights you lost control'.[9]

CLOTHES AND CONSUMPTION

Reviewing the press coverage of these writers, it seems that photographers rarely took pictures of them at work, and never created the classic scene of the author at a desk with bookshelves in the background which suggests intellectual gravitas. Shelagh Delaney was frequently photographed against the backdrop of slum terraces in Salford but with the other authors there was a tendency to take those reassuring pictures of the little lady writer at home with her husband and children, as Paris-Match had photographed the teenage Françoise Sagan in an apron putting a nourishing casserole in the oven. Where domesticity was implausible, photographers sexualised the images as much as possible. Virginia Ironside recalls 'They were always trying to get you to climb ladders so they could get a shot up your skirt'.[10] Some photographers combined the two tropes. Margaret Forster became the victim of paparazzi up-skirting although she sat beside her husband on their sofa with her children at her knee.

The writers in this survey who made their debuts later seem to have taken note of this process and restricted the images of them in circulation, with varying success. Margaret Forster was also interviewed as 'The Wife with Too Much Money,' by the *Daily Mail* who were quick to reassure their readers that, 'she cooks and cleans every morning, pram pushes in Hampstead Heath every afternoon, and writes her novels while the children have their mid-day rest and between putting them to bed and welcoming her journalist husband home from work'.[11]

The content of these works was rarely discussed and reportage focused on fitting the writer into a chosen mould, either relating her to other publishing phenomena or focusing on her as an emblem of hedonistic youth. Sometimes, both together:

'Spend, spend spend. Quickly, rashly A fast sports car with an open top. New clothes for brother Joe. Lots of holidays for Mum. These are the New Year resolutions of 19-year-old Shelagh Delaney, the factory girl who became Britain's Françoise Sagan overnight'.[12]

The *Daily Mail*'s critic concluded his first-night review of *A Taste of Honey* with the judgment, 'If there's anything worse than an Angry Young Man it's an Angry Young Woman'.[13] The *Mail*, encouraged by the play's producer, Gerry Raffles, also focused on the sexual content of the play, while other reporters asked the writer about clothes and money. While no comment was ever passed on the nondescript clothes worn by the Angry Young Men, Delaney was ridiculed for her lack of narcissism. One newspaper described her as looking 'like a kennel maid on her day off' while another sneered at her 'lumbering through the grey wastes (of East London) in a windcheater and jeans'. Journalists repeatedly hinted that her height and casual style suggested masculinity, and a reporter who interviewed her over lunch disparaged her for actually eating the food.[14] One newspaper, claiming to be offended by Delaney's habitually casual clothes, gave her a couture fashion make-over.

A young woman writer who did not much care how she looked was attacked for it, but one who did take care to bring her appearance in line with contemporary ideas of sexual attractiveness put her writing reputation at risk. As Edna O'Brien observed,

> I'm not that attractive, but on a good day I can muster it. [... interviewer mentions the image of the colleen.] Yes, yes. More codology, that sort of colleen image, being very pretty and unblemished, sitting at the hearth. [...] but again and again and again some snide remarks crop up. That infuriates me. If you happen to have your hair done, well, then you can't be a serious writer. It's so narrow, really.[15]

In the absence of husband, family or casserole, fashion was the great neutraliser employed by the press to trivialise the women's writing. A glossy magazine carried a feature headlined, 'Dressed to Write' which interviewed Edna O'Brien and Virginia Ironside at length about their fashion philosophy. Ironside, in a pinstriped suit, is quoted saying, 'My ideas are probably not synonymous with being a serious woman writer, but the popular idea of the way a woman novelist dresses is so awful that I am not going to give up my way of thinking,' O'Brien, in bespoke ostrich-feather trimmings and a tweed cap belonging to Nell Dunn, paraphrased Shakespeare, saying, 'The apparel always proclaims the man, and I'd hate any man or woman to think that I was a good, normal or consistent woman, as that would be untrue'[16].

By the mid-sixties young women writers were an observable phenomenon and were often grouped together in features predicated on trivial hedonism. In a feature headlined 'Living it up with the booted birds' one journalist paired Ironside with the 21-year-old Annabel Dilke and reported, 'The Chelsea birds are in full voice. They are the latest literary fashion, the young ladies who look back in disillusionment, with all the wisdom of their 20-odd years, on nights of living it up among the kinky boots and swinging swells'.[17] The idea that there might be anything at all disturbing in their writing was thus well obscured.

LOSING IT AT THE MOVES:
SCREEN ADAPTATION

Several of the most memorable British films of the decade were adaptations of the Rebel Writers' works. The film industry is always hungry for product, and the proportion of films based upon books currently is around 25 per cent. At this time, however, the British film industry was about to rise like a phoenix from its own ashes and, with screenwriting almost a secret profession, was hungry for plays and novels to adapt. Screen adaptations increased the audience for the writing from mere thousands to millions all over the world and allowed these writers to bypass London's literary elite in finding an audience.

Some of the most gifted creative people of the time were involved in the process, and reaped considerable rewards. Shelagh Delaney, the leading actors and the director of the film *A Taste of Honey* between them collected two prizes at Cannes, four BAFTAs and a Golden Globe, as well as two Writers' Guild awards. Tough messages about conflicted girlhood suddenly became crowd-pleasing. *Georgy Girl* was blessed with a title song by the hugely popular Australian group, The Seekers, which sold 3.5 million copies worldwide and topped charts in the US, Britain and Australia.

While screen adaptations undoubtedly widened the audience for these writers, they also traduced the works, in major as well as minor ways, diluting themes, eviscerating narratives and fitting characters into moulds that were often stereotypical. A debut writer is almost completely powerless in the adaptation process. Once a creative work is sent out into the world it has a life of its own and what was once an individual idea becomes a shared concept. The author's intentions are subsumed by the response of the audience, and the relationship between writer and reader is mediated not only by directors, actors and producers but also by a stratum of critics and fellow professionals who will frame the expectation of the audience at large.

As noted above with *Up The Junction*, there are often radical differences between the text and the screen adaptation. The process was uncomfortable for all the writers, and for some it was so traumatic that they were to steer their careers decisively away from commercial exploitation.

THE LAST DAYS OF THE BRITISH FILM INDUSTRY

To understand what happened it is important to know that the British film industry of the late 1950s and early 1960s was fragile, fragmented and endangered. The pre-war glory days of Alexander Korda, when British films had matched the best of Hollywood in both quality and profits, were over, the big studios on the western fringes of London were empty and amiable comedies, low-budget horror movies and nostalgic war films such as the original *Dunkirk* (1958) were all that the industry had to meet the perceived threat of television, 'the monster that was gobbling up its audiences'.[1]

The industry was in every kind of trouble. Profits were dwindling, people were deserting the cinema and the domestic market could not pull in an audience large enough to justify the investment needed for a feature film. In 1957 the worst box-office slump in British history saw over a thousand film industry workers lose their jobs in the first three months of the following year. Once-famous studios closed, once-familiar production companies went bust. Entertainments tax of 50 per cent took half all box-office takings in the UK, while the only non-commercial source of investment, the

National Film Finance Corporation, also suffered in its turn because it was financed by a levy on cinema admissions.

Audiences were falling, resources had vanished and creative talent struggled to develop. While the war years, with the need for propaganda, information and entertainment for the troops, had paradoxically given a great technical education to a generation of film, television and radio artists, the rising generation had to rely on trade apprenticeships which, with production stalling, were disappearing. There was not yet a national film school, there were no screenwriting courses and the BBC offered the only alternative professional training for film-makers. The late 1950s was a time of great danger for film making in Britain, when the entire industry could have been lost forever.

In 1959, amid this wreckage, a group of independent producers formed Bryanston Films, a co-operative under the chairmanship of the veteran Sir Michael Balcon, believing that their combined track records would enable them to raise the finance for quality, small-budget films from independent British producers. Their early fortunes were divided between cosy small-scale successes, the adventurous (financial) disaster that was the film of *Look Back in Anger*, the play by John Osborne that was the keynote work of the Angry Young Men, and the outright flop of Osborne's next adaptation, *The Entertainer*, despite Sir Laurence Olivier as its star. The director of both was Tony Richardson, a figure who, more than any other, would lead the renaissance of British drama on screen and stage. At this time, however, he was hearing earnest pleas from the English Stage Company at the Royal Court Theatre to come back to them and leave the film industry to its lingering death.

THE TRIUMPH OF *A TASTE OF HONEY*

But the cinema was Richardson's first love. Just after leaving Oxford he had connected with other recent graduates – Lindsay Anderson, Gavin Lambert and Karel Reisz – who shared a passion for European social-realist films and a determination to create avant-garde cinema in Britain. By 1956 they had enough product to win a series of screenings under the name of Free Cinema at the National Film Theatre. Richardson wrote a manifesto:

As film-makers we believe that
    No film can be too personal.
    The Image speaks. Sound amplifies and comments. Size is
irrelevant.
    Perfection is not an aim.
    An attitude means a style. A style means an attitude[2]

The Royal Court claimed Richardson for a few years, but he had set up a company, Woodfall Films, with John Osborne and a middle-aged, Canadian-born, internationally-based maverick, Harry Saltzman, to produce *Look Bank in Anger*. He directed the Broadway production of *A Taste of Honey*, casting both Angela Lansbury and Joan Plowright, who, as Olivier's partner, had become a friend during the making of *The Entertainer*. He also acquired the film rights to Shelagh Delaney's play, only to discover that Saltzman had tried to sell them on to another producer behind his back. Saltzman, by instinct a realist and by training a showman, believed that the Salford location of *A Taste of Honey* made it unbankable. He seems to have been looking for the light, Euro-Hollywood style of Sagan's *Bonjour Tristesse*.

   'I felt the story was too provincial and too English. [...] It really had little appeal or popular identification for people in other countries. As I saw it, it should have been set in France, with Simone Signoret as the mother and Leslie Caron as the girl, which would have made it into an international picture. But Tony couldn't see it that way, so our partnership was dissolved'.[3]

   Darryl Zanuck, the legendary former head of Twentieth Century Fox, offered finance on condition that the baby died and the film had a 'happy' ending. Audrey Hepburn was suggested for Jo. Fortunately,

Woodfall had a box-office hit with Karel Reisz's adaptation of Alan Sillitoe's *Saturday Night and Sunday Morning,* on the back of which Bryanston were able to raise the very modest finance to start filming *A Taste of Honey* on 14 September 1962.

Richardson and Delaney collaborated on the script. They shared the screenwriting credit and later the awards. The Free Cinema ethos of location shooting and complete naturalism finally freed the play from Joan Littlewood's music-hall vision, a transition which Delaney took as a reclamation of her own work. Narrative was not particularly esteemed in the European New Wave cinema, so no move was made to impose a trajectory on Jo beyond the implied development of her pregnancy.

While Richardson's decisions as director transformed the play even further, the work as a whole retained its spirit. The cramped studio rooms of the play were partly recreated in the loft at the Royal Court and also in the top of floor a semi-derelict house in Fulham, rented for £20 a week as both set and production office. In addition, the script allowed for all the implied exterior sequences, and more besides, which were filmed in Salford. The lighting cameraman was one of the Free Cinema team, Walter Lasally, who, coming from documentary tradition, used naturalistic lighting and grainy film stock, and enjoyed Richardson's improvisational directing style. For them both, serendipitous events, even unpredictable weather, added to the dynamism of the film.

Shot in black-and-white, *A Taste of Honey* has a dream-like quality which strongly references key New Wave titles like *Last Year in Marienbad* or *Le Grand Meaulnes* – not that the British critics saw this as a virtue, rather, as *The Times* had it, a weakness that was 'all from the play'.[4]

In casting the role of Jo, Richardson saw 'well over two thousand girls'. For the cinema there was no possibility of the Broadway casting of Joan Plowright, now in her mid-thirties and unable to carry off a close-up as a 15-year-old. After Richardson had compiled a shortlist a young actress from Liverpool arrived at his office, accompanied by her mother. 'Out of kindness' he let her read, then improvise but decided she was 'too spiky, too hard-edged' for the part of a spiky, hard-edged teenager. He went on to do six screen-tests but still 'that little hedgehog' stuck in his mind and, disappointed with his choices, he did one final test with her. 'Five seconds later a close-up of Rita (Tushingham) with her all-speaking eyes was on the screen and the search was over'.[5]

Rita Tushingham was to become the face of the decade. She won the 1962 Cannes Film Festival Award for Best Actress for her performance in *A Taste of Honey*, as well as the Most Promising Newcomer at the Golden Globe and the BAFTA Awards. The film won four BAFTAs in all, Best British Film, for Richardson and Delaney for Best British Screenplay and for Dora Bryan won Best Actress. Murray Melvin, who recreated in Stratford role of Geof, won Best Actor at the Cannes Film Festival and Richardson was nominated for the 1963 Directors Guild of America award. Delaney and Richardson also won a Writers' Guild of Great Britain award.

The film was also a commercial success, both in the UK and in America, although it was banned or censored in some territories, including New Zealand. 'It seemed as if Woodfall had made a breakthrough,' Richardson remembered, looking back on the production as a wholly happy experience. Woodfall soon became part of the much larger and internationally financed British Lion group and, with the proof that a British film on a British theme with British actors could make money, began to develop a flurry of new projects, which meant securing options to as many promising novels as possible.

GREEN EYES

Woodfall optioned Edna O'Brien's *The Country Girls* for £4,000, an event was to become the decisive moment in the failure of her marriage to Ernest Gébler, but it was her second novel, *The Lonely Girl*, that was filmed first. The producers changed the title to *Girl With*

Green Eyes. Released in 1964, it was directed by Desmond Davis, the camera operator on both *A Taste of Honey* and Richardson's next film, *Tom Jones,* making such a successful debut that he won the US National Board of Review award for Best Director. Rita Tushingham played the more vulnerable Kate, while Lynne Redgrave, sister of Richardson' then wife Vanessa (his original choice for the part,) played the worldly and confident Baba. They began a lifelong friendship and a screen partnership that inspired a later film comedy, *Smashing Time* (1967) also directed by Davis and intended to capture the essence of late-sixties London. Edna O'Brien's fifth novel, *Casualties of Peace*, is dedicated to Rita Tushingham.

The scriptwriting credit for *Girl With Green Eyes* is given to Edna O'Brien, who was already writing both stage plays and film scripts in parallel with her novels. Nevertheless, in 1963, seemingly when the film was still in production, her estranged husband Ernest Gébler sent a typescript of the screen adaptation to her new publisher, Tom Maschler at Jonathan Cape, claiming that he wrote it and owned the publishing rights, and also claiming that he had written 'whole sections' of the original book. 'The script [...] is very readable particularly for those who liked the girlie stuff of *The Lonely Girl*', he wrote.[6] Maschler declined immediately.

Film producers bid for all O'Brien's early novels. At the start of the process of adapting a work for the screen the writer and producer sign a contract defining their business relationship, which begins with an option period, in which the producer can use the original work to commission a screenplay and raise money to make the film. If the producer does not succeed in getting the finance needed in the time agreed, the option expires. All Edna O'Brien's early novels were optioned, and Leslie Caron negotiated for *August Is A Wicked Month*. The *Girl With Green Eyes* was well received, but did not match either the critical or commercial success of *A Taste of Honey*. No more film adaptations of O'Brien's work appeared until *The Country Girls* finally made it to the screen in 1983, with Desmond Davis again directing. *The Girl With Green Eyes* did, however, establish the author as a screenwriter. An American producer, Charlie Feldman, asked her to adapt Mary McCarthy's *The Group* as a film, which she turned down because she felt she did not have the experience to tackle it. The script was eventually written by the 64-year-old producer, Sidney Buckman and the film, released in 1966, established the career of Candice Bergman.

O'Brien adapted her own novel for the film *Zee & Co* (1972), which starred Elizabeth Taylor at the height of her fame in the self-referential role of a socialite diva. This was a major achievement in itself. By fits and starts the British film industry had regenerated itself, but it was an industry that was almost entirely male. Apart from actors and stunt performers, the only woman on a film set would typically be the script supervisor (once known as the continuity girl) and the make-up artists. In the production process women costume designers and casting directors began to appear but women directors, writers or producers were almost unknown. All the key decisions about a film were most definitely made by men.

NOT REALLY *THE L-SHAPED ROOM*

The film adaptation of *The L-Shaped Room* was a much less harmonious experience and one which alienated the author from her own work, and from the film industry, for many years. In a preface to the second novel in the trilogy, which was to follow ten years later, Banks wrote that the radical changes made to the story by the producer and director, 'upset my equilibrium' so much that she never wanted to return to the same characters, Banks, a former actress and a dramatist before she was a novelist, did not write the script.

The producers were the veteran brothers John and James (Jimmie) Woolf, second-generation movie moguls and as near as Britain could come to Hollywood royalty. Jimmie asked Bryan Forbes, a young actor with ambitions to write and direct, to adapt the novel.

At that point Woolf expected that Jack Clayton, who had directed the film adaptation of John Braine's *Room at the Top,* would also direct his new project. Forbes, noted for playing sparky soldiers in many World War II action movies, had formed a production company with another, similarly-typecast, actor, Richard Attenborough, who would in the coming decades become a great statesman of British cinema and a life peer. Jimmie Woolf took the approach outlined by Harry Saltzman of injecting European glamour into the scenario. The French actress Leslie Caron, a former ballerina acclaimed in the Fifties for roles in three Hollywood musicals, was cast as Jane. According to Forbes, 'Jack (Clayton) then went cold on the whole idea and didn't even consider my finished script'.[7]

Woolf then asked Forbes to direct. After 'much thought' he agreed, and later reasoned that Caron 'lifted the film out of the parochial kitchen-sink rut'and found some contemporary relevance as, 'the problems of au pair girls living in our major cities at that time was frequently the subject of headlines'.

The wholesale translation of the story began. The location of the room itself was moved from shabby Fulham to a slightly more boho district, Notting Hill. The character of Mavis, the neat, reserved and wise retired costume designer, became a campy lesbian actress. Toby Cohen, Jane's lover, in the book a middle-class intellectual sacrificing lifestyle for his writing, was played by Tom Bell, then a menacingly charismatic newcomer, as an embittered, working-class boy struggling to become a writer. The pivotal roles of Jane's father and Aunt Addy were completely cut, so the narrative became more about a love affair than a woman searching for herself. The film was shot in black and white, and a Brahms' piano concerto used on the soundtrack, a reference to a French New Wave triumph, Louis Malle's *Les Amants*, released in 1958.

The film poster carried the image of Caron and Bell in bed, under the tag line, 'Sex is not a forbidden word'. The author was traumatised, but powerless. 'The film was taken away from me like they do. Bryan Forbes showed me the script and I was turning over

the pages ... absolutely astonished.... . When I first saw it I was
utterly shattered. The ending and everything – it was a shocking and
a travesty of my book'.[8]

For all the violence that Woolf and Forbes did to Lynne Reid
Banks' story in pursuit of an international market, they did not
entirely surrender to the demands of the industry. The film censor,
John Trevelyan, Secretary of British Board of Film Classification
sent four pages of notes detailing changes required and then, after
the film was screened for the BBFC, demanded that the scenes
in which Jane discusses an abortion be cut. Forbes and Woolf
protested. Trevelyan then put forward a suggestion which testified
to his willingness to move with changing times. A trial screening
was organised for an audience of randomly-selected women, and
their opinion asked on the scenes relating to abortion. None of
the audience objected and the film-makers won their point. The
objection can only be seen as misogynistic, however, as a far more
explicit and distressing abortion sequence in *Alfie*, which starred
Michael Caine as a promiscuous Cockney chauffeur occasionally
startled by his own heartlessness, had been accepted without cuts
the previous year.[9]

After the censor was appeased, the distributors, exhibitors and
financiers all demanded substantial cuts to the film on the vague
grounds that, at over two hours, it was too long. Jimmie Woolf
responded with an incandescent dismissal of their demands, which
Forbes seconded, and the film was subsequently shown without
these cuts.

As a film, *The L-Shaped Room* was a critical success, largely
because of Caron who won Best Actress Awards at both the Golden
Globes and BAFTA. Tom Bell enhanced his growing reputation
as a rebel by heckling Prince Philip. At the Academy Awards
Caron was nominated in the same category and the film itself
nominated as Best Picture. Although casting Lesley Caron made
it possible for the producers to finance the film, it was conceived
as a low-budget, art-house movie, not likely to have mass audience

appeal. Nevertheless, the sales of the novel increased ten-fold after the film was released.

HEY THERE, *GEORGY GIRL*

Margaret Forster's *Georgy Girl* was aimed at the same modest audience, but in fact was a huge commercial success, taking almost $ 17 million in the US in its first year, the fourteenth highest-grossing film of 1967.[10] Timing made the difference. Its first appearance at the Berlin Film Festival came less than three months after the famous *Time* magazine cover of 15 April 1966 that christened London 'the swinging city,' identifying the pop culture revolution that made the city briefly 'the epicentre of the world's creativity'. A slightly surreal story about sexy young women exploring alternative ways of living in London, with a theme song that shot to the top of the charts and Charlotte Rampling's wardrobe designed by Mary Quant, was exactly what the world wanted to see from a British movie. The breezy, almost giggling tone of the film proved even more appealing than the bitter humour of *Alfie*, the big hit of the previous year.

At the beginning of what writers know as 'development hell' there was no indication that *Georgy Girl* as a film would succeed at any level. The producers took two years to put the finance together[11] and even after they had attached James Mason, one of the most distinguished British actors to have a Hollywood profile, still had barely enough finance to go to work. Lynne Redgrave, now with as good a track record as a young actress could have had at that point in her career, was cast in the title role, with Charlotte Rampling, a model who had small parts in Richard Lester pictures, and Alan Bates, award nominated but still inexperienced, as Meredith and Jos. This cast of appealing novices did not impress the international financers. As Lynn Redgrave remembered:

> They kept pulling the plug on the film because they said that James and I and Alan Bates didn't add up to much at the box

office, but in the end we got it made because of James (Mason's) enthusiasm for the quirkiness of the story, and the chance it gave him to go back to his Yorkshire accent. He took very little money for it, and we all thought it was just going to be a low-budget release, so when it became such a huge success it was all the more lovely for those of us who'd always had faith in it.[12]

The director chosen was Silvio Narizzano, who had established an excellent career in television both in his native Canada and in Britain, but his feature film experience amounted to one bizarre low-budget horror movie with Tallulah Bankhead. Narizzano admired British realist directors including Tony Richardson and John Schlesinger, and also Richard Lester, whose gift for surreal comedy launched a million music videos with the Beatles' 'A Hard Day's Night'. Narizzano shot in black and white, used the zany street sequences and jittery editing that were Lester hallmarks and made the most successful film of his career.

After its selection for Berlin, *Georgy Girl* began to garner awards while storming away at the box office. Lynne Redgrave won the New York Film Critics Award, a Golden Globe, and an Oscar nomination. James Mason was also nominated for the Academy Award for Best Supporting Actor, Ken Higgins for Best Cinematography and the film itself for Best Music.

The only person not enchanted by *Georgy Girl* seems to have been the author. Margaret Forster, at the time pregnant with her second child, was asked to write the screenplay, and went to three drafts before the playwright Peter Nichols was asked to write the fourth. The producer suggested that she should invite Charlotte Rampling to tea, and give the actress her baby daughter Caitlin to hold to since this aspect of motherhood was hard for her – although, of course, it should have been far outside the skillset of the glacial Meredith. Perhaps the producer had sensed that the author was turning away from her story. Forster's husband, Hunter Davies, recalls that 'Margaret did not go to the world premiere [...] in the West End [...] I am not sure she even got invited. Not that she was bothered. Or would have gone anyway. She did not see a future for herself in writing scripts and was just glad not to be involved any more'.

Margaret Forster earned only £3,000 from the film whereas her husband, with the same literary agency, Curtis Brown, was paid £20,000 'up front' for the adaptation of his novel *Here We Go Round The Mulberry Bush*, and was invited to the premiere, although the film flopped and is now seldom remembered.

SMALL SCREEN, BIG IMPACT

The film industry was right to worry about the impact of television, then a new mass medium. But it was not only audiences that television was stealing, but also talent. While working in film meant the ceaseless strife of international production, working in television offered young directors and writers a specifically British management unconcerned with global box office figures. Drama production was dominated by the public service company, the BBC, founded on the principles of its first director-general, Lord Reith, to 'educate, inform and entertain'. Note the order of those imperatives. At the start of the 1960s the BBC broadcast on one channel only in black and white, but a second channel, offering more challenging, demanding or niche programming was launched in 1964 and programmes were screened in colour from 1967.

Single plays were offered by both the BBC and the only commercial channel, ITV, and the BBC's *Wednesday Play*, launched in 1964, quickly became famous for original, ground-breaking and even avant-garde productions. Under the producer James MacTaggart, the series quickly established a reputation for political drama and launched the careers of writers such as Dennis Potter and David Mercer.

This, rather than the boppy strand of Swinging London cinema in which *Georgy Girl* was prominent, was the destination for Nell Dunn's work. Rather than allow an agent to sell her books into production, she networked to link up with the ideal director for her. Among her friends was a fellow contributor to the left-wing political journal,[13] the *New Statesman*, the poet Christopher Logue, and he introduced her to Ken Loach, a young television director with credits for *The Wednesday Play*.

Loach was persuaded to read *Up the Junction*, which became a *Wednesday Play* under his direction, with MacTaggart as producer. Nell Dunn worked with him on the adaptation, although his contribution is not credited. 'He lived in Barnes and I lived in Putney and he'd come over and I'd do a bit and he'd leave me with homework', she recalls, 'he was in charge of the picture and the story and I was in charge of all the dialogue. It was such a laugh'[14]. As a TV drama *Up the Junction* retained its episodic structure, with no clear protagonist or narrative arc. Among the cast was Carol White, a young actress who was to work with Loach again.

Ten million people watched the play when it was screened on 3 November 1966, deliberately timed to coincide with a parliamentary debate on the Abortion Law Reform Bill, which was to begin the process of making abortion legal in England. The BBC received about 400 complaints about the drama, from Christian groups and pro-life campaigners, but also from those concerned on both the political right and the left that drama had intervened overly in the political process.

Some complaints were about a growing movement in television to blend fact and fiction. *Up the Junction,* like *A Taste of Honey* and *The L-Shaped Room*, was shot in a documentary style, on location on the streets with naturalistic acting and design. Loach was one of many directors to take this approach, saying 'we were very anxious for our plays not to be considered dramas but as continuations of the news'.

Because the play was timed to contribute to the political process, it was considered to have contravened the BBC's commitment to impartiality, and MacTaggart was replaced at *The Wednesday Play's* producer. The higher management of the BBC refused to schedule the customary repeat screening, after a trade unionist among the Governors, who had never seen it, advanced the opinion that its portrayal of working-class life was unnecessarily negative.

Undeterred, Loach began to work on a screenplay by Dunn's husband, Jeremy Sandford, this time produced by Tony Garnett, who was to become a long-term collaborator. This play again starred Carol White as a young mother who is abandoned by her husband and becomes homeless. *Cathy Come Home*, has been acclaimed as one of the best television plays of all time, and was to lead directly to changes in housing and welfare legislation.

Loach then began work on *Poor Cow* as his first feature film, with Carol White once more, in the role of Joy. For the producer, Joseph Janni, it was intended to be a small film of high integrity to atone for his success with the 'roadshow' movies demanded by Hollywood, but with international finance still needed compromises were inevitable. Loach's *cinema-verite* style had to give way to the producer's demand for a film made in colour, and the quintessentially glamorous Terence Stamp was cast as Joy's lover. He recalled that Loach was evolving his improvisational style as a director.

> We didn't really have a script. That was one of the things that was interesting about it. It was just wholly improvised. He had the idea, he had the overall trajectory in his mind, but we didn't have a script. And, consequently, it had to be Take One because each of us had cameras on us. So before a take, he'd say something to Carol, and then he would say something to me, and we only discovered once the camera was rolling that he'd given us completely different directions. That's why he needed two cameras, because he needed the confusion and the spontaneity.[15]

Dunn was disillusioned and, although she was to write successful stage plays, never again wrote for the screen. *Poor Cow* was made for £210,000 and earned $1,400,000 in the US alone in its first year, while White was nominated for a Golden Globe. This was enough success for *Up The Junction* to be remade into a feature, although, as we have seen, Dunn took no part in the process and was horrified to discover that a character intended to be her had been transplanted into the story and made the focus of it, to the detriment of the working class women who had been her subjects. The advice, 'Never judge a book by its movie,' is well taken for the work of the Rebel Writers.

A STAIN UPON WOMANHOOD

Women were not supposed to write. If they did write, they were not supposed to be truthful. If their writing seemed truthful, then it couldn't be considered fiction. That was the message from the negative, almost violent reactions to the Rebel Writers. Arguments from Satanic possession to mere venality were formulated to decry their work. Attacks upon the writers ranged from anonymous abuse and personal complaints through unsympathetic criticism to political campaigns of suppression orchestrated at the highest level.

The overall thrust of all these assaults was to deny these women the role of a writer. Ann Quin, a novelist of a different stamp in that she was interested primarily in experimental fiction, was interviewed in Nell Dunn's next book, *Talking to Women*, and expressed the very clear sense she had that she was doing wrong by writing. She said, 'I find difficulty in being a writer and a woman where lots of men are very unsure of me and they are liable to sort of put me down and treat me from a physical angle which gets me very frustrated and I then try to assert myself and hate myself at the same time for having to do this and I hate the man'.

While some saw their work diminished as autobiographical, others, who were not overtly writing autobiography, were more perplexing to the literary establishment. Critics were troubled by the idea that Nell Dunn's novels seemed authentic evocations of working-class life. Their presumed authenticity was considered a shortcoming. Her acute ear for dialogue was turned against her, and the episodic structure of her novels taken as evidence that she was not writing fiction at all, merely reportage. '*Up the Junction* might have been called "I am a Tape-recorder,"' grumbled the 30-year-old novelist David Lodge, writing in the *Listener*. 'There is no attempt to weld the episodes into a novel. [...] Miss Dunn's occasional attempts to create significance out of a pattern of events are not successful'.[1] Claire Tomalin in *The Observer* wrote of *Poor Cow*, 'Nell Dunn's reportage is as good as ever.'[2] While another anonymous reviewer asserted that, 'The letters between Joy and her imprisoned lover must, surely, be non-fiction,' and went on to complain, 'The basic flaw in *Poor Cow* is the same as that in the television version of *Up the Junction*, the absence of the author from the story. [...] It would be good if she could move forward from the self-deceiving "I-am-a-camera angle" and find some way to bring a version of herself into her fiction. This is a serious and moving little book, but it is scarcely a novel, nor, quite, an original substitute for one.'

Another difficulty, noted but barely articulated, was that the women in her works had very little agency. In the *Spectator*, 'the book hangs on the central misconception that passive suffering in itself is interesting ... Moreover, *Poor Cow* also displays almost a curious voyeurism, which emerges not only in the treatment of the central character's sexual ruminations, which one would expect, but in its intense preoccupations with the social and class minutiae of poor Joy's world'.[3] Again, the critic seems unable to consider the possibility that the author might have chosen to demonstrate the powerlessness of a woman like Joy in order to provoke a response in the reader. Reviewers also did not relate these novels to modernist ideals or to the contemporary social realism, beyond occasional citation of the 'kitchen sink'.

Some critics did not understand these works as coming-of-age stories in which young women were seeking identity and testing societal expectations. '*Georgy Girl* is a much more faithful attempt at describing the egocentric idiocy of warring women,'[4] wrote Jeremy Rundall in *The Sunday Times*. If critics did recognise that one of these writers was concerned with what it meant to be a woman was enough for some critics to condemn the topic as illegitimate. 'The idea that "women novelists" form an easily identifiable and usually inferior category of writer is certainly as vulgar and stupid as Brigid Brophy is always telling us it is. All the same, Edna O'Brien's new novel, like the previous four, is written with an extreme consciousness of what her heroine thinks of as "female-dom".'[5]

NYMPHOMANIACS ANONYMOUS

The topic that was even more offensive than womanhood was, course, women's experience of sex. The literary establishment responded to accounts of women feeling desire or pleasure with distaste, condemnation and outright horror. At Jonathan Cape, the reader who to whom it fell to write a report on Edna O'Brien's *August Is a Wicked Month*, confessed, 'I am really very troubled about this book. It's difficult to know what to say about it from the "pornographic" point of view. It is a very good book about an unhappy nymphomaniac separated from her husband in search of a man in the South of France. It is beautifully written, totally realistic and as a study of this woman it can't be faulted from a literary point of view BUT it is very nasty in places and I feel [...]that it might, from the angle of the average man in the street, be considered in places as likely to "influence and corrupt" the young.'[6] Clearly the angle of the average woman in the street was not a consideration. The author uses 'Influence and corrupt,' an archaic form of words replaced in the censorship legislation by 'deprave and corrupt'.

Cape's reader was neither the first nor the most distinguished man to have termed a character in one of Edna O'Brien's books a nymphomaniac. The term, which is vernacular and not medical, entered the language in the late eighteenth century and describes a hypersexual woman, usually in a negative sense. *The Country Girls,* about two teenagers, both virgins, one in a grooming relationship with an older man and the other flirting for opportunities to get food, was dismissed as 'a skittish story of two Irish nymphomaniacs' by the septuagenarian author of *The Go-Between*, L.P. Hartley.[7] There was, it seems, no acceptable level of sexual activity at all for a woman.

CENSORSHIP AND OFFENCE

The Cape reader was referring to the possibility that the book might be prosecuted under the Obscene Publications Act of 1959. This law reformed the legal basis for censorship of publications in Britain and was the result of a campaign by the Society of Authors in the fifties. This new legislation allowed artistic or social merit to be advanced in defence of obscene texts, and was famously tested when Penguin Books won their case for the publication of D.H. Lawrence's *Lady Chatterley's Lover* in 1961. The definition of obscenity, however, remained that of older legislation: 'an article shall be deemed to be obscene if its effect [...] is such as to tend to deprave and corrupt persons who are likely, having regard to all relevant circumstances, to read, see or hear the matter contained or embodied in it'.[8]

When Ken Loach's adaptation of *Up the Junction* was televised, the same concerns were raised by the wide range of people who complained about it. Twenty doctors sent a telegram to the secretary of the British Medical Association to say, 'In view of the present increase in venereal disease, promiscuity and the increase of sexual violence, we are urgently requesting you to make strong representations to the BBC to reverse its present policy [...] in presenting moral laxity as normal'.[9]

In Britain, apart from the misgivings of the British Board of Film Certification about the film adaptations of Rebel Writers' works, the state censors did not take any action against them. In Ireland, however, the Catholic Church and the Censorship of Publications Board lined up to ban Edna O'Brien's books. *The Country Girls* was well received by some reviewers, who praised its colleen qualities of freshness and innocence. It was banned from sale in Ireland in June 1960 by the Censorship of Publications Board.

Her mother wrote to tell her of the shock, hurt and disgust their neighbours in Tuamgraney were feeling. 'The postmistress, who happened to be Protestant, told my father that a fitting punishment would be for me to be kicked naked through the town. Stoning would be next'.

She was unaware at that time that the Archbishop of Dublin had written to the Minister for Justice, Charles Haughey, and that the two had agreed that the book was a 'stain upon Irish womanhood' and should be banned. They 'shared their indignation' with the Archbishop of Westminster. Their disapproval was enough to inhibit some booksellers. Even a bookshop in the genteel British seaside town of Eastbourne considered *The Country Girls* too hard a sell.

The Archbishop of Dublin at that time was John Charles McQuaid, who held the post between 1940 to 1972. McQuaid, remembered for his 'purity crusade,' was an extreme misogynist who, early in his career in 1934, had denounced the participation of women in athletic events, declaring, 'mixed athletics and all cognate immodesties are abuses that right-minded people reprobate, wherever and whenever they exist.' Mixed athletics were 'un-Irish and un-Catholic', a social and moral abuse.

A personal friend of Eamon De Valera, the president and former Taoiseach (prime minister and head of government of Ireland), McQuaid regarded political interference as his duty, and a decade later was writing to Ministry of Health officials to persuade them of the moral dangers of tampons. [At the] 'Low Week meetings of the Bishops, I explained very fully the evidence concerning the use of internal sanitary tampons, in particular, that called Tampax. On the medical evidence made available, the bishops very strongly disapproved of the use of these appliances, more particularly in the case of unmarried persons'. The danger resided in the possibility that a woman who used Tampax might feel sexual stimulation. He was to oppose the Mother & Child Scheme several years later, which would have provided free healthcare to newborns and their mothers, fearing that doctors 'trained in institutions in which we have no confidence' might offer contraceptive advice.[10] This was at a time when infant mortality in Ireland was around 50 deaths per 1,000 live births, more than ten times the rate in Britain today.[11]

A man more hostile to women would have been hard to find. When *The Lonely Girl* was published, and Baba and Cait were virgins no more, Fr Peter Connolly, a priest who was also a professor of English at Maynooth College, wrote a glowing appreciation of both novels, praising their less contentious concerns with nature and rural Irish life. Official action was taken and *The Lonely Girl* received a Prohibition Order on the 4 June 1962. According to the Register of Prohibitions, this was appealed to the Censorship of Publications Appeals Board in August 1962 but the appeal was dismissed.[12] The Prohibition was revoked under Section 2(1) of the Censorship of Publications Act 1967, which meant that the ban lasted twelve years. In practice, it meant that Irish booksellers would not carry any of her novels in that period. It was an honour she shared with Honore de Balzac, J.D. Salinger, Graham Greene, Aldous Huxley and a great many others, among them her fellow-countrymen, James Joyce, Samuel Beckett and Brendan Behan. Most shamefully, McQuaid's influence on the Censorship Board was soon afterwards to cost John McGahern his job as a school teacher after his novel *Death* was banned in 1965.

Nevertheless, some copies of Edna O'Brien's books were acquired and had dire effects on people. 'Some woman who had read it got terribly ill, and felt she was possessed by the devil, and the priest had to come to her house'[13]. O'Brien also received anonymous letters claiming that she too was possessed by Satan. Her mother told her that copies of her books had been burned in the church yard, although the parish curate was later to deny this. O'Brien had sent her mother a copy of *The Country Girls*, with a hand-written dedication. After her mother's death, she found the mutilated volume hidden in a bolster, with pages torn out and passages concealed with black ink.

The personal abuse 'wounded' her and she has described internalising the shame felt by her parents. 'They were ashamed so I was ashamed and believed I had done something awful. [...] One gets very confused, you know, by accusations. I was young, and I was frightened, still am to a great extent! If people tell you you've written dirt, even if you know you haven't, some of it stays with you. I wanted to go away very far. Australia even'.[14]

Even London, less than an hour's flight away, was too far for her detractors, however. The worst crime an Irish writer can commit is not obscenity but emigration. The Irish people were already notorious for their condemnation of writers who, persecuted at home, had chosen to live abroad, and here was another one. An arts organisation in Limerick staged a public debate at which Fr Connolly was an eloquent advocate of Edna O'Brien's writing. The audience, however, wanted mostly to attack her for living abroad. Although the event degenerated into a shouting match, it did prompt the *Irish Times*, in reporting it, to say that censorship of Irish writers 'marked the more shameful aspects' of the independent republic.

Ireland was not the only country to ban Edna O'Brien's books, however. When it came to the third novel in the trilogy, *Girls in their Married Bliss,* the original printers, the Chaucer Press, an old-established family business that printed religious books for larger customers, deemed it 'contentious' and refused to print it.[15] It was banned in South Africa and what was then Southern Rhodesia. In Australia, copies were impounded at customs while the book was considered by the authorities, but eventually allowed into the country.

SMALL TOWN VENDETTA

'I'm not particularly degrading anybody, I'm just writing a play,' protested Shelagh Delaney when the news of the rage of the civic dignitaries of Salford reached New York before *A Taste of Honey* opened on Broadway. By this time half of the city seemed to be up in arms defending itself against the disgraceful suggestion that gay men and whorish women might be found there. Or rather, that was the impression that the local newspaper, the *Salford City Reporter*, was giving.

The row began as a reaction to Shelagh Delaney's perfectly truthful admission that she had failed the 11-plus exam four times At that time, the 11-plus was an exam sat by English schoolchildren in their eleventh year of age to assess their academic potential. A child who

passed would go to a grammar school for an academic education
while a child who failed would attend a vocationally–oriented
secondary modern school. It was, on the face of it, surprising that a
woman who had become a leading playwright before her twentieth
birthday would have been classified as a second-class intellect by the
local educational system. With a childhood disrupted by post-war
construction chaos and serious illness, Delaney would not have had
the level of coaching for this exam that schools provided at that
time and her failures were nobody's fault but Hitler's. However, the
Salford City Reporter, defensive to the point of paranoia, interpreted
her admission as an attack on her teachers, solicited an outraged
response from the Director of Education and ran the story under a
headline, 'Shelagh Delaney Accused of Ingratitude to her Teachers'[16].
It was a classic manoeuvre in the game of small-town politics.

The *Reporter* was a well-read weekly broadsheet, edited by Saul
Reece, who had clearly conceived a personal animosity towards
Shelagh Delaney. Occasionally employing (but not acknowledging)
family members in the fray, he proceeded to attack the young
playwright on all fronts. It was an excellent way to gain the trust
of the city fathers, who were charged with spending £34 million
on regenerating the city after the war. The support of the local
newspaper was as valuable to them as their patronage was to the
editor. His strategy was to ingratiate himself by trashing Delaney.
The *Reporter* cast doubt upon her authorship of *A Taste of Honey*,
sneered at it openly in editorials, and accused her of exaggerating
the city's deprivation for financial gain. In fact, the setting of the play
is described as 'Manchester' and so could have been anywhere in the
conurbation, Britain's largest metropolitan area outside London, of
which Salford is only one of the smaller settlements.

This last attack provoked an extraordinary chorus of support and
protest. The next week's front page was devoted to a letter from her
mother, headlined, 'Mrs Delaney Says, "Shelagh Loves Salford"'. 'Has
he never seen slums, or a white girl with a coloured baby? Has he
never heard of sex?' she demanded. The letter was a masterpiece in

its genre, suggesting that the apple had not fallen far from the tree in this family. Ian Albery, the distinguished London theatre owner, wrote to the mayor of Salford, inviting him personally to visit Wyndham's theatre, where *A Taste of Honey* had transferred. Many other ordinary people wrote to defend her, suggesting pointedly that stories such as that of Jo and Helen could be heard in the magistrates' courts every week – a shot at Reece, who was a magistrate himself. Many other readers, most of whom had neither seen nor read the play, also wrote to support the newspaper, describing the work as 'sordid filth' and using terms today seldom seen in print outside a Twitter storm.

The *Reporter* had succeeded in creating an honest-to-God public controversy of the kind that definitely sold newspapers at that time. And many people, including the victim, were well aware of the process. Shelagh Delaney herself gave as good as she got. When a *Reporter* journalist door stepped her again, she told him, 'I feel the *Reporter* has been most unfair to me, and not only the *Reporter* but others in Salford, too. People from Salford who have seen the play like it. It is unfair to condemn it without seeing it, and it's wrong to say I intended reflecting life in Salford. It could be anywhere.' She went on to accuse the paper of sensationalised crime reporting fit only to wrap fish and chips.

As the battle raged, the *Reporter* found new vulnerabilities. The city art gallery asked for the original playscript, which Delaney had given to Joan Littlewood. The paper carried this story under the headline 'Something Nasty' which provoked a magnificent response from a team of construction workers employed by the council.

> On behalf of the undersigned building workers I have been asked to come to the defence of Miss Shelagh Delaney on the basis that at the very least it's about time somebody attempted to present a reasonable argument in what we believe is the deliberately manufactured controversy about this young Salford lass who has managed to achieve fame as a playwright.
>
> Salford should surely be proud that it has produced a person who is achieving world-wide fame as a writer. We are usually

noted for having the worst slums, the highest proportion of people suffering from various diseases and other things unmentionable perhaps in a play about people.[...]

The very idea that Shelagh Delaney has cast a slur on Salford is absurd. It arises from a silly, parochial, narrow-mindedness that no citizen of any city should tolerate.

This eloquent protest was ignored and the *Reporter* continued to disparage Delaney's writing at every opportunity. This placed her in a bind. With close family bonds, she wanted to support her mother and brother emotionally as well as financially after her father's death. After the birth of her daughter, she wanted to maintain these close ties, particularly with her mother. At nineteen, she did not feel ready to leave home, and her creative environment was the city in which she had grown up. To reject Salford was to reject her family and her inspiration, so she attempted to ignore her detractors. Her first book, a collection of short fiction and essays, *Sweetly Sings the Donkey*, was first published in New York in late 1963, and barely promoted in Britain, leading some to speculate that she was looking towards America as a home.

A plan for an arts centre, with which she was involved, was torpedoed by hostile city councillor and the bitter correspondence in the *Reporter* continued with persistent misinterpretation of almost everything she wrote. Eventually she withdrew from public life, leaving Liza Minnelli, in her film *Charlie Bubbles,* to speak for her when she runs along a mountain of rubble exclaiming 'Look at the view here!' and pointing to the colliery and the gas works, seen in the distance over a vast demolition site, as if it was a glorious landscape.

14

THE ANGRY YOUNG MEN:
THE LITERARY MOVEMENT
THAT NEVER WAS

Early in 1956, in a pub ion a tiny, grimy cut-through on the southern edge of London's theatre district, George Fearon, a veteran theatre publicist, sat down with a 27-year-old actor whose play was about to be produced by the English Stage Company at the Royal Court Theatre. The conversation, as the playwright later recalled, was awkward. Fearon, 'equivocated shiftily, even for one in his trade, and then told me with some relish how much he disliked the play and how he had no idea how he could possibly publicise it successfully. The prospect began to puff him up with rare pleasure. He looked at me cheerfully as if he were Albert Pierrepoint guessing my weight. "I suppose you're really – an angry young man, aren't you?" I could see no help coming from that quarter...'[1]

The actor was John Osborne, and the play, the fourth English Stage production, was *Look Back in Anger*. And he was wrong, because Fearon's casual description was to become the defining name of a generation of writers, and a great help in terms of establishing their reputations. *Look Back in Anger* opened to a half-empty house, which Noel Coward's habitual impresario Binkie Beaumont left at the interval, nearly followed by Terence Rattigan, the king of the drawing-room dramas which Osborne was to label 'Loamshire' for their middlebrow ponderance. The daily press critics were underwhelmed and the audiences subdued. The barmaid said she was looking forward to it folding and a nice Peggy Ashcroft vehicle putting the smiles back on her customers' faces.[2]

At the weekend, however, the quality Sunday newspaper critics hailed a new revolution in British theatre. *The Observer's* critic, Kenneth Tynan, a great champion of innovation, wrote:

> *Look Back in Anger* presents post-war youth as it really is [...] To have done this at all would be a significant achievement; to have done it in a first play is a minor miracle.
>
> All the qualities are there, qualities one had despaired of ever seeing on stage – the drift towards anarchy, the instinctive leftishness, the automatic rejection 'official' attitudes, the surrealist sense of humour ... the casual promiscuity, the sense of lacking a crusade worth fighting for and, underlying all these, the determination that no one who dies shall go unmourned ... The Porters of our time deplore the tyranny of good taste and refuse to accept emotional as a term of abuse; they are classless, and they are also leaderless. Mr Osborne is their first spokesman ... I doubt if I could love anyone who did not wish to see *Look Back in Anger*.[3]

The play itself is largely a nihilistic rant by its dominating character, Jimmy Porter, a lazy market-trader who attacks his wife, Alison, because her parents are middle-class. After she leaves him, he has sex with her best friend, and in the final act Alison returns for more abuse, having lost the child she had conceived. Despite her pivotal role in the drama, Alison has few lines and spends most of the stage time ironing in her underwear. While the targets of Porter's anger are largely people he perceives as of a higher social class than him, and authority in general, the work is also relentlessly misogynistic. Tony Richardson, the director of both the play and the subsequent film, was the only person, as Osborne remembered, not surprised by the poor initial reception. He and his producer, George Devine, had spent months leaking the text to key people in British theatre, generating a word-of-mouth *success de scandale*.

Two months after the opening, when Osborne had gained acceptance as a revolutionary new theatrical force, London's influential *Evening Standard* newspaper ran an interview with him, headlined 'Angry Young Man'. Osborne himself publicly accepted the label in a TV interview few days later, middle-market dailies then took up the story and finally, on 16 October 1956, BBC television screened a twenty-minute extract from the play. This immediately brought a new audience to the Royal Court. The stage director, Michael Halifax, recalled, 'The houses were appalling. Then, after the TV extract, all these people started arriving. People you never see in theatres. Young people gazing around wondering where to go and what the rules were. A completely new audience; just what we were trying to find.'[4]

A full-length television adaptation, screened on the only commercial channel, ITV, after dire trigger warnings including 'you can send the children to bed,' followed the next month and the play moved to continue its sell-out season at another small neighbourhood theatre in London, the Lyric in Hammersmith.

Journalists began to link Osborne with Kingsley Amis, whose generational novel *Lucky Jim* had been published two years earlier, and with Amis's Oxford friend, John Wain. Colin Wilson, whose book *The Outsider* was published in the same year as *Look Back in Anger* was premiered, was another debut writer whose incandescently negative stance seemed to fit the concept, although *The Outsider* is a poorly-argued literary comparison study and Wilson soon proved to be a bizarre character whose chief talent was proclaiming his own genius. John Braine created a working-class anti-hero on the make in a northern industrial town in *Room at the Top,* which was published in 1957 and filmed shortly afterwards. Keith Waterhouse, a satirist with a background in journalism, created a gentler but still iconoclastic hero in his novel *Billy Liar,* which appeared in 1959.

In contrast, Allan Sillitoe's fiction, his novel *Saturday Night and Sunday Morning* in 1958 and a short story, *The Loneliness of a Long-Distance Runner*, in 1959, placed him firmly in the social-realist tradition, but featured angry, destructive, working-class young male protagonists confronting individuals and institutions that they despised. Arnold Wesker's plays, set in the East End Jewish communities, shared the same social-realist energy. Wesker, three years younger that Osborne, was 'oblivious' to *Look Back in Anger* when it was first staged, but caught up with it later and was inspired to write what became a trilogy of plays beginning with *Chicken Soup with Barley*, staged at the Royal Court in 1960. Britain's intelligentsia seemed deeply worried by the idea of social realism and at pains to obscure any link between British writers and the European neo-realist movement in film. Instead, the term 'kitchen sink' came into use for working-class realist writing, despite the fact that no angry young protagonist was ever depicted in the vicinity of a kitchen sink.

The keynote in this works is indeed male anger, directed against the entire status quo of British society, buttressed by class divisions and lack of social mobility and inflamed by the presence of women, who are both desired and despised. Indeed, frustration seems to be at the root of the rage, *Lucky Jim* impugns the integrity of academia while the protagonist struggles to join it. Joe Lampton in *Room at the Top* sneers at the 'zombies' in authority while craving the markers of their status: 'I wanted an Aston Martin, I wanted a three guinea linen shirt, I wanted a girl with a Riviera suntan – these were my rights, I felt, a signed and sealed legacy'. Arthur Seaton in *Saturday Night and Sunday Morning,* sees every restriction on his life as a challenge: 'That's what all those looney laws are for, yer know: to be broken by blokes like me'.

While these utterly disparate and unrelated writers were bracketed together as a literary movement, most of them were strangers to each other and they had little in common. Kingsley Amis was the only critic not to review Wilson's *The Outsider* as 'brilliant' and after his sneering criticism in the *Spectator* they met for lunch a couple of times, encounters organised by Dan Farson, a Soho flâneur whose acquaintance they had in common. The two men drank a lot but, unsurprisingly, did not bond. Undeterred, Farson – who was getting commissions from the leading middle-market newspaper, the *Daily Mail*, for Angry Young Men features – brought John Osborne and his future wife, Mary Ure, the actress who first played Alison, to a party at Wilson's house. This initiative also failed, despite high alcohol consumption. John Braine, who had used his earnings from *Room at the Top* to buy a nice house in Yorkshire for his family, rented a room in Colin Wilson's London home but, when interviewed some decades later, admitted, 'There never was a group and all the people who have been labelled Angry Young Men are all very different'[5]. Alan Sillitoe, although he soon became well-connected among writers, artists and media commentators in London, also said that he never felt part of the Angry Young Man movement, 'if such there was, and I can't think of any writers who did, for the label was used by journalists and others who wanted to classify those who wrote in ways they didn't understand or care for – to define so as to defuse'.[6]

However vehemently they rejected the label, as most of them did, it was a great marketing plus for them, creating the easy recognition with editors, publishers and producers that appeared to guarantee good sales. As Arnold Wesker admitted:

> There never was an Angry Young Man … Neither John Osborne nor we, his peers, were angry. On the contrary, we were very happy. Our work was being performed and we were earning more money in a year than in our entire lives till then. Ill-informed interviewers still ask, as though it were the most perceptive question ever, 'Are you still angry?' It's a miracle they escape being murdered on the spot.[7]

On rare but significant occasions, the group supported each other in public. They were largely united in their support for nuclear disarmament and opposition to military conflict, causes which were briefly able to unite thinkers across the political spectrum, from far-right to far-left. In August 1961, when Britain seemed on the brink of war during the Berlin Crisis, John Osborne wrote a coruscating declaration headed 'A Letter to my Fellow Countrymen' expressing his hatred for 'the men with manic fingers leading the sightless, feeble, betrayed body of my country to its death'. It was published in the centre-left periodical the *Tribune* and set off a public debate that raged throughout that summer, in which John Braine, Arnold Wesker and Shelagh Delaney all came out with unqualified support for Osborne.[8]

Humphrey Carpenter, in his admirable study *The Angry Young Men: A Literary Comedy of the Fifties*, puts forward the idea that the Angry Young Men as a literary force had roots in Oxford University, where Kingsley Amis, John Wain and Philip Larkin met during the war, all reading English Language and Literature at St John's College. They shared a middle-class but not significantly privileged background, dabbled in left-wing student politics, published each other in student magazines, discovered jazz and were to remain friends through their crucial post-graduate years, although their paths soon diverged. The right-wing journal the *Spectator* identified them, with other poets, as the Movement in 1954. Oxford-educated women, Iris Murdoch and Elizabeth Jennings, are sometimes included in this group, which was otherwise entirely male. Wain, whose tutor was C.S. Lewis – he and J.R.R. Tolkien were the two towers of the Oxford writers' group known as the Inklings. It was close to that template of a face-to-face, interactive literary movement, and this group at least shared values – anti-romantic, anti-modernist, nostalgically English – and promoted and published each other's work.

While Wain remained in academia and Larkin began his lifelong career as a librarian, Amis was alone in finding popular success as a novelist with *Lucky Jim*, a bitter campus comedy about a young university lecturer, not at the hallowed institutions of Oxford or Cambridge, but at one of the institutions established in England's industrial cities at the turn of the twentieth century, known as a 'redbrick' university. The protagonist was inspired by Larkin, to whom the book is dedicated.

The Angry Young Men belonged to a generation that grew up during World War II, and so one thing they all shared were formative years disrupted by the conflict. Unstable family lives and fragmented education were normal for most people in Britain at this time, but in many respects also the Angry Young Men were a fatherless generation, many with absent or hostile fathers, others separated from their families. Kingsley Amis went to a boarding school and managed to avoid the conflicted relationship he had with his father. John Osborne's father died of tuberculosis in 1940. Colin Wilson's father joined the army in 1939 and when he was discharged in poor health 'we remembered how much we disliked him'. Allan Sillitoe's father was illiterate, violent and often drunk, seldom held a job more than a month and the family moved constantly to avoid debts. Arnold Wesker, born in the East End of London, was evacuated twice as a schoolboy during the war and so was separated from his family for extended periods, and Keith Waterhouse's father died when the future writer was still in infancy.

Another common factor is that very few of this group shared the defining experience of men of their generation, compulsory military service. Conscription in Britain began in 1939 and during the war was mandatory for all men between the ages of eighteen and forty-one. It continued after the war until 1960, with all men between the ages of seventeen and twenty-one required to serve in the armed forces for eighteen months. Kingsley Amis and Arnold Wesker were the only two of these writers to have typical experience of National Service. The others, although they were to make their names in challenging authority, had little or no experience of the overwhelming system of military hierarchy and no viable models of masculinity.

Amis left Oxford in 1942 and served as an officer in the Royal Corps of Signals for three years before resuming his studies. Of this group, he is the only one to have served as an officer and the only one to have joined the Army. John Wain (and Philip Larkin) were found unfit for military service because of their poor eyesight. John Braine was called up in the Royal Navy and also invalided out with tuberculosis, and John Osborne, whose father had died of the disease, was already suffering from tuberculosis when he was called up. Sillitoe, like Wesker and Waterhouse, served in the ranks in the Royal Air Force, but he too was invalided out with tuberculosis and spent eighteen months in hospital. Colin Wilson joined up but soon avoided National Service by claiming to be homosexual.

The majority of these writers, therefore, did not have the full experience of military training, designed to produce unquestioning and instant obedience. This set them apart from their generation and equipped them with instincts to challenge authority rather than accept it. One more unifying characteristic of the group was their lack of formal education. Amis graduated from Oxford with a First, but again was the only one of the Angry Young Men to have progressed to higher education. Typically these writers left school in their mid-teens with almost no educational qualifications and took up unskilled jobs, some serving apprenticeships. As writers, they were self-taught, responding to the faint glimmers of art and culture that penetrated the hopeless desperation of the lower middle-classes at this time. In writing about their early experiences they were genuinely ground-breaking, strident new voices heard above the genteel murmuring of the privileged elites that had passed for national conversation for most of the century.

A young publisher took it upon himself to present the Angry Young Men as more than a newspaper headline. Tom Maschler had been born in Berlin the son on an entrepreneurial publisher whose authors included Erik Kastner, creator of the best-selling children's book *Emil and the Detectives*. His family was Jewish and, as the Nazis gained power, Maschler senior was able to relocate his business to Switzerland and moved the family to Vienna. Fortunately, he was on a business trip when Nazi officers arrived to arrest him and requisition the family home. Tom escaped to England with his mother at the age of six, and was joined later by his father. Three of his grandparents, who remained in Germany, were gassed in concentration camps.

Maschler evaded university and, after travelling in Europe, returned to London in his early twenties to enter his father's profession. He was a young editor at the respected literary house of MacGibbon & Kee, chafing at their refusal to let him sign Allan Sillitoe, when he decided to commission 'a series of manifestos from leading writers in the arts' with the non-binding suggestion that they discuss how social change could be achieved.

Declaration, edited by Maschler, appeared in 1957 and succeeded in his aim of presenting new writing in Britain as something more than a tabloid headline. He wrote, though 'most of the contributors to this volume have at some time or other been termed Angry Young Men, they do not belong to a united movement. Far from it; they attach on another directly or indirectly in these pages. Some were even reluctant to appear between the same covers with others whose views they violently oppose'. The writers he chose were Colin Wilson, John Osborne, John Wain, the drama critic Kenneth Tynan, film director Lindsay Anderson, two debut novelists and Wilson acolytes Stuart Holroyd and Bill Hopkins, and one woman, Doris Lessing. At thirty-eight, she was the oldest and best established of the authors in the anthology, with seven novels published and a Somerset Maugham Award in 1954. She had also grown up in what is now Zimbabwe and was a radical opponent of apartheid, which gave her an 'outsider's edge' with a London intellectual audience and placed her comfortably at a distance from the Angry Young Men.

Lessing remembers their meeting like this:

And now enter Tom Maschler, very young – twenty-three – handsome and ambitious, who arrived in my flat with a demand that I write a piece for a book her planned, called *Declaration*. I said that I hated writing think pieces. He said reproachfully that his whole future depended on this book [...] Besides, he had approached Iris Murdoch – he said – and she said no, and he had to have a woman in it: I could not let him down.[9]

Thus emotionally blackmailed into joining the cause of Maschler's career, Doris Lessing took the opportunity to eviscerate the Angry Young Men, observing that 'the most exciting writers we are producing in this country, for all their vitality are sunk inside [British] parochialism'. She chides Kingsley Amis for 'generalising from an emotion which is current among a section of his generation now. It is a temporary mood of disillusion'. She rebukes Colin Wilson: 'Mr Wilson may find the desire of backward people not to starve, not to remain illiterate, rather uninteresting but he and people like him should at least try and understand it exists, and what a great and creative force it is, one which will affect us all'. She observes that John Osborne's hero Jimmy Porter has concluded that 'there is nothing for it but to stagnate and submit to being sucked dry by women'. But then observes, 'when it reaches the point where we are offered the sex war as a serious substitute for social struggle, even if ironically, then it is time to examine the reasons'.

Maschler and Lessing were to become good friends, although he published her only briefly at MacGibbon & Kee. He also became a close friend of Arnold Wesker and they bought adjoining holiday homes in Wales. As he had hoped, *Declaration* turbo-charged Maschler's career and, after a short spell with Penguin, he joined Jonathan Cape in 1960, quickly becoming a legendary force in British publishing and editor, for a while, to two of the authors in this study, Edna O'Brien and Margaret Forster. Among many prominent authors, he was to sign Kingsley Amis's son, Martin, and 'I recall his telling me some years later that he was greatly impressed by my selection of girlfriends'.

One aspect of British intellectual life which most of the Angry Young Men accepted without question was misogyny. Britain in the early twentieth century was divided by gender so deeply

that men and women were separated almost as brutally as in a
system of apartheid. A writer such as Kingsley Amis, an only
child who moved from single-sex schools to an all-male academic
environment, and thence to a male-dominated publishing industry,
male-dominated media, clubs and even pubs in which only men
were welcome, would have had very limited contact with women
other than his mother, cleaners and typists, and sexual partners,
actual or potential. As most workplaces were either male, like the
metal workshop in *Saturday Night and Sunday Morning,* or female,
like the sweet factory in *Up The Junction,* working-class men and
women, while some attended mixed-sex schools, were kept apart
for much of their daily lives. So it is not surprising that female
characters in the works of the Angry Young Men are few and feeble.

Such respect as women had won in the war years had been
reversed, and in its place were commonplace attitudes of misogyny
that today seem so extreme as to be almost beyond belief. 'Women
appear to me as basically dull, but as basically pathetic too,' wrote
Amis to Larkin. 'Women get in the way of man's thinking. Particularly
so-called intelligent women with their bright chatter,' was a position
taken by Wilson but shared and quoted by several of the Angry Young
Men. There were very few female critics to challenge the position
and the media was as much of a patriarchy as any other cultural field.
While women had appeared on television as continuity announcers
in the early 1950s, they soon disappeared and there were no female
editors or news anchors and, when in 1971, the feminist group
Women in Media wrote to the Independent Television News to ask
why this was, they received the answer that women did not read the
news because if they did, 'no one would believe it'.

Those with direct experience of the fusty all-male atmosphere of
an Oxbridge college or a London club defined the tone and most of
the rest aspired to it. They regarded women with something close
to the hatred of the modern incel cult, as inherently emasculating,
acceptable only as transient sexual conquests or, in the undesirable
situation in which a woman was pregnant, burdens to be married and

divorced as quickly as possible. Women were deliberately excluded from any form of friendship, intellectual association or collegiality. Needless to say, none of their works would pass the Bechdel test.[10]

Women characters have no agency and rarely occur outside a sexual relationship with a man. They are judged on the Madonna-whore spectrum. With the honourable exception of Beatie, the heroine of Arnold Wesker's *Roots*, they are presented as despised objects to the male characters' progress, creatures to be used and abused almost as symbols of the status quo which the male protagonists attack, creatures whose existence embodies the evil establishment imperatives of marriage and family. In *Look Back in Anger* Jimmy rages at Alison, 'I want to stand up in your tears, and splash about in them, and sing. I want to be there when you grovel'.

Two tropes recur in these works: suicide appears as a manipulative move by a female character; abortion is a distressing, disrespectful act of which women are guilty. When tragedy befalls a woman, men may demonstrate their moral value by expressing remorse or assigning blame. In *Lucky Jim* the protagonist's girlfriend has deviously tried to kill herself when she was dumped by her previous fiancé; at the end of *Room At the Top*, the protagonist's married lover drives drunk into a wall after he ends their affair so he can be free for a shotgun wedding to the boss's daughter; in *Saturday Night and Sunday Morning*, the protagonist has sex with his lover's sister while she has an abortion – a scene not included in the film adaptation.

The Angry Young Men proved to be a generational title which was inevitably superseded as new voices emerged. In 1960 in Edinburgh a producer brought together four recent Oxbridge graduates, Alan Bennett, Peter Cook, Jonathan Miller and Dudley Moore in a satirical revue, *Beyond the Fringe*. It transferred to London, acclaimed by Kenneth Tynan, then went to Broadway and – with cast changes – ran until 1966, by which time the original performers had taken to television. Political satire instantly dominated the cultural high ground and traditional platforms such as the novel and the theatre were eclipsed.

Amis and Osborne continued to pursue their careers with increasing success, moving further and further to the political right as years passed. Amis, knighted in 1996, became an almost archetypal man of British letters, hardly divisible from the image as 'an arch-reactionary, misogynist, boozer and scourge of modernities in all things [...] in blimpish red-face, staring apoplectically and uncomprehendingly out of the Garrick Club bar at the fools in the street below.'[11] The career of Colin Wilson and his associates Bill Hopkins and Stuart Holroyd, declined as it became clear that he was unable to produce creative work, only to analyse that of others. John Braine never established a literary career and declined into alcoholism. Alan Sillitoe continued to write, novels, poetry, children's books and essays but, although well-reviewed, refused to have his work submitted for awards and rejected any attempt at classification. He campaigned on behalf of political prisoners, but did so with a low profile. Arnold Wesker wrote over forty plays. While his early works were constantly staged all over the world, his later output had mixed fortunes, particularly after he fell out with the National Theatre. Wesker also established Centre 42, a trade union backed arts centre designed to 'destroy the mystique and snobbery associated with the arts' which became one of London's great cultural powerhouses during the 1960s. He was knighted in 2006.

So the Angry Young Men had very little in common. The writers largely despised each other and the work is disparate, sharing little stylistically or thematically. The writers expressed the frustrations of their generation, giving vent to the uncomprehending hostility of young people towards those would never get past their wartime experiences, but had nothing to put in place of the icons they were determined to shatter. Genuine artistic innovation was bursting out elsewhere in film, television drama and pop music.

As a marketing wrapper, the name established a solid foundation for the careers of those with the talent and resilience to build on it. They generated a storm of media attention and initiated some public debate. John Osborne certainly broke the mould of British post-war theatre, but swiftly recast it a traditional form, beginning with *Luther* (1961). It is notable that some of his early plays were not at all successful but producers bore with him until he was able to produce mature writing. Shelagh Delaney, in contrast, was written-off after her second play despite the fact that her first had been far more successful as a film, both critically and financially, than any work by Osborne.

In terms of social (or even attitudinal) change, the Angry Young Men achieved very little. This odd non-movement, seemingly born of a latent craving for something new in traditional culture, eventually proved to be like Macbeth's view of life, full of sound and fury, signifying nothing.

BACKWARDS IN HIGH HEELS:
SUCCESS AND AFTER

This chapter looks at the way the Rebel Writers managed their careers after their initial success. 'Managed' is not quite the right word, as they, like their characters, were feeling their way to a new identity through a process of response and reaction. Their ambitions were very different and also changed over time as they experienced the ways in which their work was received. Margaret Forster set out with the determination to build a literary career, but with a distaste for much of the literary culture of her time. Others, while they wanted to be writers, were not as ready to negotiate the traditional structure of the industries, nor were they concerned with arcane literary aesthetics. Virginia Ironside instantly rejected the whole idea of being a novelist, while Edna O'Brien found herself writing prolifically but desperately as an unsupported single mother who needed to make a home for her children.

While writing is mostly solitary, we write to communicate, to be read, heard or seen by other people. For writers who want a public audience this will mean working with people and organisations that present writing to the world: publishers, literary agents, producers, directors, actors, television, film or theatre companies, the media, other writers, other artists.

How supportive those relationships are will determine the success of the writer, both real and perceived. At the same time, writing is often absolutely solitary and requires profound concentration. Writers are typically sensitive people whose work depends on their thin skins and sharp eyes. So for many writers the first challenge is to overcome their own temperament and instincts. In comparing the career paths of the Rebel Writers, it is striking how those who were able, and willing, to engage others were ultimately more successful, although all of them struggled in a society that was only prepared to listen to them on its own terms. We must also ask what measure of success is appropriate, however, and if professional achievement should be valued over a balanced and fulfilled life.

With seven young women making their writing debuts in the fifties and early sixties, it is impossible to discount gender in this process. The responses to their work were those of a patriarchal society to nubile young women. Nearly all their essential creative relationships were with men, so their careers were advanced by male editors, male agents, male producers, male directors and male collaborators. Or not. For a debut writer these are formative relationships in which they develop creatively and, while some of the writers in this study undoubtedly benefitted from these associations with men, others were frustrated by associates who limited them. Some women, notably the theatre producer Joan Littlewood, publisher Carmen Callil and literary agent Ursula Winant, did play significant roles in the writers' success, but the institutions in which they worked were completely controlled by men, who acted on their own ideas of what a woman was.

In other ways, as we have seen, it is clear that these young women were immediately struggling in a male environment that wanted to impose its own ideas of female identity. Thus, the airhead young wife of Charlotte Bingham's TV comedies or the free-loving single women of Edna O'Brien's middle period novels such as *August Is A Wicked Month* were acceptable, while women who were clever, older or more complex, like the characters created by Lynne Reid Banks or Margaret Forster, were not. Attempts to break these moulds, progress creatively and tackle other themes were not enabled, while male writers were free to experiment. Failure, by a woman writer, was often immediately fatal to her career, whereas failure by a man was considered an interesting experiment demonstrating his potential, and a good reason to throw money at his next project.

Critically, there are breathtaking contrasts between the reception given to male growing-up novels of about the same time, such as *The Catcher in the Rye* (1951) or *Portnoy's Complaint* (1969), which were vaunted as literary landmarks and eagerly accepted into the cultural mainstream. *The New York Times* hailed *Portnoy* with, 'If viewed as the apotheosis of a genre, the culmination of a fictional quest–and it is [...] the very novel that every American-Jewish writer has been trying to write in one guise or another since the end of World War II–then it may very well be what is called a masterpiece'[1]. In contrast, works of the Rebel Writers, commended for charm or entertainment value, marketed with an emphasis on sex and often dismissed as insignificant tales of girlhood, were very seldom considered in a genre, or related to earlier literature, although the comparisons with the Brontë sisters or with Jane Austen are begging to be made. Significant themes in these works were never identified, so Edna O'Brien, writing about a girl of eight being groomed by a middle-aged man, never found *The Country Girls* being compared to Vladimir Nabokov's *Lolita*.

SHELAGH DELANEY

From the outset of her career, Shelagh Delaney protected her privacy and rebuffed journalists' questions about her private life. She may have been adept at mythologizing herself, but she never cast her family as characters in a public narrative. So perhaps it is not surprising that so many accounts of her life miss the fact that her father, he who had fought so hard to get her the best education, died when she was eighteen, a few months before the premiere of *A Taste of Honey*. Thus her professional life began in the shadow of a major trauma. The fifties were an age of emotional repression, in which the 'stiff upper-lip' was a response to be admired. The decisions she made in the period immediately after her stellar debut can be better understood if her loss is also considered.

Delaney was lionised after the success of *A Taste of Honey*. The teenager who had never been more than a few miles from Salford went to New York for the Broadway premiere, Cannes for the film festival, and to Paris, often with Joan Littlewood who remained a friend. She went alone to Warsaw as a guest of the Polish Writers' Union. Still half a child, she ran out of spending money and couldn't afford the entry to a provincial Lenin museum. In London she was seen at first nights, Soho clubs and CND rallies with the great and good of the radical middle-class. When she was invited to attend a major peace protest in Trafalgar Square, she asked Doris Lessing's advice. The older writer recalled her saying, 'she hated demos and riots and even large numbers of people, but she supposed she had to do it?' So she went and was arrested, held in a police cell overnight and in the morning, fined £2 and left the court with the actress Vanessa Redgrave, Tony Richardson's wife.

She was frequently the token women in TV and radio debates, appearing beside Alan Sillitoe or Arnold Wester and speaking passionately for peace, justice and the reform of censorship laws. After Dan Farson, who was riding the wave of his success with the Angry Young Men, included her in a series of TV interviews titled *Success Story*, she was hailed as a 'natural screen personality'. The absolute accolade in media terms came shortly afterwards with an hour-long documentary in the prestigious *Monitor* arts series on BBC2. Directed by Ken Russell, a rising star at that time, it was shot in Salford and she talks at length about the challenges facing young people in post-industrial cities.

Delaney's second play was originally titled, *The Glory, Jest and Riddle*, the last line of a philosophical verse by the eighteenth-century poet Alexander Pope. It was finally called *The Lion in Love*, and like *A Taste of Honey* it is set in a working-class home, 'not necessarily' in Salford. At the centre of the drama was another hard-drinking woman resentful of her cheating husband only this time, unlike *Honey*, there was no sassy young daughter to talk back. The play is a picture of a dysfunctional marriage and its victims, crackling with one-liners and with a deep and bitter undertone of commentary about poverty. It is clearer that some of the women are getting by as casual prostitutes. The title comes from a tale included in the fables of the ancient Greek storyteller Aesop, about a lion who falls in love with a young woman. Her father persuades the beast to have his claws and teeth removed in case he hurts his bride, but then kills the animal when it is defenceless. The story is usually interpreted as a cautionary tale about the fatal foolishness of falling in love.

Joan Littlewood was disappointed in the play and wanted Delaney to do more work on it. Instead, she decided to sign up with a producer of a different stamp, Wolf Mankowitz. From a Russian-Jewish immigrant family, he had been associated with the English Stage Company at the Royal Court, but had found popular success with an amiable rock'n'roll musical, *Espresso Bongo*. With Oscar Lewenstein he had taken *Honey* into the West End, but as a producer he was inexperienced, and he hired a completely inexperienced director, Clive Barker, an actor from Littlewood's company.

Casting began in July 1960 when Delaney had already been working on the film script of *A Taste of Honey* with Tony Richardson. Three actors who were later to become major stars, Terence Stamp, Sean Connery and Oliver Reed, were seen but the final choice for the lead role was Kenneth Cope.[2] The play was mauled by the censor, who wanted the language toned down, and Delaney was angry enough to write a programme note explaining in particular why she resented having to write 'It's a bastard of a life,' instead of 'It's a bugger of a life'.

Mankowitz chose the traditional approach of opening the play out of London. The first reviews were poor, and, after an ominous delay, the play finally opened at the Royal Court in the absolute graveyard of the theatrical year, 21 December. The notices were mixed, and some of them harsh, in a particularly misogynistic vein.

Even John Osborne, neither a stranger to invective nor a friend of feminism, recalled the 'obtusely vicious' reception of the play as 'a classic example of a second play being demolished on the grounds of feigned admiration for a first play's privately resented success. None of the women playwrights who followed Shelagh possessed a fraction of her four-square plain gifts and poetry realism. Yet, at the age of twenty, she was savaged with such deliberation and spite that her successors would have run howling to some lunatic Equal Opportunities Tribunal'.[3]

She appeared unfazed by the criticism, although in an interview shortly after the opening she accused the British of 'a terrific, sickening hypocrisy about smut. You get theatre critics roaring their heads off at sly innuendoes. But face them with honest-to-goodness sex and they act as if they're disgusted [...] Hypocrisy is a mistaken sense of what is valuable. It is pretence for effect'. The play closed after eighteen weeks and later had a short off-Broadway run in New York.

The sensational success of the film adaptation of *A Taste of Honey* followed and she was writing prolifically, beginning new plays and publishing sketches and essays, some of which were collected into an anthology, *Sweetly Sings the Donkey*, which was first published in America in 1963. As noted earlier, she was still living principally in Salford, despite the vicious attacks on her work made by local worthies, and began to gather support for an open-access arts centre there.

Arnold Wesker's cultural initiative, Centre 42, had mounted arts festivals in several northern cities and in Salford a group of trade unionists asked for Shelagh Delaney's help in doing something similar. *Lion*'s director, Clive Barker was working for Centre 42 and became a natural partner in the venture. Plans for a community performance space were drawn up and launched to the press with Shelagh and Clive as its advocates. They drew up a business plan and identified a building, the Grade II listed Salford Hippodrome, an old music-hall build in 1904 and renamed the Windsor Theatre.

Within a few months, however, the local council bought the
building and effectively killed their plans. A councillor who had
been in favour of the scheme wrote to Barker, 'I have been surprised
[…] to find out how much prejudice there is among members of the
council against Sheila on the grounds that her plays have brought
Salford into disrepute'. The building was delisted and demolished in
1963; the initiative seems to have been written out of history, with
no reference to it in the background to the Lowry Centre, which
opened in 2000.

On April 3 1964 a local newspaper in Salford carried the
announcement that Shelagh had given birth to a baby girl in a
London nursing home. There was some speculation that the story
was a joke, as the original announcement came from her on April
Fool's Day. She confirmed the news to a London reporter a few
days later, with her mother in the background. She remained close
to her family and her daughter Charlotte, also a writer, remembers
frequent visits to her grandmother in Salford. So from that year
onward the young dramatist was also a first-time parent. From that
year also she withdrew from public life and gave no more interviews.

She returned to Salford to work with Lindsay Anderson, the
most radical of the Free Cinema directors, on an adaptation of one
of the sketches in *Sweetly Sings the Donkey*, called *The White Bus*. As if
to infuriate the civic worthies it is a surreal bus ride around the city
with Arthur Lowe in the role of mayor and tour guide. It features
Anthony Hopkins in his first film role, singing a song by Bertolt
Brecht. The short film is episodic, with scenes loosely linked by a
character based on Delaney who travels north from a London office
to revisit her home town.

While filming *The White Bus*, she met Albert Finney, the leading
young British actor of the day and also from Salford. After a few years
at the top of his profession following his debut in *Saturday Night and
Sunday Morning*, Finney had retreated from the media glare and had
set up his own production company. Shelagh had written a thirty-two
page film treatment[4] and they worked on the script together over

a year or so before taking the decision that Finney should both star and direct, as well as producer. *Charlie Bubbles*, premiered in 1968, is a delicately surreal story about a rich and famous writer returning home to Salford in a gold Rolls Royce and finding his success has estranged him from his family, his heritage and even simple pleasures like taking his son to a football match. Everyone he meets responds to him as a celebrity rather than a person, he cannot make any kind of normal human contact, even with his adoring assistant, played by Liza Minnelli in her first screen role.

At the end of the film Finney is driving, pursued by a pack of paparazzi, loses control of the car and is killed, an uncanny foreshadowing of the death of Diana, Princess of Wales. Finney used the term 'identity crisis' to describe the feelings both he and Delaney had after their early success. 'The kind if identity crisis she went through was quite considerable. Much more, I think, *much more* than mine'.

These two famous figures trying to explain the psychological damage inflicted by celebrity culture were quite beyond the understanding of the entertainment industry and the media. The film won two awards, one for Shelagh from the Writers' Guild of Great Britain for the Best British Screenplay, and the New York Critic's Circle prize for Best Supporting Actress, given to Billie Whitelaw in the role of Bubbles' wife, but was a 'commercial disappointment'.

Delaney had found her metier as a screenwriter and thereafter wrote steadily, if slowly (as she admitted) for television and radio, while also enjoying motherhood. Her daughter remembers a great railway journey made with her mother across America in 1972[5]. She contributed to an internationally successful drama series, *Seven Ages of Woman* (1974), along with Lynne Reid Banks, Elizabeth Jane Howard and Jack Rosenthal. A single drama, *The House That Jack Built* (1977) returned to the theme of marriage. *A Taste of Honey* continued to be staged, restaged and studied around the world.

Her writing also had an inspirational effect on musicians, notably Morrisey, lead singer of the Smiths, who said, 'At least fifty per cent of my reason for writing can be blamed on Shelagh Delaney'. Her photograph was used on the cover of their 1986 compilation album *Louder Than Bombs*.

Her most significant later work was *Dance With A Stranger*, a film about Ruth Ellis, the last woman to be executed by hanging in Britain, directed by Mike Newell, which won the *Prix Populaire* in Cannes in 1985. She was still writing at the time of her death from cancer in 2011.

EDNA O'BRIEN

Edna O'Brien was twenty-nine when her first novel was published and the great public success of the book was coupled by the extreme personal pain of her collapsing marriage. Ernest Gébler's paranoid jealousy created a 'fraught, even febrile' atmosphere in their home.[6] Everything she earned was paid to her by cheque, which he insisted she endorse so it could be paid into his bank account. He supported her writing in some ways, buying a garden shed for her to work in, but poured private contempt into his journal and speculated that his wife was having an affair with the editor, Ian Hamilton of Hutchinson, who was now publishing them both. Or rather, publishing O'Brien as her husband was yet to complete a new book.

So her first priority was to leave Hamilton, the editor who had made *The Country Girls* such as success, with American and many other foreign rights sold and a film option, as well as the following reviews, interviews, television and radio appearances. At this time the concept of blame was taken into account in divorce proceedings and she could not risk the possibility of losing her children if a judge considered she had had an affair. She was able to make the change advantageously.

O'Brien had a literary agent, Mark Hamilton at A.M. Heath. Tom Maschler, now building what would become a legendary list at Jonathan Cape, began to court her within months. After a false start – 'I do hope you get your domestic arrangements sorted out' – they had lunch. 'I wish I always enjoyed my lunches so much' – early in May 1961 and he wrote to her afterwards, 'it would give me a very special personal pleasure to publish you'. Hamilton conducted an auction, in which Maschler was successful and the manuscript of her second novel was sent to him before the month ended.[7]

She titled this second part of what became *The Country Girls* trilogy, *The Lost Girls*. Maschler renamed it *The Lonely Girl*. His backing proved even more successful than Hamilton's. At the same time, he was trying to establish his very first signing at Cape, an American author whose novel, *Catch 22*, was considered too American for the British market. He sent the book to Edna O'Brien, who 'embraced' it immediately, but also asked the author to read her own novel. Joseph Heller wrote:

> A beautiful, sincere, refreshing novel and I enjoyed its candor and humorous vitality from beginning to end. The love scenes in particular are presented with such honesty it is hard to believe they were written by a woman. And then, of course, one realises they could only have been written by a woman.[8]

Kingsley Amis bizarrely found that it 'takes us further into that suburban, or sub-urban, world' (which it does not) and opined that, 'what makes a wonderful man wonderful is notoriously tricky for the woman novelist,' having presumably missed the clues that 'Eugene Galliard' had psychotic aspects to his character.

In June the Irish Censorship of Publications Board banned its sale in the Republic, but in Britain it was as successful as her debut novel. The film rights were optioned by Woodfall and the arrival of their cheque, for just under £4,000, at her home sparked the final row with her husband. He threatened to strangle her unless she endorsed it to him. She did so, then fled the house, going to the police station, a hospital, and then Woodfall office. At Woodfall, she borrowed some money and someone rang the film critic Penelope Gilliatt, the same young journalist who launched *Brides* magazine,

who was by then an acclaimed film critic and married to John
Osborne, to see if she and her sons could stay there for a few days.

What followed was a year of trauma and instability, in which she
had to depend on the kindness of friends and strangers for places to
stay, and her husband tried to trick her into legally abandoning their
children.[9] As he was in possession of all her previous earnings, she
had to borrow money to survive. Just before Christmas in 1962,
Tom Maschler was asked by a suburban department store to confirm
that she was creditworthy enough to open an account with them.
The first tranche of the £750 advance for her next novel enabled
her to rent a room in a house in Putney, and a year or so later she
was able to buy a house on the same street, about six miles closer
to the centre of London, near the River Thames. Here she wrote
the third novel in the trilogy, 'often in transit on the bus when I
went to meet the children at school or at Wimbledon station, where
they came on Saturdays [...] *Girls in their Married Bliss* was deemed
not as lyrical as my earlier works. 'Indeed, her American publisher
was 'troubled' by it, 'more for what it says about her state of mind
than for any other reason'. A male reader feeling 'troubled' was to
become something of a motif in the response to O'Brien's work.

A friend had helped her to negotiate an informal shared custody
arrangement under which her sons stayed with her three nights a
week, but Gébler tried in many ways to attack her through their
children, and sometimes threatened to emigrate with them to New
Zealand. His goodwill was also desirable in case he chose to descend
from his position of lofty disdain and sue for libel. The lawyer advised
Maschler to 'publish and be damned' but he sent the manuscript
to Gébler asking him to read it and respond. Gébler wrote back
declining this 'indignity' although his sons revealed to their mother
that he had indeed read it. The news of their separation was of
little interest to the press, and although she promoted her work
energetically, she did not at that point reveal the news. In November
1962 she told an interviewer from the *Guardian* that '*The Lonely
Girl* is being made into a film and I'm writing the script with my

husband or he's doing it with me, whichever you prefer'. (This was ten months before Gébler sent the screenplay to Maschler, passing it off as his own).

In the next few years she was extraordinarily prolific. As well as the screenplay for the Woodfall's adaptation of *The Lonely Girl,* called *Girl with Green Eyes*, she was also writing plays: *A Cheap Bunch of Nice Flowers* was staged at the New Arts Theatre in November 1962 and found by the legendary critic Bernard Levin to be 'insubstantial but not entirely meritless'. *The Keys of the Café* (1965) was written for the BBC; and *The Wedding Dress*, *The Three Piece Suite* and *Waiting for a Hurt*, all for the commercial television company ATV. And there were short stories, in which she explored new themes, which began to appear in *The New Yorker* and many other magazines and periodicals.

With those four nights of the week without her family, she was able not only to write at all hours but also to accept invitations, make friends and connections, and develop both professional and personal relationships. At this point it should be noted that she was considered the most charming of young women, with an allure that to some seemed almost supernatural. A television researcher recalls a lunch meeting at which the venerable gay art historian, Sir Harold Acton, was clearly among those bewitched by her. Her life became a crazy blend of Hollywood film stars and Mayfair hotels interspersed with bus trips to the boys' school and buying second-hand chairs.

From the outset she was clear-eyed about the appeal of her first book. 'I think people like books about young girls. And it's simple, easy to read and has a kind of innocence.' The reviews of *Bliss*, and there were many, also focused on a new dimension in women's writing. As we have seen, female sexuality intrigued as many readers as it repelled, and until this time when censorship laws were relaxed, had never been depicted explicitly except in proscribed works of erotica. Her next a novel, *August Is a Wicked Month*, is about a single woman, Ellen, waiting out a long, hot August in London while her estranged husband has taken their son on holiday. A would-be lover will not commit, and she decides on a whim to travel alone to the south of France. At her hotel she falls in with exotic strangers and has sex with two of them. She realises she is craving affection, not pleasure, but then news comes of her son's death and in the final quarter of the book shows her moving numbly through grief.

By now she was on first-name terms with several London literary editors and one, from the most prestigious of the quality Sundays, who had evidently seen the raw manuscript wrote, 'Well, dear girl, I am going to say that *August Is a Wicked Month* shows you to be the Scott Fitzgerald of the 1960s. But you don't owe anything to him or anyone else either. [...] Of course, there is a certain novelty about a woman writing with such frankness and honesty [...] There will be a frightful row about it'. He also urged her to resist any attempt by Cape to tone down the text. (The letter is dated Christmas Eve). Nevertheless, they tried.

The book was banned in territories which were by now the usual suspects in censoring her work: Ireland, Rhodesia and South Africa. Her husband seized on it as evidence of 'perversion' that made her an unfit parent, but at the hearing in 1965 the judge ruled that 'boys of nine and eleven would not be interested in this kind of literature,' and awarded custody to her. Their divorce was finalised two years later, on the grounds of her desertion, with no maintenance provision for her because of her success.

By now the little house by the river in Putney had become a venue for informal parties attended by the great and good; more so a few years later when she moved to a beautiful Chelsea square. Her next novel was *Casualties of Peace* in 1966, and a substantial collection of short stories, *The Love Object* which was published in 1968. This Maschler was less wholeheartedly enthusiastic about, and there was disagreement about the cover. He was even less taken with a fantasy novel that she sent him and by January of 1969 she had moved to Weidenfeld & Nicholson and Maschler was promising eternal friendship nonetheless.

While fascinated by the bohemian beau monde of *Zee & Co*, by the end of the decade she also began to approach her Irish heritage in *A Pagan Place* and to explore a woman's sexuality more deeply in *Night* which followed in 1972. The 'deconstruction of old myths of Ireland and Irish womanhood'[10] continued to be major themes as she wrote a new novel almost bi-annually, as well as more plays, scripts, memoirs and short stories. She spent more time in Ireland and bought a home there, although London remained her base. In 2018 she was made a Dame of the British Empire and after many other national and international prizes, she was awarded the Frank O'Connor Short Story Award in 2011, she was proclaimed as 'the Solzhenitsyn of Irish life'.

LYNNE REID BANKS

Shortly after she began to write *The L-Shaped Room*, Banks had ceased to be a television reporter. She was taken off the screen because, in an interview with the American singer Paul Robeson, she asked him a political question.[11] She was sent off screen to write 'nasty, ephemeral little scripts'[12] and while she also worked on her novel, her colleagues read out sections of the text and ridiculed it. Once it was published, to good reviews, 'There I was sitting quietly in my little booth working on my scripts when all sorts of faces would appear over the top and stare at me in amazement'. When news of the film rights' sale broke Reginald Bosanquet, one of the most colourful news anchors of the day said, 'I wish I could write such rubbish'.

The American rights went to Viking and the hardback was chosen by the prestigious Book of the Month Club as their selection for November 1960, but sales were only decent and not all the reviews were good. Leonard Russell in *The Sunday Times*, who had lauded O'Brien, wondered whether she was wise to write about 'broken-down people living in an awful broken-down house in Fulham'.[13] The paperback rights were sold for £500 to Penguin, at the same time as they paid twice as much for a book by a male debut novelist from the same agent. By now the news of the 'glittering sum'(£25,000)[14] paid for the film rights was out and Penguin delayed the paperback publication to coincide with its release. It was a good decision, as the sales outstripped all projections and the book was reprinted in exponentially increasing numbers.

A few months after the hardback was published, Banks's agent wrote to the Israeli ambassador in London asking for assistance for 'our authoress' in visiting his country, and gave out that she was in Israel researching her next book. 'I went to Israel for a holiday to write it. I was crazy about the place. I always knew I'd marry a Jew one day. Call it middle-class guilt or whatever. But if I was asked what had had the greatest effect on my life, I'd say the post-war pictures of Belsen. I was one of those people who was hipped on the Jewish race. It became something of an obsession with me'.

Back in London, at the height of the success which she thoroughly enjoyed, she met and fell in love with Chaim Stephenson. Born Harry Stephenson in Liverpool to Russian-Jewish immigrant parents, he had changed his name when he joined a group of young Jewish people who entered Israel illegally in 1947 and worked to establish the new state.

She recalls that, 'During a year's leave back to England in 1960, when he studied under the sculptor Willi Soukop, he met me. I was then under contract to ITN, but some months after Chaim had returned to Israel I chased after him. We had to marry in Cyprus because a "mixed" marriage between a Jew and non-Jew, then as now, was impossible in Israel'. So in the year that her novel was published she emigrated to Israel and became a *kibbutznik*.

Chaim lived on a kibbutz at Yasur in Western Galilee, working as a shepherd and gardener The kibbutz movement began in Israel as a Utopian experiment in living as a collective community, with all decisions taken collectively and all work shared, whether industrial, agricultural or domestic. Artistic work, however, was considered a pastime. Yasur is a secular kibbutz but was run on strict rule which governed every minute of every day. She joined him and 'began my 'career' in the kibbutz as a worker in the chicken houses and the vineyards, too tired at night to do anything but fall into bed after supper – eaten in the communal dining-hall.'[15] Later she became an English teacher at a local high-school and described her life to Ian Parsons, her editor, as teaching all day and preparing classes in the evenings and weekends, with time to write only in the holidays. Between 1965 and 1969 she had three sons, Adiel, Gillon and Omri, and recalled the time in a lifestyle feature about happiness.

> We were really happy, according to my former definition of happiness as the absence of anxiety, fear or friction. We had no money worries, no rat race, no unemployment, no housing or education problems, no inflation, no household drudgery – and very few family quarrels. What was there to quarrel about? We had our little home, we enjoyed our work, our children were beautifully looked after and our relationship with them untrammelled.

Looking back about ten years later, a *Guardian* journalist said simply, 'she threw up a bright and starry career at the very beginning by going to live in Israel'. What she did not have there was time to write, or any possibility of the kind of networking that other writers undertook to establish their careers. She did not adapt her own novel for the screen and was thousands of miles apart from her editor, her agent and all the other contacts and associates connected to her. Journalists could not get hold of her and airmail letters, neatly typed to the very edge of the paper, were her only means of communication, apart from an occasional telegram when acutely anxious about something. If she wanted to visit London, she had to get permission from the kibbutz leaders to do so. The strict interpretation of kibbutzim rules requires all property to be held in common, so the organisation had rights on her earnings. She needed special dispensation even to import her modest old car.

She had completed another play, staged briefly at St Martin's Theatre, and her second novel before she left. *An End to Running* (1962) is a novel that draws directly on her life at that time, a love story narrated first by Martha, a young woman who is hired as amanuensis by Aaron, a writer whose older sister dominates him and who then moves to a kibbutz to escape the toxic relationship. It was praised for its portrayal of two contrasting worlds, smart bohemian London and idealistic Israel, but six years then passed before her next book, *Children at the Gate* (1968), was published. Set in Acre, Israel's largest port city, it is about the tender relationship that develops between a Canadian divorcée, an Arab house-painter and his child.

It was clear that all her professional relationships were wearing thin. Her books were still earning worthwhile royalties, but these diminished steadily. A year passed in which she heard nothing from her agent at all. Her editor wrote disdainfully that he pictured her with a 'gaggle' of children. By 1968 her agent had been seriously ill, as had her editor, who was semi-retired. With this weak support she wrote two more novels to complete the *L-Shaped Room* trilogy, *The Backward Shadow* (1971) and *Two is Lonely* (1973). Penguin paid £2,000 for the paperback rights to the first, which sold 6,000 copies in the first week, indicating that some fans of the first novel were loyal, but that the wholesale success of the film tie-in edition was not going to be repeated.

> I wrote this book, except the first chapter, in Israel, in intervals between teaching English to kibbutz children. I wrote it during the long summer break, under conditions of extreme heat (my writing room is in a wooden building with no plug for a fan) and pressure, knowing that come September, I would be submerged in lessons again and all would be broken off and probably lost.
>
> It was lovely to come into that little oven of a room and let my imagination take me to cool, wet, green England. Sequences of cold and rain were written with nostalgia which borders on sensuality. It is generally better, I think, to write about 'where

one is not'. Fiction-writing should be an escape, a re-creation of past emotions, or an exploration of imagined one. Writing a story about one's 'present' is more like documentary than fiction writing. That's probably why I enjoyed writing *The Backward Shadow* so much – it was like a daily visit to England, to meet old friends.[16]

These later novels continue the story of Jane and David, her baby son. She moves to the country, but not far from London, and opens a village shop with a new woman friend. Toby, her lover, reappears but again leaves her and marries another woman. Jane falls in love again with a far more stable man, but is still haunted by her attachment to Toby, who is now divorced and living in Israel. The character of John, the Jamaican musician, becomes more and more significant as the story develops and he eventually travels to Israel with Jane in search of Toby.

Lynne, Chaim and their children returned to England in 1971, to a small house in the beautiful London suburb of Kew, where the botanic garden is situated. Looking back, she identified the changes in Israel after the Six-Day War of 1967 as a decisive factor. 'It changed a very great deal. It's no good pretending otherwise. Innocence is ignorance. We lived a sort of innocent life in Israel in the 1960s, but we shouldn't have done; we shouldn't have been so happy. I was happier then than I ever was before and happier than I have ever been since. I can't unwish those years, but I feel quite guilty about them now.'[17]

For the first time they had sole responsibility for their three sons and for their household, It was stressful but productive. In eighteen months she wrote two novels, a play, three short stories and a great deal of journalism. She had begun to write novels for children and young adults, and also to research the life of the Bronte siblings for a biographical novel, *Dark Quartet*, which won the Yorkshire Arts Association Award in 1977 and was followed by a study of Charlotte Brontë's experience of fame.

Penguin continued to publish her, to a modest but faithful following. She wrote a children's fantasy novel, *The Indian in the*

Cupboard, based on a bedtime story she told her youngest son, about a magic cupboard that brings a boy's action figures to life, inspired by her wartime childhood in Canada. As the figure of the Iroquois brave ventures into the boy's world some dark and complex aspects of the scenario lift it above that of a typical children's story of the time. Through the eighties it won local awards all over the US. By the early nineties she had written four sequels and the original novel was filmed, with Frank Oz directing, in 1995. The novel has sold over 10 million copies internationally. She continued to write for children and in 2013 won the Action for Children's Arts J.M.Barrie Award for 'a lifetime's achievement in delighting children whose work [...] will stand the test of time'.

CHARLOTTE BINGHAM

Coronet Among the Weeds was more than a success, it was an international sensation. Charlotte Bingham recalls that:

> This very short book is thought to have started some sort of social upheaval, as well as being vaguely scandalous, which only shows how times have changed. It is quite simply written in the voice of a teenager making fun not just of herself and her friends, but also of life in general. I have to say that I did hope that I would sell it, and when I did I thought my cup was indeed flowing over. What I never envisaged was that it would make me famous, selling in ten countries, taking me all over the world on author tours, and engendering more publicity than could possibly be imagined outside, well, a frothy Hollywood comedy.[18]

She spent a year promoting the novel in Britain, the US and Europe. She was profiled in *Life Magazine,* photographed by Paris-Match, invited on to television shows including one with an audience of 84 million and shared a New York book signing with the veteran comedian Bob Hope.

Selling your first book at nineteen is obviously great but, on the other hand, when you live at home it can be a bit difficult. The book was taken up round the world and I was giving eight or ten interviews a day. Our house was plagued with photographers and journalists from about ten countries. My father didn't like the house being photographed because he worked for MI5, and in the end my mother put her foot down and said, 'No more photographers in the house'.[19]

This did not deter her daughter from smuggling in one more photographer through the kitchen door. Her parents were supportive in their way, although when one photographer wanted to picture her in a leopard skin bikini her father simply suggested she send the man to see him, after which the bikini was never mentioned again.[20] But while legitimate reporters made appointments, opportunistic paparazzi climbed the trees on the street outside and rented a flat in the house opposite, hoping for intimate pictures of her at home.

Much as she ridiculed finishing school education in her novel, it proved useful in that she was able to meet most of the challenges of worldwide celebrity with patience, courtesy and some confidence, and to charm everyone she met in the process. When the famous London bookshop Foyles gave a Literary Luncheon for her, at the end of which she had to give a speech, she was frightened.

Imagine never having spoken in public before, and just four months out of the typing pool finding yourself sitting surrounded by famous literary people all waiting for you to open your mouth. I went so white that the press table seated below the top table kept sending me notes saying, in very different ways, 'cheer up it will soon be over!' Happily, due, I always think, to my extreme youth, the speech received a great ovation, and the following day I was sent a bouquet from the press table, which was more than generous, and not at all deserved.

When the storm of publicity eventually subsided, she tried to begin a new book but instead found herself in a kind of limbo. There were darker sides to instant celebrity. In *Coronet Among the Grass*, the sequel to her first novel, she has the same narrator look back on the first days of success and remember crying constantly, triggered even by positive events, a recognisable indicator of depression, and rushing away to a cloakroom to vomit after the simplest act of kindness from a stranger.

Not all strangers were kind and the hostility behind many encounters was not lost on her.

> No book I had ever read told you about how rude success is – which is extraordinary because, far from people hiding their sneers beneath their urbanity, they get right up close to you, so you can see their sneers better. And while I had read once of people spitting all over Noel Coward's evening dress, it was a least because they hadn't liked the play. I mean they had actually seen it, and then spat. Whereas as far as I could see nowadays people spat first, before they'd even read what you'd written.[21]

She found herself writing her name over and over to convince herself she was still there. And then she went to the theatre to see the satirical revue *Beyond the Fringe*, in which a young actor called Terence Brady had just taken over the role created by the comedian Peter Cook. 'I went backstage and told him how wonderful I thought he was,' she recalled. 'He fell in love with me at first sight and proposed within days'. They married early in 1964 and their daughter, Candida, was born in April 1965, with their son Matthew following shortly afterwards. Her next novel, *Lucinda*, was published in 1966, but her editor was disappointed that it was not another story of a fluffy debutante. Instead it was a story about a young girl's friendship with an eccentric older woman who keeps an antique shop, with neither a hunt ball nor a tiara in sight.

BACKWARDS IN HIGH HEELS: SUCCESS AND AFTER   223

Virginia Ironside reviewed it as, 'Just as funny as *Coronet Among the Weeds*...Simple and bright, it is as refreshing and pleasant as a glass of fizzy orange on a hot day'.

Terence Brady was an extraordinary, brilliant and multi-talented man who continued his acting career while also writing and devising television drama. (In later life he was also to succeed as a painter and breeder of racehorses and eventers). As a school leaver he had had the choice between places at art school, the Royal Academy of Dramatic Art and a scholarship to St John's College, Oxford, all of which he had turned down to read History and Political Science at Trinity College, Dublin. After their marriage, the couple began to work together and embarked on a long career writing for television. Their debut was in an anthology drama series, which led to comedy series about three young women sharing a London apartment, *Take Three Girls*. It ran for two years, with a sequel that followed the characters following later.

They then devised *No-Honestly*, a comedy series about a married couple – she a writer, he an actor – which both narrate in flashbacks, demonstrating a romantic Rashomon effect as they remember key moments in their relationship differently. As a tribute to the American comedy duo George Burns and Gracie Allen, the husband ended each episode by wishing his wife goodnight. This also ran for two years, with a follow-on series. They contributed to the long-running historical drama *Upstairs Downstairs*, and wrote single plays, feature films and adaptations for stage and screen. While writing sharp social comedies, by 1980 Charlotte had returned to her first love, historical romance, and in 1996 won the Romantic Novel of the Year Award from the Romantic Novelists' Association. In 2017 Bloomsbury published *MI5 And Me,* a memoir of her days working with her father in the offices of MI5. When an interviewer remarked that she and her husband had made their own fortune while her older brother had inherited the family title, she replied, 'My brother was the heir – I got the talent!'[22]

NELL DUNN

Between the publication of *Up The Junction* and *Poor Cow*, Nell Dunn
wrote a book called *Talking to Women* (1965). It is a collection of
interviews with women in her own circle of acquaintance and,
viewed from a historical perspective, it is one of the most important
texts of second-wave feminism. The form is that of a conventional
work of oral history, although the interviewer's questions are
printed as well as the subjects' answers, in contrast to the written-
through style of the great American historian of the working-class,
Studs Terkel, and of most mainstream media of the time. The Q
& A format had been used by the literary magazine *Paris Review*
since the 1950s, and was to be adopted by the alternative press,
including *Rolling Stone*, founded 1967 and Andy Warhol's *Interview*,
launched in 1969. In 1965, however, the style of the book was
revolutionary.

So too was the content. It is a book about being a young woman.
The focus on the experience of womanhood, long before the
words 'feminist' and 'feminism' were in general use, or the idea
that women could benefit from sharing their experience became
central to the feminist movement. Late in the decade the Women's
Liberation Movement identified itself, in the US and the UK, and at
the same time the principle of conscious-raising was recognised. In
1965, however, the idea that a group of women would meet and talk
with the sole purpose of sharing thoughts and feelings, and in the
process bringing to light experiences that had been de-legitimised
or even forbidden, was ground-breaking. At one point in the book
Dunn admits that 'I started lying because I was unable to tell people
certain things,' suggesting that her personal need for authenticity
inspired the book.

The nine women interviewed were Pauline Boty, an artist and
a founder of the pop art movement in Britain; Kathy Collier, a
single mother who worked in a butter factory; Frances Chadwick,
who wrote poetry, made furniture and was the estranged wife of a
notable sculptor; Edna O'Brien; Emma Charlton, a wife, mother

and costumer maker for London's opera houses; Antonia Simon, a photographer in a failing relationship with worried about never having children; Suna Portman, heiress, model and socialite who was soon to open a legendary Chelsea boutique; Paddy Kitchen, who had just finished her first novel about having the biggest baby ever born in St Stephen's Hospital, Chelsea, and who would go on to a distinguished writing career as both a novelist and a biographer; and Ann Quin, an experimental novelist who wrote in the deconstructed style of Marguerite Duras and Alain Robbe-Grillet.

The conversations range from moral questions, knowing right from wrong or the place of fidelity in marriage, to physical experiences, emotional responses, attitudes to men, to ways of living, and to their own bodies. In her introduction, Dunn wrote:

> If these girls have anything in common it is a belief in personal fulfilment – that a woman's life should not solely be the struggle to make men happy but more than a progress to the development of one's own body and soul. As Daniel Deronda tells Gwendolen Harletch that she should sing for 'private joy' instead of the public ear, so these girls have severed themselves from some of the conventional forms of living and thinking, in trying to find what for them are the 'private joys' of life.

'I didn't have clarity about myself, which is one of the reasons I did the book,' she said later. 'Because I felt so lost, I wanted to know how other people were doing, and most of them were equally lost, really'.[23] Her subjects were, like her, rejecting the *Brides* magazine ideals and searching for new, more thoughtful, more fulfilling ways to live. The search was not easy. Of the nine, two were to commit suicide, Frances Chadwick before the book was published and Ann Quin, who drowned herself in 1971 after years of poor mental health. Pauline Boty died of a rare cancer in 1966, a few months after giving birth to a daughter; she refused to terminate the pregnancy or to have treatment that might have damaged the child.

The book is remarkable because it is written with a sense of exploration. Nell Dunn did not have a feminist agenda. In the year it was written she told a *Daily Mail* writer that 'The running of the country is better left to men. I think that finally a woman or most women would give up everything for love. Love always comes first'.[24] As an interviewer her style is conversational, and at many points in the book she puts forward her own thoughts and ideas, but she imposed no structure on her subjects, avoided identifying problems or proposing solutions. Yet at the same time her purpose was clearly to present potential alternatives to the nuclear family of the fifties.

In her own life she was trying to find a fresh approach to creating a family. She and her husband, now with three sons, had moved to the suburb of Putney, bordering the Thames in the south west of Greater London, to Deodar Road, the street on which Edna O'Brien also lived. She remembers them sitting in their gardens in the sunshine, 'talking about books they loved. Nell learned a lot from her'. She worked in a 'nursery study' which contained one desk and two cots for the younger boys and, despite her father's millions, lived on what she and her husband earned. She has said that she lived with a level of free-floating anxiety for many years. 'I'm afraid of living in a house with four walls, not worrying about anyone outside it, thinking that without a three-piece suite you've failed. [...] I'm scared to the next stage, of stopping caring about people. I'm scared of becoming a typical bourgeoise'.[25]

Women Talking defined two themes that were to persist in her writing. One was the exploration of alternative lifestyles, and after the disappointing experiences with the film industry she wrote another book of collected conversations with women, *Living Like I Do*. It was described as a 'before-its-time documentary of women's liberation' and is a collection of 'intimate case histories,' featuring both men and women talking about the ways they lived with partners and children. Some lived in a commune, others in a house-share, three were in a polygamous relationship, two were single parents and the other simply single.

In the introduction, Dunn wrote, 'I wanted to write a book about alternative families because of my own situation', citing the separation from her first husband, the process of re-partnering and the tensions, largely uncharted in any parenting guide, that arose in integrating their families – seven children between them. She also wrote about the effect on her hiding her feelings for the sake of her children. 'This fundamental flaw in my life-style kept my life as a mother totally separated from my life as a woman'. This had prompted her to find out how others negotiated similar challenges. Behind these immediate personal questions, however, lay the wider potential in society at large. 'When the nuclear family collapses, society and the social worker a re apt to think that's the end, the children and adults are lost. This isn't true – children and adults can and do survive outside the 'family' system. [...] Domestic life is the base from which all of us operated. If we don't feel alive and free, without constraints in our domestic lives, we will never feel free outside them'.

Publishers had so little faith is this book that only a paperback edition was published, while the Canadian publisher, Lorimer, brought out a hardback for their market under another title, *Different Drummers*. Undeterred, Nell Dun continued to explore ways of living in her writing and later examined the experience of being a grandmother, and a cancer survivor, in the same form of oral documentary.

Her early success did not bestow great self-confidence, nor did it guarantee the interest of publishers. Novels proved harder to write and harder to sell, too. As well as her friendship with friendship with Edna O'Brien, she also met Margaret Drabble on an Arts Council writer's tour of North Wales in 1969. Drabble had thoughtfully packed some whiskey to help get them through an itinerary that was heavy with civic dignitaries and low on audiences for their readings. She was to help her with her next novel. 'Maggie has supported my work enormously.

There's a feeling sometimes of wanting to go on being a writer, but thinking nobody believes in you. Maggie went on believing in me. She proved a tremendous friend when I was lost with a book called *Tear His Head Off His Shoulders*. She read it and said, "Push on with it until a publisher publishes it"'. Again, this title went straight to paperback. Drabble's encouragement was needed as the lack of interest that the publishing industry showed in this revolutionary writer is astonishing. Dunn seems to have lacked the quality of champion that helped to build the success of other writers in this study.

The second major theme in her work is of women talking, the enormous and disregarded field of female conversation, in which intimate disclosure can quickly lead to bonds that form over deep social divisions. With her acute ear for dialogue, drama was naturally attractive. Her play, *Steaming*, appeared in 1980 and in 1985 was made into a film featuring Vanessa Redgrave, Sarah Miles and Diana Dors. It is about six women, diverse in character and background, meeting in a Turkish bath and sharing their stories and experience of life, relationships and sex. When the baths are threatened with closure, they unite to save them. *Steaming* was to be the first of seven plays written by Dunn, and eventually she blended the dramatic form with the documentary conversations of her non-fiction books.

Her interest had always been far more in people, and the reality of our lives, than in any literary concern. Of herself as a writer, she says, 'I've always been a sidestream writer, never mainstream. I like to explore the waterweed, or look at an old duck. I'm quite like a painter and interested in portraiture. People in moments of crisis are more vivid and part of my impetus in writing has been a huge caught-upness about people'.[26]

VIRGINIA IRONSIDE

There is something very fresh and honest about it. Very slight [...] autobiographical (libel?) it still seems to me to give a hideously accurate picture not only of the aimless King's Road life, fatuity shading over into delinquency, but of the lostness, the precocious cynicism and disillusion, the throttled idealism of the present teenager.

Virginia, at eighteen, has already had too many one night stands – the one she describes, towards the end, is shocking in its absolute perfunctoriness, and very, very sad [...] In certain ways she is leading the life of an adult but her mind is almost that of a child. Yet the observation is good, the self-analysis tough and surprisingly grown up. Since the vogue, at present, seems to be precisely for this kind of book – Charlotte Bingham, Caroline Glyn, even Rosemary Erskine and Amanda Vail – I feel it should be considered seriously, and perhaps issued quickly, with suitable publicity.

This was the verdict of the publisher's reader on *Chelsea Bird*. Notice that the reader also conflates the author with her character and assumes that the work is autobiographical. His judgement was both spot-on and wrong. The vogue was indeed for confessional novels by very young women, now known as 'teenybopper authors,' and the book was fresh, honest and well-observed. It was to become clear that he had not appreciated that the genre had peaked, or that the market required innocent sauciness and naïve charm, not 'precocious cynicism and disillusion'.

At first everything seemed set for success. 'Publication day came at last. Tongue-tied, I was taken out to lunch,' Virginia Ironside recalls. The head of the publishing company, 66-year-old Fredric Warburg, veteran of Ypres and publisher of George Orwell, not only entertained her to lunch but also invited her to a party at his home later that night. 'Lonely, prickly, guarded and contemptuous' she may have been but she was also genuinely repelled by her fellow guests, who were a selection of the intellectual great and good of the day, including the novelists Elizabeth Smart and Penelope Mortimer, and the anti-liberal Christian polemicist Malcolm Muggeridge. Old and young, drunk and sober, they all seemed 'hideous'. In addition, more than fifty years later, she still shudders at the memory of the wine. 'The most revolting I have ever tasted. It was the sort that when you lean forward to sip it your eyes started watering because of the vinegary fumes that rose upward'.

The day was enough to seal her conviction that the life of a novelist was not for her. The reviewers echoed the praise of the publisher's reader, but lifestyle features far outnumbered serious notices. She too weathered a storm of publicity, featured by almost all the British press, and enjoyed the experience. 'Now that I was being photographed for myself, and not as some clone of my mother, I didn't mind at all. For a few months, I was getting almost as much publicity as my mother herself'.[27]

Harriet, the art student with the stiletto-sharp wit, was not the adorable ingénue that the industry was looking for. Film rights did not sell, and by August it was clear that American rights were a hard sell as well. 'There is little point in showing Harper and Row CHELSEA BIRD as they turned it down earlier this year,' wrote a sales executive. 'It has also been rejected by Knopf, Random House, Doubleday, Putnam, Viking, Atlantic Monthly, Prentice Hall, David McKay, Farrar Strauss, Dutton, Lippincott and Simon & Schuster. If Virginia would like to send a copy to Macmillans (to whom it has not been submitted), I suggest she does'.

Being an author, although it had upsides, did not give her the experiences she was looking for. She did not feel successful. 'The publicity meant nothing to me and the publication of *Chelsea Bird* had absolutely no effect on my low opinion of myself. I felt I had simply been lucky, that anyone could write a book if they tried. I experienced no feelings of pride and excitement; I became more depressed and distant from myself. […] I felt unreal, as if a pane of glass lay between me and the rest of the world'.

The novel's advance of £400 was enough for her to go on a trip to America by herself because, 'I thought that was the sort of thing a normal person of my age would do if they had been in my position'.

She went to New York, to Chicago where her on-off boyfriend was working at the comedy theatre, Second City, and then to New Orleans, where she was the only passenger on the plantation houses tour bus and came back to sit alone in a Creole restaurant, watching herself in a mirrored wall. 'I had no idea what I was doing there at all'. Back in London her father's household revolved around her baby half-sister and her father and step-mother decided to move and found a new house which, 'I was quick to observe, did not have room for me'. So she found herself living alone.

She had been decisively repelled by the world of books. 'It was uncool. I wanted to be cool'.[28] And the middle-market *Daily Mail*, waking up late to the youth culture revolution that was storming through London, offered her one of the coolest jobs on the planet at the time, the newly-conceived role of pop columnist. 'I was interviewed by the *Mail*, wearing the mini-est of mini-skirts, long black high-heeled boots and fish-net stockings. Mouthing a few words like "fab", "groovy", "square", "Tamla Motown", "cover version" and "backing group", I managed to persuade the astonished features editor, who had never heard such language before, to hire me on the spot'.

Her job involved choosing records from a pile of 45 rpm vinyl platters that arrived for review every week, picking the hits and interviewing a group. The establishment was now so bewitched by youth culture that the paper carried the story of her top pick on its front page. 'During my time at the *Mail*, I interviewed the Beatles, the Rolling Stones, Jimi Hendrix, James Brown, Janis Joplin, Ravi Shankar and Marc Bolan. My father said later, "I didn't know what a glamorous job it was until one day I answered the phone and it was Paul McCartney asking for her".'

Despite the day-to-day genuine thrills of her job, her mental health continued to decline. 'I was the original wild child,' she said later, remembering years in which she had sex with dozens of men, barely aware that what she wanted was affection. She gave up her pop column four years after *The Times* music critic famously compared the Beatles to Schubert. 'My only interest in pop was that it was subversive and rebellious, and now it had been endorsed by the establishment, it no longer interested me'. Instead she wrote sparkling lifestyle features. 'Woodstock was happening and hippies were dancing in the street with flowers in their hair. The truth for me was that most of the time I sat alone in my flat, worrying about my mother'.

Janey Ironside, her mother, was by now a diagnosed alcoholic who alternated suicide attempts with unsuccessful spells in a brutal rehab clinic. Her state was exacerbated by the outright persecution by the College principal, a rejected lover who cared not that she her teaching had inspired a generation of designers, the men and women who made London the world's fashion capital for a decade. Virginia found herself, like many children of dysfunctional parents, taking the role of the adult with her own mother, while her father was benignly distant, taken up with his own successes and his new family. Her depression became blacker, deeper and more frightening. Yet she met her deadlines, filed her features and showed the world a bright, hip face.

She had a year in which her mental health improved, in which she married the man she had loved since she was seventeen, Robin Grove-White, and supported him through the completion of his university degree. Then 'my anxiety increased tenfold. I began to feel I was possessed by the Devil, who was sitting on my shoulder in the shape of a bird, grinning gleefully. {...} If I sit very still even now, I can sometimes feel his dark shadow. What I was suffering from was not simply a conviction that I was worthless – a feeling reasonably easy to bear – but a conviction that I was truly evil'.

She also began to have suicidal thoughts, but the birth of her son, Will, temporarily inhibited them. Instead 'our marriage exploded like a nuclear bomb,' shortly before her mother was diagnosed with terminal cancer. Her priority then was to find a way to make a living that would allow her to care for them both, and for a while she got by financially by taking lodgers and working in a shop on Saturdays to smooth out the peaks and troughs of a freelance journalist's cash-flow.

She was thirty-three when she talked herself into her first job as an agony aunt, for the popular weekly magazine, *Woman*. This role was a national institution in itself. It meant discussing problems chosen from the weekly avalanche of letters from some four million readers. As well as writing her own advice column, she found herself in charge of a team of amateur counsellors who 'were expert at replying to readers who wanted to know how to eat an avocado pear or whether to remove their gloves when meeting a bishop. But when it came to sex questions – well, none of them was married, they were all baffled. They'd come into my office saying [...] "What is a blowjob?"'

She remained at *Woman* for eighteen years, then moved to the *Independent* newspaper for a further two decades. She also began to write books: a historical novel, a series of children's novels, the harrowing memoir of her childhood and her relationship with her mother, reflections on grief and finally a series of novels and comedies about ageing, beginning with *No, I Don't Want to Join a Book Club* in 2007. These struck such a chord with what was by then the silver generation of her contemporaries. She extended the theme into a series of one-woman shows, *Growing Old Disgracefully*, which proved a sell-out success in London and at the Edinburgh Festival. She is also the agony aunt for the *Oldie*, a free-thinking, funny magazine designed as an ageless alternative to Britian's millenial media. 'I love people asking my advice. It's flattering to feel wanted. I loved being an agony aunt. When you feel pretty depressed a lot of the time, it's lovely to see a lot of letters from people more miserable than you, and to be able to offer comfort'.

MARGARET FORSTER

For a young woman who looked on the marriages of her mother's generation as 'a rotten bargain,' Margaret Forster was very ready to take on the roles of wife and mother. Their film earnings allowed

her and her husband to leave their apartment and move to a house,
albeit a house with a sitting tenant. They stayed in Hampstead,
traditionally the London suburb that welcomed intellectuals, and
set to work restoring the building. In a later book about her homes,
My Life in Houses, she recalled the next two years as 'hectic'.

> Our house, during this period, became a place of meetings –
> directors, producers and actors – which I didn't like at all. I felt
> uncomfortable having these people in my house, though they
> were being very accommodating and kind, agreeing to come to
> me, first because I was about to have Jake and then after I'd had
> him. It wasn't, for them, a very workman-like atmosphere, sitting
> in a room full of toys and baby clothes, with one child tottering
> around and the other roaring in his cradle on just next door and
> not at all out of hearing. They were tolerant, these men, sitting
> with scripts on their knees, pointing out what would work and
> what would not, and I was the impatient one, knowing I wasn't
> suited for this and for any kind of team work.

Hunter Davies, her husband, was soon at work on a book about the
Beatles, which meant that three out of the four most famous rock stars
in the world arrived with their partners, for tea or for dinner. These
distractions were soon eclipsed, however, by the need to protect
their unexpected family fortune from the tax authorities, at the
time demanding 95 per cent of the income of high earners. Britain,
unlike countries such as Ireland or France, has never recognised that
a creative person's income can fluctuate wildly and so Margaret, her
husband and their children had either to say goodbye to most of the
money they would ever earn, or become tax exiles.

They went first to the Maltese island of Gozo, and then to the
Algarve region of Portugal where she lived up to her belief that
'anyone who really wants to write can write anywhere' by finishing
her next novel, a deliberate break with everything to do with
fashionable London, about an ill-tempered, elderly woman trying

to connect with her estranged adult children. The couple returned to London after the statutory year away, where they had one more child, their daughter, Flora.

Margaret was to write nine novels in the next fifteen years. She rarely identified herself as the author of *Georgy Girl*, nor did she accept that novel's success. It seemed as though the publishing industry was quite happy to discount her success, so her agent was still hoping for a breakthrough several books later. Her advances got smaller and her editor's enthusiasm waned. She temporarily abandoned fiction to write her first biography of Bonnie Prince Charlie. Although she did complain that, with three small children, she was too tired and busy to write much.

To add to the stress, in 1975 she was diagnosed with breast cancer, and in hospital after a mastectomy 'tried to make my bed like my desk,' although the nurses banned her fountain-pen and she had to write in biro. For a year or so she seemed to have recovered completely but the cancer, so unusual in a young mother with no family history of the disease and a healthy lifestyle, returned. She had a second mastectomy in 1977, after another tumour was removed, followed by nine months of chemotherapy. But she kept working.

She began her second biography of William Thackeray but 'realised I had no desire whatsoever to know how far Thackeray was telling the truth about himself,' and chose to write a pastiche autobiography in which she reconstructed the great Victorian novelist's voice from his diaries and other documents. Her editor didn't like the idea, so she returned the publisher's advance, completed the book, and asked her agent to offer it to him again, whereupon he bought it. Reviewers were kind but puzzled, and her novels, dynamic stories of eccentric people, had neither achieved the mass audience of *Georgy Girl* nor the status of literary fiction.

After two more novels she made a decisive change of publisher, moving from Secker & Warburg to Chatto & Windus, where the legendary feminist editor Carmen Callil was editorial director. The tentative, exploratory period of her early work ended and she at once wrote three highly acclaimed novels *Private Papers* (1986) *Have the Men Had Enough?* (1989) and *Lady's Maid* (1990). All three depict women as daughters, mothers, wives and lovers, their lives governed by their relationships, emotionally and often materially. *Lady's Maid,* Callil believed to be her finest book, is the story of Elizabeth Barrett's love affair with Robert Browning, as related by her maid.

She also returned to biography, writing the life of Elizabeth Barrett Browning (1988), which won her the Heinemann award and then a biography of Daphne du Maurier (1997) won the Fawcett book prize. In this she explored for the first time the degree to which du Maurier was bisexual. She chose her subject superstitiously after a copy of *Rebecca* fell off a shelf into her hand. As her career continued her writing became more feminist, and wider and deeper in scope, beginning in 1984 with *Significant Sisters*, a study of first-wave feminists.

She also began to explore her family history in a series of memoirs: *Hidden Lives,* about her grandmother and mother as well as herself, 1995, followed by *Precious Lives* (1998), which won the J. R. Ackerley Prize. One of her most extraordinary novels was *Diary of an Ordinary Woman: A Novel* (2003), which needed its subtitle as the meticulous account of a woman living through the twentieth century seemed so authentic that some readers assumed it was a journal.

Her husband described her writing life in his own autobiography, *A Life in the Day*:

> Around nine o'clock each morning, she would go into her office at the top of the house, on the back extension, which was like being on a ship, looking out over all the gardens. She would sit there for one and a half hours each morning, writing. She had no phone in her office, no computer, no mobile, just blank sheets of paper and her Waterman fountain pen. She never read what she had done the day before, just started each day at the top of

a blank page. She never numbered the pages, but each day she would find that she had written precisely ten pages.

When she had finished the novel, she would then read it through to see she had not changed the heroine's name or hair colour, numbered all the pages and send (sic) it to Gertrude, her typist for so many years. I would scream at her when I found she had posted the only manuscript, without making a copy. What if it gets lost in the post, destroyed or burned. Your year's work will be ruined... 'Doesn't matter,' she would say. 'I am only playing'.

For each of her twenty-six published novels, she would make no notes, never talk about it, either before, during or after. [...] Doing was the thing. [...] She had an agreement with her publisher that she would not be required to do literary festivals, [...] give talks or do signing sessions.

I am sure that our three children, when growing up, had no idea their mother wrote books. If they came into her room, she would hide the current manuscript, drop everything and attend to whatever they wanted.

In 2007 more tumours were found and, after years of hormone injections, chemotherapy and finally palliative care, in which four more novels were published, Margaret Forster died in February 2016.

16

WE WERE PIONEERS

The women in this study wanted to be a new kind of writer. They never thought of being anything but honest and they never wanted to fit into the accepted literary mould. When they made their debuts, a writer in Britain was a tweedy, privileged male in the mould of Evelyn Waugh or Kingsley Amis, coming down from Oxford or Cambridge with a network of contacts who shared their faintly nostalgic aesthetics and supported by an intellectual establishment that could only recognise a woman writer if she approximated the male ideal in heritage and lack of narcissism. If a writer wasn't like that, he could be an aggressive working-class man from the post-industrial north of England.

It was hard to swim against this patriarchal tide, but the writers in this study benefited enormously because their gender denied them the beaten path to literary achievement. They were born outside the mainstream and so, whether or not they intended to challenge the status quo, their work would be revolutionary.

Their greatest allies in the struggle were the new mass media, television, film and women's magazines. A writer of the Hampstead school would be content to reach a few thousand like-minded readers, mostly in London. The Rebel Writers reached audiences of millions all over the world, however tepid their critical reception may have been at home. At a time when women's popular fiction was entirely colonised by bodice rippers and pulp romances, these works reached the mass of women who were equally repelled by the misogynist elitism of literary fiction.

None of these writers would have called themselves feminists. The word was rarely used at the time. The fifties were a low point for women's rights, when there had been no advance on the gains of first wave feminism and the egalitarianism forced on society during World War II had been swiftly extinguished. In an interview for BBC Radio 4's Book Club, Lynne Reid Banks said, 'At the time I didn't see how important feminism was. To tell you the honest truth, at the time I thought men were the superior sex. But I think I felt it deep in my gut, that things had to change. We really were pioneers. I just didn't make a fetish of it – I wish I had'.

What these writers did do, and what unifies their work across vastly different backgrounds and ambitions, is tell the truth. They lived, they felt, they thought, they observed the lives of other women, and they wrote it all like it was. Their works are social documents that illuminated areas of life which were overlooked, ignored or even deliberately hidden by society at the time. Their preoccupations aligned with the core issues of second-wave feminism, which were equal pay, equality in education and employment opportunities, legal and free contraception and abortion. The popular success of the Rebel Writers meant that these issues had been discussed in the general population years before those demands which were handed to the prime minister on 6 March 1971 during the First International Women's Day march in London.

For some the social legacy of these works was immediate. In the year in which *Poor Cow* was published, contraception was made legally available to single women in England. The 1967 Abortion Act, the 1970 Equal Pay Act and changes to social housing regulations in favour of single parents followed shortly afterwards.

These writers wanted to change their world, even if they didn't believe they had the power to do so. Their impact was spontaneous, unconscious and enormous. They also did not intend to become a literary movement. Most consciously rejected the literary preoccupations of their time and set out to do something new and authentic, even though they were not sure what it would be.

By writing as women, they foreshadowed *l'ecriture feminine* while having no intention of defining a new literary style.

At their debuts each one was alone, although as their genre gathered strength and one young woman's success led to the next, they became aware of one other's work. In time, some would become friends and support each other as they developed. Their work is unified by its content to a much greater extent than that of the Angry Young Men. At a time when an author is a public figure with a media profile, it is not necessary for a lone writer to walk, like the Lake Poets, for a day across hill and dale to meet another and discuss their ideas. Your fellow writer is there, on the television, and she's walking you round her home town.

Their legacy also empowered many other young women who wanted to write. In the Dublin Review of Books, Maureen O'Connor acclaimed Edna O'Brien because her first novel 'made possible for both male and female writers in Ireland who followed her, a right to self-determination in representing sexuality and the body'.[1] In his obituary of Shelagh Delaney, the *Guardian's* theatre critic, Michael Billington, wrote, 'if we now think there is nothing freakish or unusual about women dramatists making a mark in their teens or coming from a working-class background, we have Shelagh Delaney to thank for it'.

Any woman in a creative profession can learn from these life stories, not only because so many of these writers triumphed over extreme adversity but because the bad things that happened to them are still happening. Women artists still have to argue with definitions of art that exclude them, and negotiate with industries whose imperatives are determined by men. The Rebel Writers have a lot to teach us about self-belief and never giving up. Jeanette Winterson, writing after Shelagh Delaney's death, summed up her personal inheritance:

Delaney was born in Salford in 1939. I was born in Manchester in 1959. Same background, same early success. She was like a lighthouse – pointing the way and warning about the rocks underneath. She was the first working-class woman playwright. She had all the talent and we let her go.

This book is written in the hope that we will not let so many talents go in the future.

EPILOGUE

And Françoise Sagan? For a few years, her literary career bloomed. She swiftly followed *Bonjour Tristesse* with a semi-sequel, *Un Certain Sourire*, about a student in Paris and her love affair with a middle-aged businessman. Less scandalous than her first novel, it was swiftly adapted as a film directed by the veteran Hollywood director, Jean Negulseco, using some European actors – in this case the Italian Rossano Brazzi and Christine Carère from France.

Hollywood was dazzled by inherently glamorous European settings at the time, which allowed film-makers to create scenarios featuring relationships that would have been considered scandalous in America itself, and the films of Sagan's first two novels were typical of cinema at the time. Sagan has a co-writer's credit for the screenplay, whereas the Hollywood adaptation of *Bonjour Tristesse*, released in the same year and directed by Otto Preminger, was written by Arthur Laurents, a playwright who had a track record with subjects Hollywood considered sensitive. This starred the British actor, David Niven, alongside a celebrated New Wave star, Jean Seberg. Although this is the more experimental film with sequences in black-and-white, *A Certain Smile* was commercially and critically more successful, with three Academy Award nominations including one for the evergreen title song recorded by Johnny Mathis.

Sagan was writing, as she seemed to do everything else at this period in her life, at a manic speed. By 1965 she had added four more novels and four stage plays to her output. Her fifth novel, *Aimez-Vous Brahms?*, is about a 40-year-old designer whose unfaithful partner of five years begins a new affair, whereupon she accepts the affections of a 24-year-old son of two of her clients. The film, co-written by Sagan and directed by Anatole Litvak, who had settled in France after a good Hollywood career, stars Ingrid Bergman, Yves Montand and Anthony Perkins, who won the award for Best Actor at Cannes Film Festival for his performance. Shot in black and white with Brahms's music on the soundtrack, it is an intense evocation of a mature love affair that is arguably the most satisfying adaptation of Sagan's work.

The author, however, was enjoying her success to excess. As well as hanging out with international film stars, she quickly formed a coterie of friends and family, moving restlessly with an entourage that included at various times her brother and sister, Florence Malraux and other golden children of France's brilliant cultural regeneration. Brattiness was expected of them, so she was fashionably late for dinner with the Rothschilds or with future political giants including Georges Pompidou and Françoise Mitterrand. She made the charming Mediterranean fishing village of St Tropez fashionable a few years before the arrival of Brigitte Bardot, then moved back north to rent a villa owned by Christian Dior in the village of Milly-la-Forêt. This is the resting-place of Jean Cocteau and it was very nearly her own final destination.

Sagan had two dangerous obsessions, which she indulged to the utmost once she was old enough to do so. Fast cars were her first. She was driving her father's Buick before she got her licence, which she was awarded five days before her eighteenth birthday, when she could legally get on the road. As soon as she had made enough money she bought a succession of rare sports cars, and in 1956 in a radio interview described playing chicken run with her brother on the Place St Sulpice. Florence recalls driving through Paris with her at 2 a.m., doing over 200 k (124 miles) per hour and at that stage in her life it seemed that she was an expert driver.

On April 13 1957, at Milly-la-Forêt, she was waiting for some guests, the Greek actress Melina Mercouri and her future husband, the American director Jules Dassin. They telephoned to say they were late, and Sagan and her friends decided to drive out to meet them. She lost control of her Aston Martin DB 2/4 Mark 2, which left the road and overturned, landing in a field. While her passengers were thrown clear, Sagan was trapped under the mass of metal. She sustained multiple fractures, her chest was crushed and she was taken, in a coma, to a nearby hospital where a priest was called to administer the last rites.

At her brother's insistence she was transferred to a hospital in Paris where the medical team fought to save her life. Her injuries included a skull fractured in three places, crushed ribs and numerous other broken bones, and she was treated with morphine derivatives to the extent that, when she left the clinic, it was to enter another to detox. She was to struggle with addictions for the rest of her life. While the crash permanently undermined her physical and mental health, it added to the glamour of her public image. The macabre romanticisation of speed, the cult of 'too fast to live, too young to die' focused on James Dean and Marlon Brando, had seized the imagination of the media six months earlier when Dean crashed his Porsche and died. Now, instead of putting the young novelist in a housewife's pinny, photographers posed her at the wheel of a sports car.

During her time in hospital she began a self-reflective journal, *Toxique,* which was to be illustrated with drawings by the fashionable artist Bernard Buffet. She also agreed to marry a man who 'fascinated' her, a young editor, Guy Schoeller, son of the CEO of the Hachette publishing house. While he recalls that 'we had a lot of fun' their lifestyles were incompatible and neither made much of an effort to build a life together. They were divorced in 1960 although she dedicated *Aimez-Vous Brahms?* to him.

Her second obsession was gambling, which she again indulged as soon as she was legally able, from the morning of her twenty-first birthday. She played *chemin-de-fer* and roulette, and she was often lucky and impulsive in equal measure. She was renting a chateau in Normandy and playing at Deauville, where, after losing heavily all week, she came home with winnings of 80,000 francs. The next morning, when the chateau owner arrived to check on the property, he told her he was putting it up for sale. When he named the price, FFr 80,000, she bought it outright.

Her luck did not hold, however. She asked French casinos to ban her, then went to London, where gambling was very tightly regulated, and managed to gain entry to the exclusive Clermont Club. The habit also earned her media attention. She told the French television arts programme, 'When I'm losing, for a split second, I see myself in a little room with a little window, in a faint light with piles of pages to fill. I have a very romantic vision of my eventual ruin – very writerly'. This too was a prescient observation.

French society, more than many others, values women primarily as objects of male desire, something that Sagan's rebellious instincts ensured she would reject. Her close friendships with women had always been important to her and after her first divorce Sagan formed a relationship with Paola St Just, a wealthy bisexual socialite. In the winter of 1960 Sagan rented a chalet at the Swiss ski resort of Klosters, which she shared with Paola. Among their guests were another bisexual couple, the French aristocrat Charles de Rohan-Chabot and his partner, an American dilettante Robert Westhoff. Within a year Charles and Paola were married, as were Françoise and Bob. This marriage was also short-lived. Their son, Denis, was born in 1962 and lived happily with Sagan's parents for months on end.

Eventually Sagan met the love of her life, *Elle* magazine's stylist and fashion designer Peggy Roche. The couple enjoyed a twenty year relationship which brought a measure of stability to Sagan's life. However, she continued to struggle with addiction and depression, to write prolifically and to support both friends and strangers with extraordinary generosity. Roche died of liver cancer in 1991. Françoise Mitterrand, President of France from 1981 to 1995, had protected Sagan from the full implications of her tangled tax affairs and unwise business deals but after he left office in 1995 her last years were overshadowed by convictions for cocaine possession and tax fraud, as well as declining health. Her last relationship was with the wealthy Ingrid Mechoulam, who bought the house in Normandy and all her papers when the tax authorities sold them at public auction.

Until her very last years, Sagan never stopped writing. When she died at the age of sixty-nine, she had produced twenty novels and nine stage plays, as well as collections of essays and short stories. Her son extracted the rights to her early work from the tax authorities and established a literary prize in her name in 2010.

THE END

ENDNOTES

INTRODUCTION

1   Dunn, N. (2013). Poor Cow. 2nd ed. London: Virago Press. P 132.
2   Amis, K. (2008). Lucky Jim (1954). 21st ed. London: Penguin Classsics: 1648 Edition, p. 5.
3   Delaney, S. (1968). Sweetly Dings the Donkey. Harmondsworth: Penguin.
4   Myrdal, A. and Klein, V. (1968). Women's Two Roles; Home and Work. London: Routledge & Kegan Paul.
5   Pyke, M. 'Family Planning'. BMJ, vol 1, no. 4766, 1952, pp. 1028-1028. BMJ, doi: 10.1136/bmj.1.4766.1028.
6   Hansard HL Deb 24 October 1956 vol 199 cc972-89.
7   Burman, Douglas D. et al. 'Sex Differences In Neural Processing Of Language Among Children'. Neuropsychologia, vol 46, no. 5, 2008, pp. 1349-1362. Elsevier BV, doi: 10.1016/j.neuropsychologia.2007.12.021. Accessed 26 Nov 2018.
8   Chrisler, Joan C, and Donald R McCreary. Handbook Of Gender Research In Psychology. Springer, 2010, p. 245.
9   Thorpe, Vanessa. 'Why Women Read More Than Men'. The Guardian, 2009, https://www.theguardian.com/books/2009/mar/22/women-reading-books-study. Accessed 26 Nov 2018.
10 Flood, Alison. 'Readers Prefer Authors Of Their Own Sex, Survey Finds'. The Guardian, 2018, https://www.theguardian.com/books/2014/nov/25/readers-prefer-authors-own-sex-goodreads-survey. Accessed 26 Nov 2018.
11 ibid

CHAPTER I

1   Salford City Reporter (1938). Quoted in Harding (2014)
2   Monitor: Shelagh Delaney's Salford, (1960). [TV programme] BBC-2: BBC.
3   Harding (2014) p 19
4   Delaney, S. (1958). A Playwright's Education. The Manchester Guardian, p. 6.
5   Delaney, S. (1958). A Playwright's Education. The Manchester Guardian, p. 6.
6   Littlewood, J., Hedley, P. and Rankin, P. (2003). Joan's book. 3rd ed. London`: Methuen Publishing Ltd. P 514-520
7   Harding (2014) p 25
8   Littlewood, Joan et al. Joan's Book. 3rd ed., Methuen Publishing Ltd, 2003. P 519
9   Littlewood et al (2003) PP514 – 520

10   Harding, P 61

11   Littlewood et al. P 523

12   Littlewood et al. P 523

13   ibid

14   Rankin, P. *Joan Littlewood:Dreams and Realities:The Official Biography*. London. Oberon Books. 2014 P129.

15   Rankin. 2014. P 129

16   Rankin. 2014. P 141

17   O'Brien, E. (2013). Country Girl:A Memoir. 2nd ed. London: Faber & Faber.

18   O'Brien. P 97

19   O'Brien, P 98

20   Not to be confused with Ian Hamilton the critic and biographer, born in 1938.

21   Guppy, Shusha (interviewer). 'Edna O'Brien, The Art Of Fiction No. 82'. The Paris Review, 2017, https://www.theparisreview.org/interviews/2978/edna-obrien-the-art-of-fiction-no-82-edna-obrien. Accessed 31 July 2017.

22   A device which allowed news anchors to read from scripts while looking at the camera, precursor of autocue.

23   Biography.jrank.org. (2017). Lynne Reid Banks (1929–) Biography - Personal, Addresses, Career, Member, Honors Awards, Writings, Adaptations, Sidelights. [online] Available at: http://biography.jrank.org/pages/1956/Reid-Banks-Lynne-1929.html#ixzz4nlRFV9P2 [Accessed 25 Jul. 2017].

24   Bookclub, (2010). [Radio programme] Radio 4: BBC.

25   Personal interview with Charlotte Bingham. (2015). Unless otherwise stated, all quotations in this section are from this source.

26   Michael Jago, The Man who was George Smiley: The Life of John Bingham (2013), reviewed by the former Director General of MI5, Stella Rimington, in The Spectator, 2 March 2013, p. 36

27   ibid

28   'A Woman's War'. 2018, https://lady.co.uk/womans-war. Accessed 9 Dec 2018.

29   Ironside, V. (2013). Nell Dunn: I never used to think about death etc. [online] Available at: Virginia, I. (2003). Nell Dunn: I never used to think about death, until I was 50. I was never going to die. I was immortal. But now I think about death every day. The Independent. [online] Available at: https://www.independent.co.uk/arts-entertainment/theatre-dance/features/nell-dunn-i-never-used-to-think-about-death-until-i-was-50-i-was-never-going-to-die-i-was-immortal-105000.html [Accessed 2 Aug. 2017].

30   Fisher, P. (2016). Playwright and author Nell Dunn in conversation about her career - theatreVOICE. [online] theatreVOICE. Available at: http://www.theatrevoice.com/audio/interview-nell-dunn/ [Accessed 2 Aug. 2017].

31   Daily Mail. 'Tanfield's Diary'. 17 January 1957.

32   Dunn, N. (2013). Poor Cow. 2nd ed. London: Virago Press. P xiv

33   Fisher, P. (2016). Playwright and author Nell Dunn in conversation about her career - theatreVOICE. [online] theatreVOICE. Available at: http://www.theatrevoice.com/audio/interview-nell-dunn/ [Accessed 2 Aug. 2017].

34   Nell Dunn, *Up The Junction*, Virago, London, 2013. P ix

35   Gross, John. 'Sylvie, Rube And Nell'. The Observer, 2018.

36   Ironside, V. (2004). Janey and Me: Growing up with My Mother. 1st ed. London: Harper Perennial. P 1

37   Ironside, V. P16

38   Ironside, V. P154.

39   Ironside, V. P 160.

40   Ironside, V. P 193.

41   Ironside, V. P196.

42   Ironside, V. P 200.

43   Forster, M. (1995). Hidden Lives: A Family Memoir. 1st ed. London: Viking. P 198.

44   In Britain, public housing projects, for which local governments or councils are responsible, are known as 'council housing' or 'council estates.'

45   Forster, M. P 155.

46   Forster, M. P 156.

47   Davies, Hunter. A Life in the Day (London, Simon & Schuster, 2017).

48   Wood, Harriet. 2018, https://www.thebookseller.com/news/trade-pays-tribute-godfather-industry-sissons-850426. Accessed 22 Dec 2018.

49   The Guardian. 2018, p. 12.

CHAPTER 2

1   Daily Telegraph, 'Jeremy Sandford – Obituary', 2003. http://www.telegraph.co.uk/news/obituaries/1429962/jeremy-sandford.htm. Accessed 2 Aug 2017.

CHAPTER 3

1   Max Roser and Esteban Ortiz-Ospina (2018) - 'Literacy'. Published online at OurWorldInData.org. Retrieved from: 'https://ourworldindata.org/literacy' [Online Resource]

2   Michael Jago, The Man Who Was George Smiley: The Life of John Bingham. (London, Biteback Publishing Ltd, 2013) P 53

CHAPTER 4

1   Although first recorded by Fred Astaire and Ginger Rogers in 1937, Let's Call The Whole Thing Off surged in popularity from 1957 to 1960, when it was covered by Ella Fitzgerald and Louis Armstrong, and Rosemary Clooney and Bing Crosby, among many others. It was written by George and Ira Gershwin for the film Let's Dance.

2   Ibid. P 523.

CHAPTER 5

1   Ibid P 317.

2   This is the nickname the girls give to one of their number who has a scoliosis.

CHAPTER 6

1 Virginia Nicholson, Perfect Wives in Ideal Homes (London, Viking 2015) P 69
2 Sheila Hardy, Marriage and Homemaking in the 1950s (Stroud, The History Press 2012 (2013))
3 Edna O'Brien, The Lonely Girl (London, Jonathan Cape 1962 (1986)) P316.
4 https://www.theguardian.com/books/2010/oct/22/dh-lawrence-lady-chatterley-trial
5 ibid

CHAPTER 7

1 Edna O'Brien, The Country Girls (London, Hutchinson 1960 (1986)) P 347
2 Margaret Drabble, The Millstone (London, Weidenfeld & Nicholson, 1965 (2010) P 110.
3 Philip Hope-Wallace, Shelagh Delaney's 'A Taste of Honey' at Wyndham's. The Manchester Guardian, 1959.
4 Drabble, P 74.
5 Pat Thane and Tanya Evans. Sinners? Scroungers? Saints? Unmarried Motherhood in Twentieth Century England. (Oxford, Oxford University Press 2010) P 134.

CHAPTER 8

1 Virginia Nicholson, Perfect Wives in Ideal Homes, (London. Viking 2015) P 169.
2 In England and Wales state education was structured on the Tripartite System defined by the 1947 Education Act. At the age of 11 children sat a three-part examination in mathematics, English and 'general reasoning' and on the basis of their results were sent either to a grammar school for a traditional academic education delivered with high expectations or a secondary modern school for vocation-oriented learning. Although it succeeded in creating considerable social mobility, as the early biography of Margaret Forster demonstrates, the system was bitterly criticised for perpetuating elitism and largely abandoned in the 1970s.
3 Thelma Veness, School Leavers: Their Aspirations and Expectations (London, Methuen 1962) quoted in Nicholson, P 165.

CHAPTER 9

1 Travis, Alan. 'After 44 Years Secret Papers Reveal Truth About Five Nights Of Violence In Notting Hill'. The Guardian, 2002, https://www.theguardian.com/uk/2002/aug/24/artsandhumanities.nottinghillcarnival2002. Accessed 11 Jan 2019.
2 Beard, Mary. 'A Don's Life: Roman Britain in Black and White', The Times Literary Supplement, 2017.
3 In the UK a 'public school' means an independent fee-paying school.
4 At the time of writing, the Windrush generation was prominent in news headlines in Britain following a shameful attempt by the government to deport some of them following a change to immigration rules.
5 The Guardian, December 2 2014.

CHAPTER 11

1 Leonard Russell, letter to Edna O'Brien, December 24 1965, Random House Archive, JC534
2 The Guardian, May 23 (The Guardian & Observer, London, 2018.)
3 Wimbledon here refers to the genteel outer-London suburb when O'Brien and her family first lived after leaving Dublin
4 Michelle Woods, *Red, Un-Read and Edna*, in *Edna O'Brien: New Critical Perspectives* (Carysfort Press, Dublin, 2006) P 57 Stan Gébler Davies earlier made this claim in an *Evening Standard* article, *The Trouble with Edna*, October 19 1992
5 Interview in *Banned in Ireland*, edited by Julia Carlson.
6 Charlotte Bingham, letter dated London, 1963. RHA
7 Christopher Ironside, letter October 26 1963. RHA
8 Virginia Ironside, letter to James Gilbert, April 13 1964. RHA.
9 Nell Dunn, email to the author, July 4 2018.
10 Virginia Ironside, interview with the author, July 17 2018
11 ,Daily Mail, November 30 1966
12 The Daily Mail. January 2. (Associated Newspapers, London, 1959)
13 Daily Mail, May 2 (Associated Newspapers, London, 1958)
14 John Hardin, *Sweetly Sings Delaney*.
15 *Banned in Ireland,*
16 Unattributed press cutting, Virginia Ironside private collection.
17 Unattributed press cutting, Virginia Ironside private collection.

CHAPTER 12

1 Alexander Walker, *Hollywood, England*..
2 Tony Richardson, *The Long-Distance Runner*.
3 Alexander Walker, op cit. Around the same time, however, Harry Saltzman read *Goldfinger* by Ian Fleming, and with partner Cubby Broccoli acquired the rights to James Bond and the novels about him.
4 John Harding, op cit,
5 Tony Richardson, op cit.
6 Ernest Gébler, letter to Tom Maschler, September 30 1963. Random House archives JC7/12.
7 Forbes, Bryan. *Notes For A Life*. Collins, 1974. P 307.
8 "Bookclub". BBC, 2010.
9 http://www.bbfc.co.uk/case-studies/alfie Accessed June 20 2018.
10 "Georgy Girl, Box Office Information". The Numbers. Accessed inApril 16, 2012.
11 Hunter Davies, A Life in the Day (2017)
12 https://www.imdb.com/title/tt0060453/trivia?ref_=tt_trv_trv Accessed July 21 2018.
13 Cranston, Ros. "BFI Screenonline: Up The Junction (1965)". *Screenonline.Org.Uk*, 2019, http://www.screenonline.org.uk/tv/id/440997/index.html. Accessed 18 July 2018.

14   Robertson, Selina. "It Was Such A Laugh!" Writer Nell Dunn In Conversation - The F-Word". *Thefword.Org.Uk*, 2016, https://www.thefword.org.uk/2016/06/it-was-such-a-laugh-writer-nell-dunn-in-conversation/. Accessed 2 Aug 2017.

15   Sam Adams, *AV Film,* October 7 2013. https://film.avclub.com/terence-stamp-on-accents-first-takes-and-playing-a-tr-1798239122 Accessed MJuly 25 2018.

CHAPTER 13

1   David Lodge, *The Listener,* November 21 1963.
2   Claire Tomalin in The Observer, April 30 1967.
3   David Rees, '*New Novels'. The Spectator*, 2018,
4   Jeremy Rundall, *The Sunday Times*, January 17 1965.
5   S ephen Wall, *Keeping Sex at bay, The Observer*, November 6, 1966.
6   Reader's Report, May 7 1965, Cape papers., RHA..
7   Edna O'Brien, *Country Girl*.
8   Obscene Publications Act 1959, Clause 1 (1)
9   Daily Mail, November 9 1965,
10   History Ireland, 20th Century Social Perspectives, 20th-century / Contemporary History, Features, Issue 6 (Nov/Dec 2007), Volume 15
11   Liam Delaney et al. From Angela's Ashes to the Celtic Tiger: Early Life Conditions and Adult Health in Ireland,
12   Censorship of Publications Board records, at the Irish Film Classification Office.
13   Edna O'Brien, op cit.
14   Julia Carlson, ed.. *Banned in Ireland,*.
15   Letter from Tom Maschler to Edna O'Brien, September 17 1964. Jonathan Cape files, RHA.
16   John Harding, op cit. Unless otherwise indicated, quotations in this section are from this source.

CHAPTER 14

1   ohn Osborne, Almost A Gentleman: An Autobiography, Faber & Faber (1981)
2   Humphrey Carpenter, The Angry Young Men, Allen Lane: Penguin, (2002)
3   Kenneth Tynan in 'The Observer', 13 May 1956:
4   Irving Wardle, The Theatres of George Devine, quoted in Carpenter, op cit.
5   Dale Salwak, *Interviews with Britain's Angry Young Men* (1984) quoted in Carpenter Op Cit.
6   Alan Sillitoe, *Life Without Armour*, London, Flamingo (1996)
7   Humphrey Carpenter, Op Cit.
8   John Osborne, Op Cit.
9   Tom Maschler, *Publisher.* P 10 London, Picador, (2005) Tom Maschler, *Publisher.* P 10 London, Picador, (2005)
10   The Bechdel Test, defined by the American cartoonist Alison Bechdel, measures the gender balance in fiction by requiring at least one scene in which two women talk to each other about something other than a man.
11   Eric Jacobs. *Sir Kingsley Amis Obituary.* The Guardian. 23 October 1995.

CHAPTER 15

1 John Greenfield, New York Times, February 23 1966.
2 Cope subsequently had a long and successful career in television, notably in the comedy crime series *Randall & Hopkirk (Deceased.)*
3 John Osborne, *Op Cit.*
4 Alexander Walker, Hollywood, England.
5 http://www.salfordstar.com/article.asp?id=3529 Accessed August 10 2018.
6 Carlo Gébler, *The Projectionist.*
7 Tom Maschler, letters to Edna O'Brien, Edna O'Brien papers, Emory University.
8 Quoted in letter from Edna O'Brien to Tom Maschler, undated., RHA.
9 Carlo Gébler, Op Cit.
10 Iris Lindahl-Raitilla, in *Affecting Irishness.*
11 Carol Dix, The Road from L, The Guardian, March 28 1974.
12 Lynn Reid, Banks. 'Interview'. Lynnereidbanks.Com, 2018, http://www.lynnereidbanks.com/interview.html. Accessed 8 Dec 2 018.
13 Leonard Russell, Mainly About Books, The Sunday Times, November 27 1960.
14 Daily Mail, November 21 1963.
15 *Life and Style, The Guardian*, March 17 2017.
16 Lynne Reid Banks, Introduction for Book Club Bulletin, 1971.
17 Jonathan Derbyshire, *The Books Interview, The New Stateman*, September 10 2010.
18 http://www.charlottebingham.com/My-First-Success.html Accessed August 16 2018.
19 *The Independent*, June 19 1993.
20 *The Tatler*, March 7 2018.
21 Charlotte Bingham, *Coronet Among The Grass,* (1972)
22 *The Tatler,* March 7 2018.
23 https://www.newyorker.com/books/page-turner/the-secrets-of-the-forgotten-1965-classic-talking-to-women Accesse.d August 20 2018.
24 *Daily Mail,* July 8 1964.
25 *Daily Mail,* July 3 1965.
26 *The Independent*, May 17 2003.
27 Virginia Ironside, *Janey and Me.* (2003)
28 Interview with the author, 2018.

CHAPTER 16

1 Dublin Review of Books, Issue 102, 28 July 2018.

BIBLIOGRAPHY

CORE TEXTS

These are the editions used in the review section, Chapters 2 to 10.
Banks, Lynne Reid. *The L-Shaped Room*. 2nd ed., Chatto & Windus, 1960.
Bingham, Charlotte. *Coronet Among The Weeds*. William Heinemann, 1962.
Delaney, Shelagh. *Taste Of Honey*. Bloomsbury Methuen, Bloomsbury Publishing UK, 2014.
Drabble, Margaret. *The Millstone*. Penguin Decades, 2010.
Dunn, Nell. *Up The Junction*. MacGibbon & Kee Ltd, 1963.
Dunn, Nell. *Poor Cow*. MacGibbon & Kee Ltd, 1967.
Forster, Margaret. *Georgy Girl*. 2nd ed., Panther, 1966.
Ironside, Virginia. *Chelsea Bird*. Quercus Kindle Edition, 2019.
O'Brien, Edna. *The Country Girls Trilogy With A New Epilogue*. Penguin Books Ltd, 1988.

OTHER FICTION

Amis, Kingsley. *Lucky Jim* (1954). 21st ed., Penguin Classsics:1648 Edition, 2008.
Banks, Lynne Reid. *An End To Running*. Chatto & Windus, 1962.
Banks, Lynne Reid. *Children At The Gate*. Chatto & Windus, 1968.
Banks, Lynne Reid. *The Backward Shadow*. Chatto & Windus, 1970.
Banks, Lynne Reid. *Two Is Lonely*. Chatto & Windus, 1974.
Banks, Lynne Reid. *Dark Quartet: The Story Of The Brontes*. Weidenfeld & Nicholson, 1976. [note to editor – this is a biographical novel)
Banks, Lynne Reid. *The Indian In The Cupboard*. 1st ed., Doubleday, 1980.
Banks, Lynne Reid. *Uprooted: A Canadian War Story*. Harper Collins Children's Books, 2014.
Bingham, Charlotte. *Lucinda*. William Heinemann Ltd, 1966.
Bingham, Charlotte. *Coronet Among The Grass*. Heinemann, 1972.
Braine, John. *Room At The Top*. Eyre & Spottiswoode, 1957.
Delaney, Shelagh. *Sweetly Sings The Donkey*. Penguin, 1968.
Forster, Margaret. *The Bogeyman*. Secker & Warburg, 1965.
Forster, Margaret. *The Travels Of Maudie Tipstaff*. Secker & Warburg, 1967.
Forster, Margaret. *The Park*. Secker & Warburg, 1968.
Forster, Margaret. *Miss Owen- Owen Is At Home*. Secker & Warburg, 1969.
Forster, Margaret. *Fenella Phizackerley*. Secker & Warburg, 1970.
French, Marilyn. *The Women's Room*. Simon & Schuster, 1977.
Lamming, George. *The Emigrants*. Michael Joseph, 1954.

MacInnes, Colin. *City Of Spades*. MacGibbon & Kee Ltd, 1957.

MacInnes, Colin. *Absolute Beginners*. MacGibbon & Kee Ltd, 1959.

MacInnes, Colin. *Mr. Love And Justice*. MacGibbon & Kee Ltd, 1960.

Maschler, Tom(ed.) *Declaration*. MacGibbon & Kee, 1958.

McCarthy, Mary. *The Group*. New American Library, 1963.

Morrison, Majbritt. *Jungle West 11*. Tandem, 1964.

O'Brien, Edna. *August is a Wicked Month*. Jonathan Cape, 1965.

O'Brien, Edna. *The Love Object And Other Stories*. Jonathan Cape, 1968.

Sagan, Francoise. *Bonjour Tristesse*. Editions Juillard, 1954.

Sagan, Francoise. *Un Certain Sourire*. Editions Juillard, 1955.

Sagan, Francoise. *Aimez-Vous Brahms?*. Editions Juillard, 1959.

Selvon, Samuel. *The Lonely Londoners*. Longmans, 1956.

Sillitoe, Alan. *Saturday Night & Sunday Morning*. W H Allen & Co Ltd, 1958.

Sillitoe, Alan. *The Loneliness Of The Long Distance Runner*. W H Allen & Co Ltd, 1959.

Weldon, Fay. *Down Among The Women*. 1971.

Wesker, Arnold. *The Kitchen*, (1957) Oberon Modern Plays, 2011.

Wesker, Arnold. *Plays: The Wesker Trilogy: Chicken Soup with Barley; Roots; I'm Talking About Jerusalem v. 1.* (1958–62) Berg, 2001.

NON-FICTION

Adam, Ruth. *A Woman's Place 1910-1975*. Persephone, 2000.

Bingham, Charlotte. *MI5 And Me: A Coronet Among The Spooks*. Bloomsbury Publishing Plc, 2018.

Bowlby, John. *Maternal Care And Mental Health*. 2nd ed., J. Aronson (WHO 1951), 1995.

Carpenter, Humphrey. *The Angry Young Men: A Literary Comedy Of The 1950S*. Allen Lane: The Penguin Press, 2002.

Davies, Hunter. *A Life In The Day*. Simon & Schuster, 2017.

Dunn, Nell. *Talking To Women*. MacGibbon & Kee, 1965.

Dunn, Nell. *Different Drummers*. Lorrimer, 1977.

Dunn, Nell. *Living Like I Do*. Futura, 1977.

Dunn, Nell, and Ali Smith. *Talking To Women*. Silver Press, 2018.

Forbes, Bryan. *Notes For A Life*. Collins, 1974.

Forster, Margaret. *Hidden Lives: A Family Memoir*. 1st ed., Viking, 1995.

Forster, Margaret. *My Life In Houses*. Vintage, 2014.

Francoise, Sagan, and David Macey (translator). *Reponses: The Autobiography Of Francoise Sagan*. 2019.

Gaffney, John, and Diana Holmes. *Stardom In Postwar France*. Berghahn Books, 2011.

Gébler, Carlo. *The Projectionist: The Story Of Ernest Gébler*. New Island Books, 2015.

Gottfried, Martin. *Balancing Act: The Authorized Biography Of Angela Lansbury*. Littlre, Brown, 1999.

Harding, John. *Sweetly Sings Delaney*. Greenwich Exchange, 2014.

Hardy, Sheila. *A 1950S Housewife: Marriage And Homemaking In The 1950S*. Baker & Taylor, 2013.

Holdsworth, Nadine. *Joan Littlewood*. 1st ed., Routledge, 2006.

Ironside, Virginia. *Janey And Me:Growing Up With My Mother*. 1st ed., Harper Perennial, 2004.

Jago, Michael. *The Man Who Was George Smiley:The Life Of John Bingham*. 1st ed., Biteback Publishing Ltd, 2013.

Lelievre, Marie-Dominique. *Sagan A Tout Allure*. Editions Denoel, 2008.

Lewis, Jane. *The End Of Marriage*. Elgar, 2001.

Littlewood, Joan et al. *Joan's Book*. 3rd ed., Methuen Publishing Ltd, 2003.

Maschler, Tom. *Publisher*. Picador, 2005.

Myrdal, Alva, and Viola Klein. *Women's Two Roles; Home And Work*. Routledge & Kegan Paul, 1968.

Nicholson, Virginia. *Perfect Wives In Ideal Homes:The Story Of Women In The 1950S.*. Viking, 2005.

O'Brien, Edna. *Country Girl:A Memoir*. 2nd ed., Faber & Faber, 2013.

Osborne, John. *Almost A Gentleman*. Faber & Faber, 1991.

Rankin, Peter. *Joan Littlewood: Dreams And Realities – The Official Biography*. Oberon Books Ltd, 2014.

Rebetello, Dan. *1956 And All That:The Making Of Modern British Drama*. Routledge, 2017.

Richardson, Tony et al. *The Long-Distance Runner*. William Morrow And Co, 1993.

Sagan, Francoise. *Je Ne Renie Rien:Entretiens 1954-1992*. Stock, 2014.

Sagan, Francoise, and David Macey (translator). *Reponses:The Autobiography Of Francoise Sagan*. Black Sheep Books:The Ram Publishing Co Ltd, 1979.

Sagan, Francoise, and Denis Westhoff. *Chronique 1954-2003*. Le Livre De Poche, 2016.

Walker, Alexander. *Hollywood England:The British Film Industry In The Sixties*. Orion Books Ltd, 1975.

Westhoff, Denis. *Françoise Sagan, Ma Mère*. Flammarion, 2012.

Whitehead, Andrew. *London Fictions*. 1st ed., Five Leaves Publications, 2013, pp. 181–189.

Wilson, Colin. *The Angry Years:The Rise And Fall Of The Angry Young Men*. Robson Books, 2007.

Wolfe, Tom. "*Radical Chic:That Party At Lenny's*". New York Magazine, 3 June 1970.

Wynn, Margaret. Fatherless Families. Michael Joseph, 1968.

ARTICLES

"A Country Girl's Abode – Former Home Of Edna O'brien – Farmireland.Ie". Farmireland.Ie, 2014, http://www.independent.ie/business/farming/a-country-girls-abode-former-home-of-edna-obrien-30377292.html. Accessed 31 July 2017.

"Margaret Forster Remembered". Penguin.Co.Uk, 2017, https://www.penguin.co.uk/articles/on-writing/times-and-life/2016/mar/remembering-margaret-forster/. Accessed Feb 2016.

"A Woman's War". 2018, https://lady.co.uk/womans-war. Accessed 9 Dec 2018.

Beard, Mary. "A Don's Life :Roman Britain In Black And White". *The Times Literary Supplement*, 3 August 2017, Accessed 11 Jan 2019.

Bradshaw, Peter. "Poor Cow Review". *The Guardian*, 2016, https://www.theguardian.com/film/2016/jun/23/poor-cow-review-ken-loach-debut-masterpiece. Accessed 3 Aug 2017.

Burman, Douglas D. et al. "Sex Differences In Neural Processing Of Language Among Children". *Neuropsychologia*, vol 46, no. 5, 2008, pp. 1349–1362. *Elsevier BV*, doi:10.1016/j.neuropsychologia.2007.12.021. Accessed 26 Nov 2018.

Byrne, James P et al. *Affecting Irishness*. Peter Lang AG, Internationaler Verlag Der Wissenschaften, 2011.

Carlson (ed), Julia. *Banned In Ireland:Censorship And The Irish Writer*. Routledge, 1990.

Carlson, Katherine et al. "The Female Bildungsroman". *The Bildungsroman Project*, 2014, http://bildungsromanproject.com/female-bildungsroman/. Accessed 1 Feb 2018.

Chrisler, Joan C, and Donald R McCreary. *Handbook Of Gender Research In Psychology*. Springer, 2010, p. 245.

Churchill, Rhona. "The Wife With Too Much Money". *The Daily Mail*, 1966, p. 8, Accessed 29 Aug 2017.

Cima, Rosie. "The Gender Balance Of The New York Times Best Seller List". *The Pudding*, 2018, https://pudding.cool/2017/06/best-sellers/. Accessed 26 Nov 2018.

Collins, Lauren. "Where She Was From". *The New Yorker*, 2013, http://www.newyorker.com/magazine/2013/05/20/where-she-was-from. Accessed 31 July 2017.

Cranston, Ros. "BFI Screenonline: Up The Junction (1965)". *Screenonline.Org.Uk*, 2019, http://www.screenonline.org.uk/tv/id/440997/index.html. Accessed 18 July 2018

Davies, Hunter. "Hunter Davies: My Wife Margaret Forster Valued Privacy – Should I Publish Her Diaries?". *The Guardian*, 2017, https://www.theguardian.com/books/2017/jul/29/margaret-forster-hunter-davies-diaries. Accessed 2 Aug 2017.

Delaney, Shelagh. "A Playwright's Education". *The Manchester Guardian*, 1958, p. 6, Accessed 28 Aug 2017.

Espiner, Mark. "Obituary:Christopher Logue". *The Guardian*, 2011, https://www.theguardian.com/books/2011/dec/03/christopher-logue. Accessed 2 Aug 2017.

Flood, Alison. "Readers Prefer Authors Of Their Own Sex, Survey Finds". *The Guardian*, 2018, https://www.theguardian.com/books/2014/nov/25/readers-prefer-authors-own-sex-goodreads-survey. Accessed 26 Nov 2018.

Gross, John. "Sylvie, Rube And Nell". *The Observier*, 2018, Accessed 13 Dec 2018.

Guppy, Shusha (interviewer). "Edna O'Brien, The Art Of Fiction No. 82". *The Paris Review*, 2017, https://www.theparisreview.org/interviews/2978/edna-obrien-the-art-of-fiction-no-82-edna-obrien. Accessed 31 July 2017.

Hayward, Anthony. "Jeremy Sandford:Writer Of Cathy Come Home". *The Independent*, 2003, http://www.independent.co.uk/news/obituaries/jeremy-sandford-36532.html. Accessed 2 Aug 2017.

Herbert, Hugh. "Arts Guardian:Georgy Girl". *The Guardian*, 1973, Accessed 29 Aug 2017.

Hope-Wallace, Philip. "Shelagh Delaney's "A Taste Of Honey" At Wyndham's.". *The Manchester Guardian*, 1959, Accessed 19 Sept 2017.

Hugh-Jones, Siriol. "A Favourite Girl – & Others". *The Tatler*, Accessed 19 Jan 2019.

Ironside, Virginia. "Nell Dunn: I Never Used To Think About Death Etc". 2013, Virginia, I. (2003). Nell Dunn: I never used to think about death, until I was 50. I was never going to die. I was immortal. But now I think about death every day. The Independent. [online] https://www.independent.co.uk/arts-entertainment/

theatre-dance/features/nell-dunn-i-never-used-to-think-about-death-until-i-was-
50-i-was-never-going-to-die-i-was-immortal-105000.html. Accessed 2 Aug 2017.

Kersnowski, Alice Hughes. *Conversations With Edna O'brien*. Univ. Press Of Mississippi,
2013.

Kitayama, Shinobu. "Journal Of Personality And Social Psychology: Attitudes And
Social Cognition". *Journal Of Personality And Social Psychology*, vol 112, no. 3, 2017,
pp. 357-360. *American Psychological Association (APA)*, doi:10.1037/pspa0000077.

Lambert, Angela. "Life-Style/From Georgy Girl To The Man In Daphne". *The
Independent*, 1993, http://www.independent.co.uk/life-style/from-georgy-
girl-to-the-man-in-daphne-margaret-forster-the-author-who-revealed-the-half-
breed-1498180.html. Accessed 29 Aug 2017.

"Obituary: James MacGibbon". *The Guardian*, 2000, https://www.theguardian.com/
news/2000/mar/04/guardianobituaries. Accessed 2 Aug 2017

Pyke, M. "Family Planning". *BMJ*, vol 1, no. 4766, 1952, pp. 1028–1028. *BMJ*, Rees,
David. "New Novels". The Spectator, 2018, p. P 15, Accessed 13 Dec 2018.

Rees, David. "New Novels". The Spectator, 2018, p. P 15, Accessed 13 Dec 2018.

Tennen, Howardn, and Sharon Hertzberger. "Depression, Self-Esteem, And The
Absence Of Self-Protective Attributional Biases.". *Journal Of Personality & Social
Psychology*, Vol 52(1), Jan 1987, 72-80, 2019, Accessed 5 Jan 2019.

Tepper, Steven J. "Steven J. Tepper". "Reading in America: Why do Women Read
More Fiction?" (2000). *Poetics: Journal of Empirical Research on Culture, the Media and
the Arts,* Vol. 27, No. 4, 255–275.

The Daily Mail. "Now A Robot That Dances". 1957, Accessed 28 Aug 2017.

The Daily Mail. "Tanfield's Diary: The Honeymoon Will Start In A Gas-Filled
Balloon". 1957, Accessed 28 Aug 2017.

The Daily Mail. "Shelagh's Taste Of Money". 1959, p. p3, Accessed 28 Aug 2017.

The Daily Mail. "Writers Boycott Colour Bar Theatres". 1963, p. 3, Accessed 28 Aug
2017.

The Daily Mail. "Novels While She Works". 1965, p. 4, Accessed 29 Aug 2017.

The Daily Telegraph. "Jeremy Sandford – Obituary". 2003, http://www.telegraph.
co.uk/news/obituaries/1429962/Jeremy-Sandford.htm. Accessed 2 Aug 2017.

The Daily Telegraph. "Jeremy Sandford – Obituary". 2003, http://www.telegraph.
co.uk/news/obituaries/1429962/Jeremy-Sandford.html. Accessed 2 Aug 2017.

The Guardian. 2018, p. 12, Accessed 22 Dec 2018.

The Manchester Guardian. "Miss Delaney Gets Her Own Taste Of Honey". 1958,
p. 5, Accessed 28 Aug 2017.

The Sunday Times. "Dwarf's Eye". 1965, p. 48, Accessed 29 Aug 2017.

Thorpe, Vanessa. "Why Women Read More Than Men". *The Guardian*, 2009, https://
www.theguardian.com/books/2009/mar/22/women-reading-books-study.
Accessed 26 Nov 2018.

Tindall, Gillian. "Novels In Brief". *The Observer*, 1964, p. 28, Accessed 29 Aug 2017.

Topping, Keith J. "Fiction And Non-Fiction Reading And Comprehension In
Preferred Books". *Reading Psychology*, vol 36, no. 4, 2014, pp. 350–387. *Informa
UK Limited*, doi:10.1080/02702711.2013.865692.

Travis, Alan. "After 44 Years Secret Papers Reveal Truth About Five Nights Of
Violence In Notting Hill". *The Guardian*, 2002, https://www.theguardian.com/

uk/2002/aug/24/artsandhumanities.nottinghillcarnival2002. Accessed 11 Jan 2019.

Walsh, John. "A Problem Shared". *The Independent*, 2013, Accessed 28 Aug 2017.

Weiner, Eric. "Why Women Read More Than Men:NPR Choice Page". *Npr.Org*, 2007, https://www.npr.org/templates/story/story. php?storyId=14175229&t=1543235448844. Accessed 26 Nov 2018.

Williams, Richard. "Francois Sagan: 'She Did What She Wanted.'"". *The Guardian*, 2014, https://www.theguardian.com/books/2014/feb/28/francois-sagan-bonjour-tristesse. Accessed 6 Sept 2017.

Wood, Harriet. 2018, https://www.thebookseller.com/news/trade-pays-tribute-godfather-industry-sissons-850426. Accessed 22 Dec 2018.

OTHER SOURCES

"Charlotte Bingham – About Charlotte". 2017. http://www.charlottebingham.com/About-Charlotte.html. Accessed 26 July 2017.

"Charlotte Bingham – My First Success". 2017, http://www.charlottebingham.com/My-First-Success.html. Accessed 28 July 2017.

"Lynne Reid Banks (1929–) *Biography.Jrank.Org*, 2017, http://biography.jrank.org/pages/1956/Reid-Banks-Lynne-1929.html#ixzz4nlRFV9P2. Accessed 25 July 2017.

"Portrait – National Portrait Gallery". *Npg.Org.Uk*, 2017, http://www.npg.org.uk/collections/search/portrait/mw18393/Nell-Dunn?search=sp&sText=nell+dun n&rNo=0. Accessed 2 Aug 2017.

"Book Club:Lynne Reid Banks". BBC Radio 4, June 10 2010.

Fisher, Philip. "Playwright And Author Nell Dunn In Conversation About Her Career - Theatrevoice". *Theatrevoice*, 2016, http://www.theatrevoice.com/audio/interview-nell-dunn/. Accessed 2 Aug 2017.

Hansard. *HL Deb 24 October 1956 Vol 199*. HM Government, London, 1956, p. 980.

Lynne Reid Banks. "Interview". *Lynnereidbanks.Com*, 2018, http://www.lynnereidbanks.com/interview.html. Accessed 8 Dec 2018.

"Monitor:Shelagh Delaney's Salford, (1960). [TV Programme] BBC-2: BBC.". BBC, 1960.

Robertson, Selina. "'It Was Such A Laugh!' Writer Nell Dunn In Conversation - The F-Word". *Thefword.Org.Uk*, 2016, https://www.thefword.org.uk/2016/06/it-was-such-a-laugh-writer-nell-dunn-in-conversation/. Accessed 2 Aug 2017.

Sierz, Aleks. "Angry Young Men". *Aleks Sierz:New Writing For The British Stage*, 2010, http://www.sierz.co.uk/writings/angry-young-men-2010/. Accessed 6 June 2016.

ACKNOWLEDGMENTS

First of all, I would like to thank the Rebel Writers themselves, Lynne Reid Banks, Charlotte Bingham, Nell Dunn, Virginia Ironside and Edna O'Brien for their help with this study, whether it was with patiently answered questions, kindly given permissions or, as with Charlotte and Virginia, generous amounts of time spent in delightful conversation. I would also like to thank Caitlin Davies for allowing me to consult archive material relating to her mother, Margaret Forster, and the literary agents Caroline Michel and Rachel Calder for handling my queries.

I am most grateful to the librarians archivists who helped me identify and consult the valuable resources in their charge, including Greg Buzzwell at the British Library, Kathy Shoemaker, Reference co-ordinator for the Stuart A Rose Manuscript Archives at Emory University in Georgia, USA; Eugene Roche at the James Joyce Library at University College Dublin; Danni Caulfield and Ceri Lumley at the Special Collections at the University of Reading; Kirby Smith at the Penguin Random House UK Archives in Rushden, Northamptonshire; Sam Maddra at the University of Glasgow where the MacGibbon & Kee files are; Matthew Geoghegan at the Irish Film Classification Office, which holds the records of the Censorship of Publications Board, and the great team at the Bodleian Library in Oxford. As ever, I am thankful for the encouragement and support of my agent, Jonathan Lloyd and the intrepid team of Curtis Brown.

In addition, I'm indebted to two assiduous researchers, Nathan Blansett in Atlanta, Georgia who searched Edna O'Brien's papers for me and Daphne Power in London who helped with press coverage and picture research.

The help, in cash and kind, of Bath Spa University enabled me to extend my research much further than I would have otherwise been able to do, and also to carry out the substantial initial research needed to prepare this book as a proposal. I am particularly grateful to my colleagues Mark Loon, Richard Kerridge, Paul Meyer and Professor John Strachan and Katie Rickard for their support and to Professor Phil Tew of Brunel University London for his wise advice.

After developing the idea for this book over five years, it was a wonderful moment when Tatiana Wilde at I.B.Tauris responded so positively to my proposal and seemed to love the idea as much as I did. I'm deeply appreciative of her enthusiasm and also of her care and thoroughness in editing the manuscript. When Bloomsbury Publishing took over the project I was thrilled with the flair and energy with which Jayne Parsons, non-fiction publishing director, moved the process to completion. I am also most grateful for expertise and vision of Jude Drake in publicising the book. My thanks are also due to our managing editor, Claire Browne, for her masterful command of the book's creation.

In working on a book about writers, it has been marvellous to have the encouragement of so many fellow writers and bookish friends. I am particularly grateful for Helen Rappaport for her astute historian's eye and kind advice, and to Julia Bell, Amanda Craig, Deborah Levy, Tanya Bruce-Lockhart, Daisy Parente, Professor Dame Marina Warner and Professor Fay Weldon among many others, for cheering me on. Chloe Brayfield has contributed her 20-20 judgment on many occasions, read endless drafts and inspired many a light-bulb moment. Finally, I am grateful for Joan Barker for her friendship and companionship along the way.

INDEX